Learning Nagios 3.0

A detailed tutorial to setting up, configuring, and managing this easy and effective system monitoring software

Wojciech Kocjan

BIRMINGHAM - MUMBAI

Learning Nagios 3.0

First published: October 2008

Production Reference: 1101008

Published by Packt Publishing Ltd.
32 Lincoln Road
Olton
Birmingham, B27 6PA, UK.

ISBN 978-1-84719-518-0

www.packtpub.com

Cover Image by Vinayak Chittar (vinayak.chittar@gmail.com)

Credits

Author
Wojciech Kocjan

Reviewer
Manish Sapariya

Acquisition Editor
Adil Ahmed

Development Editor
Swapna Verlekar

Technical Editor
Aanchal Kumar

Editorial Team Leader
Akshara Aware

Project Manager
Abhijeet Deobhakta

Project Coordinator
Rajashree Hamine

Indexer
Monica Ajmera

Proofreader
Dirk Manuel

Production Coordinator
Rajni Thorat

Cover Designer
Rajni Thorat

About the Author

Wojciech Kocjan is an experienced system administrator, IT professional, and software engineer. He has ten years of experience in the IT industry, and his resume includes international corporations such as IBM and Motorola. He also has several years of experience in a variety of open source projects. His expertise includes managing Linux, Sun, and IBM systems.

I'd like to thank my wife Joanna and my son Kacper for all of the help and support during the writing of this book. I would also like to thank people at Packt as they have given me a lot of help and plenty of practical advice.

About the Reviewer

Manish Sapariya has nine years of experience in software development and testing. He has worked on various technologies such as C++/ATL-COM, Windows, and Linux device drivers, and OS platforms such as Windows, FreeBSD, and Linux. He started his career with Zensar Technologies, Pune, working for the Fujitsu Ltd. division. While working for Fujitsu Ltd, Manish worked on various test simulation tools for the testing of hardware devices, including high-end servers, switches and routers. For the last four years, he has been working with Great Software Laboratory Pvt. Ltd., Pune, where he is currently responsible for testing products developed at GSLab.

I would like to thank my wife Dharmishtha, and my family for all their support while I have been reviewing this book.

Table of Content

Preface

This book is a practical guide to setting up the Nagios 3.0 open source network monitoring tool. Nagios 3 is a system that watches to see whether hosts and services are working properly, and notifies users when problems occur. This book covers installing and configuring Nagios 3 on various operating systems, but focuses primarily on the Ubuntu Linux operating system.

This book takes the reader through the steps from compiling Nagios from the source, through installing and configuring it up to advanced features such as setting up redundant monitoring. It also mentions how to monitor various services such as e-mail, WWW, databases, and file sharing. This book describes what SNMP is and how it can be used to monitor various devices. It also provides details on monitoring Microsoft Windows computers. This book contains troubleshooting sections that aid the reader in case any problems arise when setting up Nagios functionality.

No previous experience with network monitoring is required, although a basic understanding of UNIX systems is assumed. This book provides examples for extending Nagios in several languages including Perl, Python, Tcl, and Java so that readers familiar with at least one of these technologies can benefit from extending Nagios.

When you finish this book, you'll be able to set up Nagios to monitor your network, and have a good understanding of what can be monitored and in which ways.

What This Book Covers

Chapter 1 talks about the Nagios application and system monitoring in general. It shows the benefits of using system monitoring software, and the advantages of Nagios in particular. It also introduces the basic concepts of Nagios.

Chapter 2 covers installing Nagios both when compiling from source code and when using pre-built packages. Details of how to configure users, hosts, and services are also given, as well as information on how Nagios sends notifications to users.

Chapter 3 talks about how to set up the Nagios Web interface, and what this offers to the user. It describes basic views for hosts and services, and detailed information on each individual item. It also introduces additional features such as scheduled downtimes, detailed information, and reports.

In *Chapter 4*, we go through Nagios plugins that allow the performing of checks of various services. It shows how you can check for standard services such as e-mail, Web, file, and database servers. It also describes how to monitor resources such as CPU usage, storage, and memory usage.

Chapter 5 focuses on managing large configurations and using templates. We see how dependencies between hosts and services can be defined, what are custom variables, and what adaptive monitoring is. We also look at flapping—services that start and stop randomly - and how Nagios detects this.

Chapter 6 describes the notification system in more details. It focuses on effective ways of communicating problems to users and how to set up problem escalations; it also shows how events work in Nagios and how they can be used to perform the automatic recovery of services.

Chapter 7 describes passive checks in detail. We give practical examples of when and how they can be used. It also shows how to use NSCA (Nagios Service Check Acceptor) for sending notifications.

Chapter 8 covers how Nagios checks can be run on remote machines. It walks through the details of deploying checks remotely over SSH using public-key authentication. It also shows how NRPE (Nagios Remote Plugin Executor) can be used for deploying plugins remotely.

In *Chapter 9*, we learn about SNMP (Simple Network Management Protocol) and how it can be used from Nagios. We start with an overview of SNMP and its versions; then we go through reading SNMP values from SNMP-aware devices and cover how this can then be used for performing checks from Nagios.

The first part of *Chapter 10* looks at distributed monitoring. It talks about how Nagios can be set up on multiple hosts and how that information could be gathered on a central server. The second part of the chapter covers how to monitor computers that are running the Microsoft Windows operating system.

Chapter 11 shows you how to extend Nagios. We talk about how you can write your own check commands, add your own ways of notifying users, and use passive checks and NSCA to integrate your solutions with Nagios.

What You Need for This Book

No previous experience with network monitoring is required, although a basic understanding of UNIX systems is assumed. This book also provides examples for extending Nagios in several languages including Perl, Python, Tcl, and Java, so that readers familiar with at least one of these technologies can benefit from extending Nagios.

Who is This Book For

The target readers for this book are System Administrators interested in using Nagios. This book will teach Nagios beginners the basics of installation and configuration of version 3; it will show professionals who have already worked on earlier versions of Nagios the new features of Nagios, such as inheritance and new internal functions like better check scheduling.

Conventions

In this book, you will find a number of styles of text that distinguish between different kinds of information. Here are some examples of these styles, and an explanation of their meaning.

Code words in text are shown as follows: "The development packages always have the `-dev` suffix in their package name—in this case, it would be the `libssl-dev` package".

A block of code is set as follows:

```
define host
{
  host_name     somemachine
  address       10.0.0.1
  check_command check-host-alive
}
```

When we wish to draw your attention to a particular part of a code block, the relevant lines or items are shown in bold:

```
define host
{
  host_name     somemachine
  address       10.0.0.1
  _MAC          12:12:12:12:12:12
  check_command check-host-by-mac
}
```

Any command-line input or output is shown as follows:

```
/opt/nagios/plugins/check_ping -H 10.0.0.1 -w 3000.0,80%
-c 5000.0,100% -p 5
```

New terms and **important words** are introduced in a bold-type font. Words that you see on the screen, in menus or dialog boxes for example, appear in our text like this: "It can be accessed by clicking on the **Tactical Overview** link in the left-side menu".

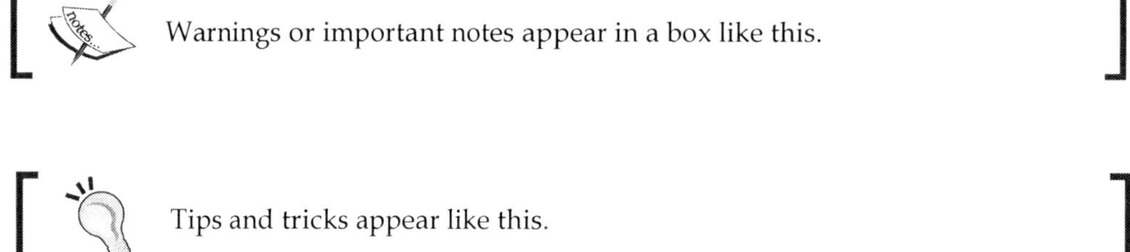

Warnings or important notes appear in a box like this.
Tips and tricks appear like this.

Reader Feedback

Feedback from our readers is always welcome. Let us know what you think about this book—what you liked or may have disliked. Reader feedback is important for us to develop titles that you really get the most out of.

To send us general feedback, simply send an email to `feedback@packtpub.com`, mentioning the book title in the subject of your message.

If there is a book that you need and would like to see us publish, please send us a note in the **SUGGEST A TITLE** form on `www.packtpub.com` or email `suggest@packtpub.com`.

If there is a topic that you have expertise in and you are interested in either writing or contributing to a book on this topic, see our author guide on `www.packtpub.com/authors`.

Customer Support

Now that you are the proud owner of a Packt book, we have a number of things to help you to get the most from your purchase.

Downloading the Example Code for the Book

Visit http://www.packtpub.com/files/code/5180_Code.zip to directly download the example code.

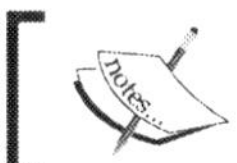

The downloadable files contain instructions on how to use them.

Errata

Although we have taken every care to ensure the accuracy of our contents, mistakes do happen. If you find a mistake in one of our books—maybe a mistake in text or code—we would be grateful if you would report this to us. By doing so you can save other readers from frustration, and help to improve subsequent versions of this book. If you find any errata, report them by visiting http://www.packtpub.com/support, selecting your book, clicking on the **let us know** link, and entering the details of your errata. Once your errata are verified, your submission will be accepted and the errata added to the list of existing errata. Any existing errata can be viewed by selecting your title from http://www.packtpub.com/support.

Piracy

Piracy of copyright material on the Internet is an ongoing problem. At Packt, we take the protection of our copyright and licenses very seriously. If you come across any illegal copies of our works in any form on the Internet, please provide the location address or website name immediately so we can pursue a remedy.

Please contact us at copyright@packtpub.com with a link to the suspected pirated material.

We appreciate your help in protecting our authors, and our ability to bring you valuable content.

Questions

You can contact us at questions@packtpub.com if you are having a problem with some aspect of the book, and we will do our best to address it.

1
Introduction

Imagine you're working as an administrator of a large IT infrastructure. You have just started receiving emails that a web application has stopped working. When you try to access the same page, it just doesn't load. What are the possibilities? Is it the router? Or the firewall? Perhaps the machine hosting the page is down? Before you even start thinking rationally about what is to be done, your boss calls about the critical situation and demands an explanation. In this panic situation, you'll probably start plugging everything in and out of the network, rebooting the machine and so on, and that doesn't help.

After hours of nervously digging into the issue you finally find the solution— the web server was working properly, but was timing out on communication with the database server. This was because the machine with the database was not getting a correct IP as yet another box had run out of memory and **Dynamic Host Configuration Protocol** (**DHCP**) server had stopped working. Imagine how much time it would take to find all that out manually. It would be a nightmare if the database server was in another branch of the company, in a different time zone, and perhaps the people over there were still sleeping.

And what if you had Nagios up and running across your entire company? You would just need to go to the web interface, see that there are no problems with the web server and the machine it is running on. There would also be a list of what's wrong - that the machine serving IP addresses to the entire company is not doing its job and that the database is down. If the set-up also monitored the DHCP server, you would get a warning email that very little swap memory is available on it, or that too many processes are running. Maybe it would even have an event handler for such cases to just kill or restart noncritical processes. Also, Nagios would try to restart the DHCP server process over the network, in case it is down.

In the worst case, Nagios would speed up hours of investigation to 10 minutes. In the best case, you would just get an email that there was a problem, followed by another one saying that the problem is already fixed. You would just disable a few services and increase the swap size for the DHCP machine and solve the problem once for all. And nobody would even notice there was a problem.

Introduction to Nagios

According to WikiPedia (`http://en.wikipedia.org/wiki/System_Monitoring`) *Nagios is a tool for system monitoring*. This means that it constantly checks the status of machines and various services on those machines. The main purpose of system monitoring is to detect and report on any system not working properly, as soon as possible, so that, you are aware of the problem before the user runs into it.

Nagios does not perform any host or service checks on its own. It uses plugins to perform the actual checks. This makes it a very modular and flexible solution for performing machine and service checks.

Objects monitored by Nagios are split into two categories: hosts and services. Hosts are physical machines (servers, routers, workstations, printers and so on), while services are particular functionalities, for example, a web server (an httpd process on a machine) can be defined as a service to be monitored. Each service is associated with a host it is running on. In addition, both machines and services can be grouped into host and service groups, accordingly. We will look into the details of each of these types of objects in the next section.

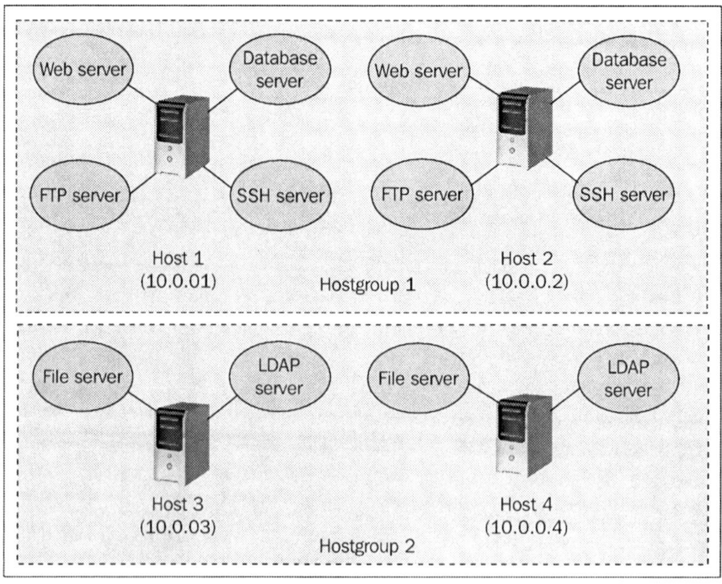

Nagios has two major strengths when it comes to scanning—first of all, instead of monitoring values, it only uses four states to describe status: `OK`, `WARNING`, `CRITICAL`, and `UNKNOWN`. The approach of only offering abstract states allows administrators to ignore monitoring values and just decide on what the warning/critical limits are. Having a strict limit to watch out for is much better as you always catch a problem regardless of whether it turns from a warning to a critical limit in 15 minutes or in a week. This is exactly what Nagios does. If you are monitoring a numeric value such as the amount of disk space and CPU usage, you can define thresholds for the values which are considered correct, a warning, or a failure. For example, system administrators tend to ignore things such as a slow decline in storage space. People often ignore it until a critical process runs out of disk space.

Another benefit is that a report states the number of services that are up and running in both `warning` state and `critical` state. Such a report offers a good overview of your infrastructure status. Nagios also offers similar reports for host groups and service groups, say when any critical service or database server is down. Such a report can also help prioritize what needs to be dealt with first, and which problems can be handled later.

Nagios performs all of its checks using plugins. These are external components to which Nagios passes information on what should be checked and what the warning and critical limits are. Plugins are responsible for doing the checks and analyzing the results. The output from such a check is a status (`OK`, `WARNING`, `CRITICAL`, or `UNKNOWN`) and additional text providing information on the service in detail. This text is primarily intended for system administrators to be able to read a detailed status of a service.

Nagios not only offers a core system for monitoring, but also offers a set of standard plugins in a separate package (see `http://nagiosplugins.org/` for more details). These plugins allow checks for almost all of the services your company might have. Refer to Chapter 4, *Overview of Nagios Plugins*, for detailed information on plugins that are developed along with Nagios. If you need to perform a specific check (for example, to connect to a web service and invoke methods), it is very easy to write your own plugins. And that's not all—they can be written in any language, and it takes less than a quarter of the time it takes to write a complete check command! Chapter 11 *Extending Nagios* talks about this in more detail.

Benefits of Monitoring Resources

There are many reasons why you should make sure that all of your resources are working as expected. If you're still not convinced after reading the introduction to this chapter, here are a few main points why it is important to monitor your infrastructure.

The main advantage is the improvement in quality. If your IT staff can notice failures more quickly, they will also be able to respond to them much faster. Sometimes, it takes hours or days to get the first report of a failure even if many users are bumping into errors. Nagios will make sure that if something is not working, you know about it.

It is also possible to make Nagios perform recovery actions automatically. This is done using event handlers. These are commands that are run after the status of a host or service has changed—this way when a primary router is down, Nagios will switch to a backup solution until the primary one is fixed. A typical case would be to start a dial-up connection as a fallback, in case VPN is down.

Another advantage is much better problem determination. Very often, what the users report as a failure is far from the root cause of the problem—an email system being down due to LDAP service not working correctly. If you define dependencies between hosts correctly, Nagios will point out that the POP3 email server is assumed to be not working because the LDAP service, which it depends upon, has a problem. Nagios will start checking the email server as soon as the problem with LDAP has been resolved.

Nagios is also very flexible when it comes to notifying people about what isn't functioning correctly. You can set it up to send emails to different people depending on what is not functioning properly. In most of the cases, your company has a large IT team or multiple teams. Usually you want some people to handle servers, and others to handle network switches/routers/modems. You can even use Nagios' web interface to manage who is working on what issue. You can also configure how Nagios sends notifications via email, pager over Jabber, MSN, or by using your own scripts.

Monitoring resources is not only useful for identifying problems; it can also save you from running into them. Nagios handles warnings and critical situations differently. This means that it's possible to recognize potentially problematic situations quickly. For example, if your disk storage on an email server is running out, it's better to be aware of this situation before it becomes a critical issue.

Monitoring can also be set up on multiple machines across various locations that can communicate all their results to a central Nagios server. This way, information on all hosts and services in your system can be accessed from a single machine. This gives you a more complete picture of your IT infrastructure, and also allows for testing of more complex things such as firewalls.

Main Features

Nagios' main strength is its flexibility—it can be configured to monitor your IT infrastructure in the way you want. It also has a mechanism to automatically react to problems, and a powerful notification system. All of this is based on a clear object definition system and on a few object types:

1. **Commands** are definitions of how Nagios should perform particular types of checks; they are an abstraction layer on top of the actual plugins that allow you to group similar types of operations.
2. **Time periods** are date and time spans within which an operation should or should not be performed; for example: Monday to Friday between 09:00 and 17:00.
3. **Contacts and contact groups** are people who should be notified, along with information on how and when they should be contacted. Contacts can be grouped and a single contact can be a member of more than one group.
4. **Host** are physical machines, along with information on who should be contacted, how checks should be performed, and when. Hosts can be grouped; into **host groups** each host may be a member of more than one host group.
5. **Services** are various functionalities or resources to monitor a specific host, along with information on who should be contacted, how the checks should be performed, and when. Services can be grouped into **service groups**; each service may be a member of more than one service group.
6. **Host and service escalations** define the specific time period after which additional people should be notified of certain events - for example a critical server being down for more than 4 hours should alert IT management so that they start tracking the issue. These people are defined in addition to the normal notifications configured in the host and service objects.

An important benefit that you will gain by using Nagios is a mature dependency system. For any administrator, it is obvious that if your router is down, all machines accessed through it will fail. Some systems don't take that into account and in such a case, you would get a list of several failing machines and services. Nagios allows you to define dependencies between hosts to reflect your actual network topology. For example, if a switch that connects you to a router is down, Nagios will not perform any checks on the router or on the machines that are dependant on the router. This is illustrated in the following example:

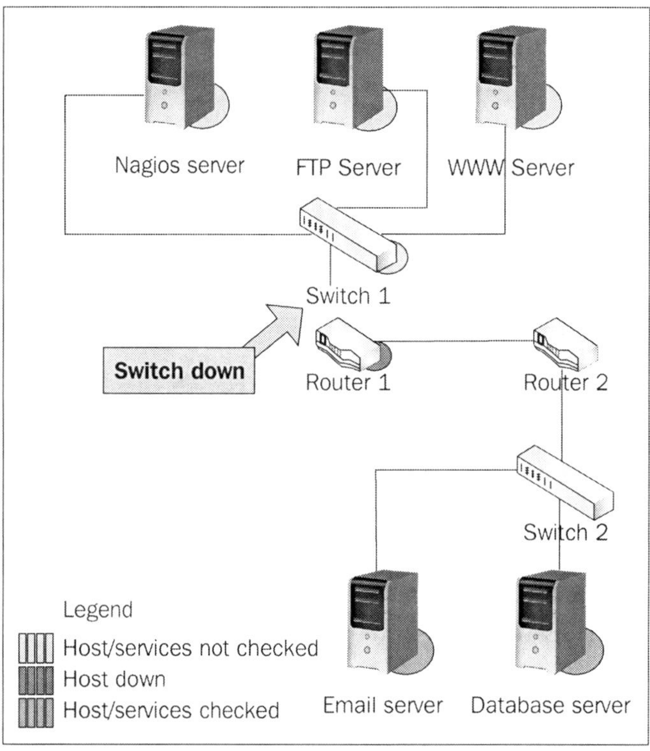

You can also define that one particular service depends on another service; either on the same host or on a different host. If one of the services is down, a check for a service that depends on it is not performed. For example, for your company's intranet application to function properly, both an underlying web server and a database server must be running. So, if a database service is not working properly, Nagios will not perform checks on your application. The database server might be on the same host or on a different host. In such a case, if the machine is down or not accessible, notifications for all services dependent on the database service will not be sent out either.

Nagios offers a consistent system of macro definitions. These are the variables that can be put into all object definitions, depending on what the context is. They can be put inside commands, and depending on host, service, and many other parameters, values are substituted accordingly. For example, a command definition might use the IP address of the host it is currently checking in all remote tests. This also makes it possible to put information such as the previous and current statuses of a service in a notification email. Nagios 3 also offers various extensions to macro definitions, which makes it an even more powerful mechanism. This is described in detail in the last section of this chapter.

Nagios also offers mechanisms for scheduling planned downtimes. You can schedule that a particular host or service is planned to be unavailable. This will prevent Nagios from notifying people to be contacted regarding the problems related to these objects. Nagios can also notify people of planned downtimes automatically. This is mainly used when maintenance of the IT infrastructure is to be carried out, and the servers and/or services they provide are unavailable for a long time. This allows the creation of an integrated process of scheduling downtimes that will also handle informing the users.

Soft and Hard States

Nagios works by checking if a particular host or service is working correctly and storing its status. Because the status of a service is only one of the four possible values, it is crucial that it actually reflects what the current status is. In order to avoid detecting random and temporary problems, Nagios uses soft and hard states to describe what the current status of a host or service is.

Imagine that an administrator is restarting a web server and this operation makes connection to the web pages unavailable for five seconds. As, usually, such restarts are done at night to lower the number of users affected, this is an acceptable period of time. However, a problem might arise when Nagios tries to connect to the server and notices that it is actually down. If it relies only on a single result, Nagios would trigger an alert that a web server is down. It would actually be up and running again in a few seconds, but it could take a couple of minutes for Nagios to find that out.

To handle situations when a service is down for a very short time, or the test has temporarily failed, soft states were introduced. When the status of a check is unknown, or it is different from the previous one, Nagios will retest the host or service several times to make sure that the change is persistent. The number of checks is specified in the host or service configuration. Nagios assumes that the new result is a soft state. After additional tests have verified that the new state is permanent, it is considered a hard state.

Each host and service definition specifies the number of retries to be performed before it can be assumed that a change is permanent. This allows more flexibility over how many failures should be treated as an actual problem instead of a temporary one. Setting the number of checks to one will cause all changes to be treated as hard instantly. The following is an illustration of soft and hard state changes, assuming that number of checks to be performed is set to three:

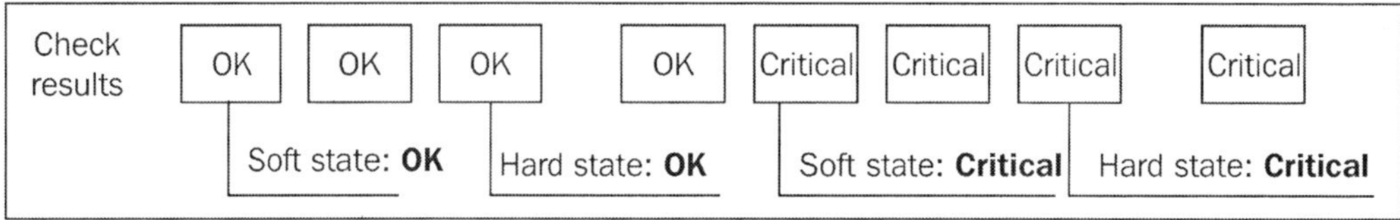

This feature allows ignoring short outages of a service. It is also very useful for performing checks that can periodically fail even if everything is working correctly. Monitoring devices over SNMP is also an example where a single check might fail, but the check will eventually succeed during the second or third check.

What's New in Nagios 3.0?

> This section is primarily intended for people who are already familiar with Nagios functionality and want to know what has been added in the new version. If you are not experienced with Nagios, not all issues mentioned in this section may be clear to you.

The new Nagios version comes with a bunch of new functionality and fixes. However, this section covers only the most important ones. It is recommended that you view the complete `Changelog` file that comes with all distributions of Nagios, or the Nagios documentation.

Macro handling is one area where there have been numerous changes. The most important improvement you might notice is that 40 new macros have been added. A notable incompatible change is that the `$NOTIFICATIONNUMBER$` macro has been removed in favor of the `$HOSTNOTIFICATIONNUMBER$` and `$SERVICENOTIFICATIONNUMBER$` macros. Moreover, macros have now been set as environment variables so that your scripts can access them easily. Because this can cause performance issues, there is also an option to disable the environment variables settings of all Nagios macros.

There have been significant changes to how Nagios stores information. The main reason behind this is that Nagios now allows plugins to return multiple lines with information or performance data. This allows more detailed information about hosts and services to be stored. The format of Nagios information and retention files has changed to adapt to this functionality. In the previous format for storing status and many other files, each line was used to represent a single object. This information is now stored in a format similar to Nagios configuration. This requires changes for all applications that read service statuses directly from the Nagios files.

The previous versions of Nagios stored scheduled downtimes as well as host and service comments in separate files. Version 3.x introduced a retention file that stores various information related to hosts and services. This file now contains a list of scheduled downtimes and comments related to each item. It also allows the storage of more information on Nagios restarts, which would be useful when performing frequent restarts.

The embedded Perl interpreter is where a lot has changed under the hood as well. You can now decide whether or not to use embedded Perl in the configuration at compilation time, as it was with 1.x and 2.x. In addition, individual plugins may decide if they want to force enabling or disabling embedded Perl usage. This would mainly be useful if a few of your Perl plugins cause problems with embedded Perl and you don't want to lose the functionality of other plugins that also have embedded Perl.

Now, it is also possible to change the frequency of monitoring hosts or services on the fly. This can be done by sending proper commands to the Nagios daemon. This functionality can be used to modify how often an object should be checked, as well as the time periods during which checks should be performed and notifications should be sent out.

A large improvement has been made in terms of host and service definitions. The major difference is that inheritance can now be done from more than object—this means that your host definition can inherit some attributes from one template and the remaining attributes from another. Services also inherit all contact and notification settings from the host they are running on, unless otherwise specified.

Starting with Nagios 3, it is possible to specify group members by specifying other groups. All objects that are members of specified groups will also be members of this group. For example, when defining a host group, it is possible to specify other host groups. All hosts who are members of such a group will also be members of the currently-described group.

Host checks have also been improved in various ways. Starting with Nagios 3, all checks will be done in parallel, which speeds up Nagios performance enormously. Host check retry handling has also been improved, and now uses the same logic as the service checks.

The dependency system has also been improved in Nagios 3. It is now much easier to configure complex dependencies. This also allows defining dependencies between services on the same host by not specifying dependent host name. It is also possible to set up periods for which dependencies are valid. If nothing is specified, a dependency is valid all the time.

Nagios 3 also introduces support for pre-caching object information. This means that instead of reading all parameters from the configuration file and creating a dependency set for all types of objects, Nagios is able to save its internal representation of the data, so that the next time it starts, it reads the cache instead of re-analyzing the configuration.

Defining time periods also is more powerful now. It is possible to specify date exceptions. For example, combining a definition of Monday to Friday from 9 AM to 5 PM with national holidays will offer a more precise definition of working hours. It is also possible to use a skip date in the time period; for example, 'every 3 days'.

For a complete list of changes, please visit Nagios 3.0 documentation website: `http://nagios.sourceforge.net/docs/3_0/whatsnew.html`.

Summary

There are many benefits of using system monitoring. It makes sure that services are working correctly. It helps in detecting problems earlier and ensuring that the appropriate people are notified when something goes wrong. Ensuring that all of your services work properly is essential. In case of problems, such systems help in giving a clear picture of what's working, and what's not.

Nagios is a very powerful application for monitoring resources. It fits both small-sized and enterprise-level environments. It can help your organization maintain a higher quality of services. Nagios also helps in determining the root cause of problems. It includes very flexible mechanisms for monitoring your infrastructure and notifying the IT staff of potentially critical problems.

Nagios features a rich configuration system with many features such as grouping hosts and services, setting up dependencies and escalations. All of these make it possible to configure both a small network and a huge IT infrastructure spanning the entire globe.

Nagios is extremely powerful as it can be configured in almost any way you want. Furthermore, it can also be extended to perform any type of operation needed for your company.

2

Installation and Configuration

This chapter describes how to install Nagios and standard Nagios plugins. The process described here does not take advantage of any of the packaging systems that are currently available on the majority of operating systems.

It is recommended that you consult your operating system and software distribution mechanisms to see if they are already offering Nagios packages. Obtaining and installing Nagios as a binary distribution, suited to a particular platform, is always a better choice as it also offers automated upgrades and ensures that all dependencies are met.

Manual installation is recommended for system administrators who want more power over where their software is installed, and want to manage software upgrades and configurations on their own.

This chapter also covers the basics of Nagios configuration, and what types of objects can be configured.

Installation

This section discusses the installation of Nagios 3. The following points are discussed:

- Upgrading from previous versions
- Prerequisites
- Obtaining Nagios
- Setting up users and groups
- Nagios compilation
- Registering Nagios as a system service

Let us look at each point in detail.

Upgrading from Previous Versions

If you already have Nagios 1 or 2, upgrading to Nagios 3 would be worthwhile. In such cases, you should proceed with the same steps as when performing a fresh installation. You need to use the same user name, groups and directories that you have used for previous Nagios installations.

It is also necessary to stop all Nagios processes before performing an upgrade. This can usually be done by invoking the following command:

```
/etc/init.d/nagios stop
```

This way, both Nagios and the plugins will install smoothly. As Nagios 3 configuration parameters are backwards compatible, your current configuration will work fine after upgrading.

Prerequisites

This section applies to people compiling Nagios from sources and installing them manually. Almost all modern Linux distributions include Nagios (1.x, 2.x or 3.0) in their packages. The Nagios website also offers instructions for automated installation on several operating systems. In such cases, all related packages will be installed by the underlying system (such as APT in Debian and Ubuntu systems). Usually, a system with the development set of packages already installed contains all the packages needed to build Nagios.

Building Nagios from sources requires a C compiler, standard C library development files and the `make`/`imake` command. Additionally, the development files for OpenSSL should be installed so that the network-based plugins will be able to communicate over the SSL layer. The MySQL and PostgreSQL development packages should also be installed so that database checks can be run.

First of all, if we are planning to build the Nagios system, a compiler along with several build tools such as `gcc`, `make`, `cpp`, and `binutils` are required. It will also need the standard C library development files. Although these packages usually come installed, make sure that they are actually there before compilation.

Nagios by itself does not have a large number of packages that offer some of the basic functionalities that you would want on your system. So, if you want to use all the functionalities that Nagios can offer, you will have to install additional software.

OpenSSL development files (includes and libraries) are required for Nagios plugins to communicate over SSL. If you plan to monitor MySQL or PostgreSQL databases, you should install header files and libraries for these databases. This will allow building check plugins to monitor databases.

If we want to use the Nagios web interface, a web server capable of serving CGI scripts is required. Apache web server (1.x or 2.x) is recommended, and is also the most popular web server on a Linux installation. Although Nagios works with any web server that supports CGI, this book covers configuring Apache.

Additionally, several plugins from the Nagios standard distribution are written in Perl, and will not work if Perl is not installed. Some plugins also need Perl's `Net::Snmp` package to communicate with devices over SNMP protocol.

Moreover, the GD graphics library is needed for the Nagios web interface to create a status map and trends images. We will also need to install libraries for JPEG and PNG images so that GD can create images in these formats.

All of the packages mentioned above are usually installed with many operating systems, and most of them are already available for almost any UNIX based platform.

Throughout this chapter, we will use the Ubuntu Linux 7.10 'Gutsy' distribution, as it is very popular. All newer Ubuntu platforms use the same package names, so commands used here will work without any problems.

We will also install Apache 2.2.4 and Perl 5.8.8 from Ubuntu packages. For different operating systems, the packages are similar though they may have different names. The following is a command to install all the packages for our chosen distribution:

```
apt-get install gcc make binutils cpp libpq-dev libmysqlclient15-dev\
                libssl0.9.8 libssl-dev pkg-config apache2 \
                libgd2-xpm libgd2-xpm-dev libgd-tools \
                libpng12-dev libjpeg62-dev \
                perl libperl-dev libperl5.8 libnet-snmp-perl
```

Package names may also be different for other operating systems and distributions. The command to install corresponding packages may also be different. For RPM packages, the naming convention is a bit different—the development packages have a suffix of `devel`. Libraries themselves are also named in a slightly different manner.

For Red Hat Enterprise Linux and Fedora Core operating systems with `yum` installed, the command to install all prerequisites would be:

```
yum install gcc imake binutils cpp postgresql-devel \
            libmysql15lib mysql15-devel \
            openssl openssl-devel pkg-config httpd \
            libgd2 libgd2-devel libgd-progs libpng libpng-devel \
            libjpeg libjpeg-devel perl perl-devel perl-Net-SNMP
```

A system with the development packages already installed, usually, contains all the packages needed to build Nagios.

Obtaining Nagios

Nagios is an open-source application, which means that the source code of all Nagios components is freely available from the Nagios home page. Nagios is distributed under **GNU GPL** (**General Public License**) version 2 (visit `http://www.gnu.org/licenses/old-licenses/gpl-2.0.html`), which means that Nagios source code can be redistributed and modified freely under the condition that all changes are also distributed as source code. Nagios also has a standard set of plugins. They are not only developed independently as SourceForge projects (see `http://sourceforge.net/projects/nagiosplug/`), but are also distributed under GPL version 2 license.

First of all, many operating systems already have binary distributions of Nagios. If you are not an IT expert and just want to try out or learn Nagios in your environment, it is best to use binary distributions instead of compiling Nagios by yourself. Therefore, it is recommended that you check to see if your distribution has a compiled version of Nagios 3 available.

For Red Hat and Fedora Linux systems, the Nagios download page contains RPMs that can simply be installed onto your system. For other distributions, their package repository may contain binary Nagios packages. The Nagios Exchange website `http://www.nagiosexchange.org/` also hosts Nagios builds for various platforms such as AIX or SUSE Linux. All binary distributions of Nagios are split into packages (rpm, dpkg, pkg, or bin file) that contain the Nagios daemon. It is usually called Nagios, and the standard set of plugins is usually called **Nagios Plugins**.

If you are an experienced user and want to control software installed on your machines, it's recommended that you install Nagios from the source. In this case, you should also download sources of both Nagios and the Nagios plugins.

In order to download the Nagios source packages, please go to the Nagios download page at `http://www.nagios.org/download/`. All Nagios downloads are hosted on SourceForge, so the download links will redirect you to the SourceForge download pages. The download process should begin automatically.

You should start by downloading the source tarball of the latest Nagios 3.x branch. It is available under the *Step 1: Get Nagios* section. Please make sure that you download a stable version (such as 3.0, 3.1, and so on), instead of the most recent CVS snapshot, as these versions might not always be as stable as the users expect. The filename of the source tarball should be similar to `nagios-3.0.tar.gz`, depending on the exact version you are attempting to download.

You should also download the source tarball of the latest official Nagios plugins from the same downloads page. It is available under the *Step 2: Get Plugins* section. The filename for the plugins should be similar to `nagios-plugins-1.4.11.tar.gz`, again depending on the exact version.

These files are used in the next section of this chapter to build Nagios from the source.

Setting up Users and Groups

This section describes how to compile and install Nagios and standard Nagios plugins from source tarballs. If you plan to install Nagios from binary distributions, you should skip this section and proceed to the next sections that describe exact Nagios configurations. You might also need to adjust the parameters mentioned in this book to specify the directories your Nagios installation uses.

If you are upgrading from a previous Nagios version, you will have all of the users and groups set up already. In this case, you should proceed to the next section.

The first thing that needs to be done is to decide where to install Nagios. In this section, we will install the Nagios binaries in the `/opt/nagios` directory, and all configuration files will be based on these locations. This is a location for all Nagios binaries, plugins, and additional files. Nagios data will be stored in the `/var/nagios` directory, where it keeps information about its current and historical status. It can be part of the Nagios binaries installation directory or a separate directory, as in our case. Nagios configuration will be put into `/etc/nagios`.

After we have decided on our directory structure, we need to set up users and groups for Nagios data. We will also create a system user and a group, `nagios`, which will be used by the daemon. We will also set up a group, `nagioscmd`, which can communicate with the daemon. The system user will be a member of the `nagios` and `nagioscmd` groups.

The following commands will create the groups and user mentioned above:

```
groupadd -g 5000 nagios
groupadd -g 5001 nagioscmd
useradd -u 5000 -g nagios -G nagioscmd -d /opt/nagios nagios
```

We create a new user and groups because Nagios processes run as separate users. This increases the security and allows a more flexible set up. Nagios also communicates with external components over a Unix socket - this is a socket that works in a similar way to a file on your file system. All commands are passed to Nagios via the pipe, and therefore, if you want your processes to be able to send reports or changes to Nagios, you need to make sure that they have access to the socket. One of the common uses for this is that the Nagios web interface needs to be able to send commands to the monitoring process.

If you want to use the web interface, it is necessary to add the user that your web server runs as, to the `nagioscmd` group. This will allow the web interface to send commands to Nagios.

The user that the web server is working as is usually `www-data`, `apache` or `httpd`. It can be checked with a simple `grep` command:

```
root@ubuntu:~# grep ^User /etc/apache*/* /etc/httpd*/*
/etc/apache2/apache2.conf:User www-data
```

For our preceding example, we now know the user name is `www-data`. So now, we'll add this user to the group `nagioscmd`. This requires a simple command to be run:

```
usermod -G nagioscmd www-data
```

Nagios Compilation

The next step is to set up Nagios destination directories and change their owners accordingly. The following commands will create the directories, and change their owner, user, and group to `nagios`.

```
mkdir -p /opt/nagios /etc/nagios /var/nagios
chown nagios.nagios /opt/nagios /etc/nagios /var/nagios
```

We will now create a source directory where all of our builds will take place. For the purpose of this book, this will be `/usr/src/nagios3`. We need to extract our Nagios and standard plugins into that directory. The extraction will create `nagios-3.0` and `nagios-plugins-1.4.11` subdirectories (or similar ones, depending on your source versions).

Now, let's go to the directory where the Nagios source is located - in our case, this is `/usr/src/nagios3/nagios-3.0`. We'll configure Nagios parameters for the directories we plan to install into by running the `configure` script. Some of the options that the script accepts are described here:

Option	Description
--prefix=<dir>	Specifies the main directory into which all Nagios binaries are installed; defaults to `/usr/local/nagios`
--sysconfdir=<dir>	Specifies the directory where all Nagios configuration will be stored; defaults to `[PREFIX]/etc`
--localstatedir=<dir>	Specifies the directory where all Nagios status and other information will be kept; defaults to `[PREFIX]/var`

Option	Description
--enable-embedded-perl	Informs Nagios to use the embedded Perl interpreter; see below for more details; the option is disabled if not specified
--with-nagios-user=<user>	Specifies the Unix user to use for the Nagios daemon; defaults to `nagios`
--with-nagios-group=<grp>	Specifies the Unix group to use for the Nagios daemon; defaults to `nagios`
--with-mail=<path>	Specifies the path to the `mail` program used for sending emails
--with-httpd-conf=<path>	Specifies the path to the Apache configuration directory; can be used to generate Apache configuration files
--with-init-dir=<path>	Specifies the directory into which all scripts required for setting up a system service should be installed; defaults to `/etc/rc.d/init.d`

The `--enable-embedded-perl` option will cause Nagios to use the embedded Perl interpreter instead of forking child processes to run plugins written in Perl. This option is not needed for Nagios to function, but in case you plan to run many plugins written in Perl, it might improve Nagios's overall performance. You can also enable it during compilation, and if your Nagios setup seems to behave incorrectly, you can always turn embedded Perl off in Nagios's main configuration file. If you are new to Nagios, it is not recommended that you turn this option on.

For the directory structure that was described earlier in this section, the following configure script should be used:

```
sh configure \
    --prefix=/opt/nagios \
    --sysconfdir=/etc/nagios \
    --localstatedir=/var/nagios \
    --libexecdir=/opt/nagios/plugins \
    --with-command-group=nagioscmd
```

The script may take time to complete as it will try to guess the configuration of your machine, and verify how to build Nagios.

If the `configure` script failed, the most probable reason is that one or more prerequisites are missing. At that point, you will need to analyze which test failed, and install or configure additional packages. Most of the times, the output is quite clear, and it is easy to understand what went wrong.

Assuming the `configure` command works, we now need to build Nagios. The build process uses `make` command, similar to almost all Unix programs. The following commands can be used to build or install Nagios:

Command	Description
make all	Compiles Nagios; this is the first thing you should be doing
make install	Installs main program, CGI and HTML files
make install-commandmode	Installs and configures external command file
make install-config	Installs sample Nagios configuration; this target should only be used for fresh installations
make install-init	Installs scripts to set up Nagios as a system service

First, we'll need to build every module within Nagios. To do this, simply run the following command:

```
make all
```

An error may occur in case some header files are missing, or when a development package is not installed.

The following is a sample output from a successful Nagios build. It finishes with a friendly message saying that it has completed successfully.

```
cd ./base && make
make[1]: Entering directory '/usr/src/nagios3/base'
[...]
*** Compile finished ***
[...]
*************************************************************
Enjoy.
```

In case an error occurs during the build, the information about the same is also shown. For example, consider the following sample output from build:

```
[...]
In file included from checks.c:40:
../include/config.h:163:18: error: ssl.h: No such file or directory
[...]
make[1]: *** [checks.o] Error 1
make[1]: Leaving directory '/usr/src/nagios3/base'
make: *** [all] Error 2
```

If this or a similar error occurs, please make sure that you have all the prerequisites, mentioned earlier, installed. Also, please make sure that you have enough memory and storage space during compilation, as this might also cause unexpected crashes during builds.

On Ubuntu systems, it is possible to look for development packages using the `apt-cache search` command. For example, `apt-cache search ssl` will find all packages related to OpenSSL. The development packages always have the `-dev` suffix in their package name—in this case, it would be the `libssl-dev` package.

Now, we need to install Nagios by running the commands:

```
make install
make install-commandmode
```

For a fresh install, it is recommended to also install sample configuration files that will be used later for configuring Nagios.

```
make install-config
```

The installation of Nagios is now complete. It is recommended that you keep all your Nagios sources as well as prepare dedicated scripts that install Nagios. This is just in case you decide to enable/disable specific options and don't want to guess exactly how Nagios was configured to build the last time it was installed.

The next step to be carried out is compilation of standard Nagios plugins.

Now, let's go to the directory where Nagios plugins source code is located—in our case, it is `/usr/src/nagios3/nagios-plugins-1.4.11`. We will configure Nagios plugins parameters for the directories we plan to install it into by running the `configure` script. Some of the options that the script accepts are described here:

Option	**Description**
--prefix=<dir>	Specifies the main directory all Nagios binaries are installed in; defaults to `/usr/local/nagios`
--sysconfdir=<dir>	Specifies the directory where all Nagios configuration will be stored; defaults to `[PREFIX]/etc`
--libexecdir=<dir>	Specifies the directory where all Nagios plugins will be installed; defaults to `[PREFIX]/libexec`
--localstatedir=<dir>	Specifies the directory where all Nagios status and other information will be kept; defaults to `[PREFIX]/var`
--enable-perl-modules	Installs `Nagios::Plugin` package along with all dependant packages
--with-nagios-user=<user>	Specifies Unix user to use for Nagios daemon; defaults to `nagios`
--with-nagios-group=<grp>	Specifies Unix group to use for Nagios daemon; defaults to `nagios`

Option	Description
--with-pgsql=<path>	Specifies path to PostgreSQL installation; required for building of PostgreSQL testing plugins
--with-mysql=<path>	Specifies path to MySQL installation; required for building of MySQL testing plugins

The option `--enable-perl-modules` allows installing additional Perl modules that aid in developing your own Nagios plugins in Perl. It is useful to enable this option if you are familiar with Perl.

Options `--with-pgsql` and `--with-mysql` allow us to specify the locations for the installation of PostgreSQL and/or MySQL databases. It is used to create plugins for monitoring PostgreSQL and/or MySQL. If not specified, the build process will look for the development files for these databases in their default locations. Installing development files for these databases is described in the *Prerequisites* section.

For the directory structure that was described earlier in this section, the following `configure` script should be used:

```
sh configure \
     --prefix=/opt/nagios \
     --sysconfdir=/etc/nagios \
     --localstatedir=/var/nagios \
     --libexecdir=/opt/nagios/plugins \
     --enable-perl-modules
```

The script should run for some time and succeed, assuming that all prerequisites are installed. If not, the script should indicate what the missing component is.

The build process also uses the `make` command in a manner similar to the way Nagios is compiled. In this case, only the targets `all` and `install` will be used. Therefore, the next step is to run `make` commands as shown here:

```
make all
make install
```

If any of these steps fail, an investigation on what exactly has failed is needed, and if it is due to a missing library or a development package, they will have to be installed and the commands tried again.

If all of the above commands have succeeded, you now have a fully installed Nagios setup. Congratulations!

Registering Nagios as a System Service

After installing Nagios, it is worth making sure that the daemon is running as a system service, and will start up properly during system boot.

In order to do that, go to the source directory (in our case it is be `/usr/src/nagios3/ nagios-3.0`) and then run the following command:

```
make install-init
```

This will install a script in our `init.d` directory (this usually is `/etc/init.d` or `/etc/rc.d/init.d`). The script is automatically created, and will contain the usernames and paths that were created when the `configure` script was run.

The next step is to set up a system to stop and start this service automatically. Depending on your system, the command to do that can be one of the following:

```
chkconfig --add nagios ; chkconfig nagios on
update-rc.d nagios defaults
```

After Nagios has been set up as a system service, it is recommended that you reboot your system to verify that it is actually starting. After your system has fully restarted, making sure Nagios is running can be done by checking the process list as follows:

```
root@ubuntu:~# ps -ef|grep ^nagios
nagios 796 1  0 00:00:00 /opt/nagios/bin/nagios -d /etc/nagios
/nagios.cfg
```

If at least one process is found, it means that Nagios has been properly started. If not, please read the Nagios log file (whose name is `/var/nagios/nagios.log` assuming a Nagios installation as described earlier) and see exactly why it is failing. This usually relates to incorrect permissions. In such a case, you should perform all of the steps mentioned in the previous sections and reinstall Nagios from the beginning.

The results of the startup is mentioned at the end of the log file and an error indication should also be present of what the issue might be. For example, a part of the log for an error related to incorrect permissions is as follows:

```
[1217273964] Nagios 3.0 starting... (PID=5509)
[1217273964] Local time is Mon Jul 28 21:39:24 CEST 2008
[1217273964] LOG VERSION: 2.0
 [1217273964] Finished daemonizing... (New PID=5510)
[1217273964] Error: Could not create external command file '/var/
nagios/rw/nagios.cmd' as named pipe: (13) -> Permission denied.  If
this file already exists and you are sure that another copy of Nagios
is not running, you should delete this file.
[1217273964] Bailing out due to errors encountered while trying to
initialize the external command file... (PID=5510)
```

By default, Nagios also sends its logs to the syslog daemon. So if the Nagios log file does not exist, looking in the system log (usually `/var/log/messages`) might provide some information about the problem.

If you wish to start or stop Nagios manually, please run the `nagios` script from the `init.d` directory with one of the parameters shown.

```
/etc/init.d/nagios stop|start|restart
```

Please note that path to the `init.d` directory might be different for your operating system.

Nagios Configuration

Nagios stores its configuration in a separate directory. Usually it's either in `/etc/nagios` or `/usr/local/etc/nagios`. If you followed the steps for a manual installation, (as described above) it would be in `/etc/nagios`.

Main Configuration File

The main configuration file is called `nagios.cfg`, which is the main file that is loaded during Nagios startup. Its syntax is simple—a line beginning with # is a comment, and all lines in the form `<parameter>=<value>` will set a value. In some cases, a value might be repeated (such as specifying additional files/directories to read).

The following is a sample of Nagios's main configuration file:

```
# log file to use
log_file=/var/nagios/nagios.log
# object configuration directory
cfg_dir=/etc/nagios/objects
# storage information
resource_file=/etc/nagios/resource.cfg
status_file=/var/nagios/status.dat
status_update_interval=10
(...)
```

The main configuration file needs to define a log file to use, and that has to be passed as the first option in the file. It also configures various Nagios parameters that tune Nagios's its behavior and performance. The following are some of the commonly-changed options:

Option	Description
log_file	Specifies the log file to use; defaults to `[localstatedir]/nagios.log`
cfg_file	Specifies the configuration file to read for object definitions; might be specified multiple times
cfg_dir	Specifies the configuration directory which contains all files that should be read for object definitions; might be specified multiple times
resource_file	Specifies the that stores additional macro definitions; `[sysconfdir]/resource.cfg`
temp_file	Specifies the path to the temporary file that is used for temporary data; defaults to `[localstatedir]/nagios.tmp`
lock_file	Specifies the to the file that is used for synchronization; defaults to `[localstatedir]/nagios.lock`
temp_path	Specifies the directory in which Nagios can create temporary files; defaults to `/tmp`
status_file	Specifies the path to the file that stores the current status of all hosts and services; defaults to `[localstatedir]/status.dat`
status_update_interval	Specifies how often (in seconds) the status file should be updated; defaults to `10` (seconds)
nagios_user	Specifies the user to run the daemon as
nagios_group	Group to run the daemon as
command_file	Specifies the path to the external command line that is used by other processes to control Nagios's daemon; defaults to `[localstatedir]/rw/nagios.cmd`
use_syslog	Specifies whether Nagios should log messages to syslog as well as to the Nagios log file; defaults to `1` (yes)
state_retention_file	Specifies the path to the file that stores state information across shutdowns; defaults to `[localstatedir]/retention.dat`
retention_update_interval	Specifies how often (in seconds) the retention file should be updated; defaults to `60` (seconds)
service_check_timeout	Specifies the number of seconds after which it should a service check has failed; defaults to `60` (seconds)
host_check_timeout	Specifies the number of seconds after which it should be assumed that a host check it has failed; defaults to `30` (seconds)
event_handler_timeout	Specifies the number of seconds after which it should an event handler should be terminated; defaults to `30` (seconds)

Option	Description
notification_timeout	Specifies the number of seconds after which it should be assumed that a notification attempt has failed; defaults to `30` (seconds)
enable_embedded_perl	Whether an embedded Perl interpreter should be used, if enabled at compilation; defaults to `1` (yes)
use_embedded_perl_implicitly	If embedded Perl is supported and enabled, whether all Perl plugins should be read with the embedded interpreter unless they specify otherwise; defaults to `1` (yes)
enable_environment_macros	Whether Nagios should pass all macros to plugins as environment variables as well; defaults to `1` (yes)
interval_length	Specifies the number of seconds a "unit interval" is; defaults to `60` which means that an interval is one minute; it is not recommended that this option is changed in any way as it might result in undesirable behavior

For a complete list of accepted parameters, please consult the Nagios documentation on `http://nagios.sourceforge.net/docs/3_0/configmain.html`.

The Nagios option `resource_file` defines the file in which all user variables are to be stored. This file can be used to store additional information that can be accessed in all object definitions. This file usually contains sensitive data as it can only be used in object definitions, and it is not possible to read these variables from the web interface. This makes it possible to hide passwords of various sensitive services from Nagios administrators who do not have adequate privileges. There can be up to 32 macros, named `$USER1$`, `$USER2$` ... `$USER32$`. Macro definition `$USER1$` defines the path to the Nagios plugins and is commonly used in check command definitions.

Options `cfg_file` and `cfg_dir` are used to specify the files that should be read for object definitions. The first option specifies a single file to read and the second specifies the directory in which all files should be read. Each file may contain different types of objects. The following sections describe each type of definition that Nagios uses.

One of the first things that needs to be decided is how your Nagios configuration should be stored. In order to create a configuration that is maintainable as your IT infrastructure changes, it is worth investing some time in planning out how you want your host definitions set up and how they could be most easily placed in a configuration file structure. Throughout this book, various approaches on how to make your configuration maintainable are discussed. It's also recommended that you set up a small Nagios system to get a better understanding of Nagios configuration, before proceeding to larger setups.

Sometimes, it is best to have configuration grouped into separate directories defined according to the locations that hosts and/or services are in. In other cases, it might be best to keep definitions of all servers with similar functionalities in one directory.

A good directory separation makes it much easier to control Nagios configuration to, for example, massively disable all objects related to a particular part of the IT infrastructure. Even though it is recommended to use downtimes, it is sometimes useful to just remove all entries from Nagios configuration.

Throughout all configuration examples in this book, we use a directory structure. A separate directory is used for each object type and similar objects are grouped within a single file. For example, all command definitions are stored in the `commands/` subdirectory. All host definitions are stored in the `hosts/<hostname>.cfg` files.

In order for Nagios to read configuration from these directories, edit your main Nagios configuration file (`/etc/nagios/nagios.cfg`), remove all `cfg_file` and `cfg_dir` entries, and add the following ones:

```
cfg_dir=/etc/nagios/commands
cfg_dir=/etc/nagios/timeperiods
cfg_dir=/etc/nagios/contacts
cfg_dir=/etc/nagios/hosts
cfg_dir=/etc/nagios/services
```

In order to use the default Nagios plugins, copy the default Nagios command definitions file `/etc/nagios/objects/commands.cfg` to `/etc/nagios/commands/default.cfg`.

In addition, please make sure that the following options are set as shown in your `nagios.cfg` file:

```
check_external_commands=1
interval_length=60
accept_passive_service_checks=1
accept_passive_host_checks=1
```

If any of the options are set to a different value, change them, and add them to the end of the file, if they are not currently present in it.

After such changes in the Nagios set up, you can move on to the next sections and prepare a working configuration for your Nagios installation.

Macro Definitions

The ability to use macro definitions is one of the key features of Nagios. Macros offer a lot of flexibility in object and command definitions. Nagios 3 provides custom macro definitions, which gives you a greater possibility to use object templates for specifying parameters common to a group of similar objects.

All command definitions can use macros. Macro definitions allow parameters from other objects, such as hosts, services, and contacts, to be referenced so that a command does not need to have everything passed as an argument. Each macro invocation begins and ends with a `$` sign.

A typical example is a `HOSTADDRESS` macro, which references the address field from the host object. All host definitions provide the value of the `address` parameter. For the following host and command definition:

```
define host
{
  host_name     somemachine
  address       10.0.0.1
  check_command check-host-alive
}
define command
{
  command_name  check-host-alive
  command_line  $USER1$/check_ping -H $HOSTADDRESS$
                -w 3000.0,80% -c 5000.0,100% -p 5
}
```

this command will be invoked:

```
/opt/nagios/plugins/check_ping -H 10.0.0.1 -w 3000.0,80% -c
5000.0,100% -p 5
```

In addition, please note that the `USER1` macro was also used and expanded as the path to Nagios plugins directory. This is a macro definition that references data contained in the file that is passed as the `resource_file` configuration directive. Even though it is not necessary for `USER1` macro to point to the plugins directory, all standard command definitions that come with Nagios use this macro, and so it is recommended that you do not change it.

Some of the macro definitions are listed in the following table:

Macro	Description
HOSTNAME	Short, unique name of the host; maps to `host_name` directive in the host object
HOSTADDRESS	IP or hostname of the host; maps to `address` directive in the host object
HOSTDISPLAYNAME	Description of the host; maps to `alias` directive in the host object
HOSTSTATE	Current state of the host (one of `UP`, `DOWN`, and `UNREACHABLE`)

Macro	Description
HOSTGROUPNAMES	Short names of all host groups a host belongs to, separated by commas
LASTHOSTCHECK	Date and time of last check of the host, in Unix timestamp for (number of seconds since 1970-01-01)
LASTHOSTSTATE	Last known state of the host (one of `UP`, `DOWN`, and `UNREACHABLE`)
SERVICEDESC	Description of the service; maps to the `description` directive in the service object
SERVICESTATE	Current state of the service (one of `OK`, `WARNING`, `UNKNOWN`, and `CRITICAL`)
SERVICEGROUPNAMES	Short names of all service groups a service belongs to, separated by commas
CONTACTNAME	Short, unique name of the contact; maps to the `contact_name` directive in the contact object
CONTACTALIAS	Description of the contact; maps to the `alias` directive in the contact object
CONTACTEMAIL	E-mail address of the contact; maps to the `email` directive in the contact object
CONTACTGROUPNAMES	Short names of all contact groups a contact belongs to, separated by commas

This table is not complete and only covers commonly used macro definitions. A complete list of available macros can be found in the Nagios documentation at `http://nagios.sourceforge.net/docs/3_0/macros.html`. Moreover, remember that all macro definitions need to be prefixed and suffixed with a `$` sign—for example, `$HOSTADDRESS$` maps to the `HOSTADDRESS` macro definition.

An additional functionality is the **on-demand macro definitions**. These are macros that are not defined, not exported as environment variables, but if found in a command definition, will be parsed and substituted accordingly. These macros accept one or more arguments inside the macro definition name, each passed after a colon. This is mainly used to read specific values not related to the current object. In order to read the contact email for user jdoe, regardless of who the current contact person is, the macro would be as follows: `$CONTACTEMAIL:jdoe$`, which means getting a `CONTACTEMAIL` macro definition in the context of the `jdoe` contact.

Nagios 3 also offers custom macro definitions. This works in a way that allows administrators to define additional attributes in each type of object, and the macro can then be used inside a command. This is used to store additional parameters related to an object—for example, you can store a MAC address in a host definition and use it in certain types of host checks.

It works in such a way that an object has a directive that starts with an underscore and is written in uppercase. It is referenced in one of the following ways, based on the object type it is defined in:

- `$_HOST<variable>$` - for directives defined within a host object
- `$_SERVICE<variable>$` - for directives defined within a service object
- `$_CONTACT<variable>$` - for directives defined within a contact object

A sample host definition that includes an additional directive with a MAC address would be as follows:

```
define host
{
  host_name     somemachine
  address       10.0.0.1
  _MAC          12:12:12:12:12:12
  check_command check-host-by-mac
}
```

and a corresponding `check` command that uses this attribute inside a check:

```
define command
{
  command_name  check-host-by-mac
  command_line  $USER1$/check_hostmac -H $HOSTADDRESS$ -m
  $_HOSTMAC$
}
```

Since Nagios 3, a majority of standard macro definitions are exported to check commands as environment variables. The environment variable names are the same as macros, but are prefixed with `NAGIOS_`—for example, `HOSTADDRESS` is passed as the `NAGIOS_HOSTADDRESS` variable. On-demand variables are not made available. For security reasons, the `$USERn$` variables are also not passed to commands as environment variables.

Configuring Hosts

Hosts are objects that describe machines that should be monitored—either physical hardware or virtual machines. A host consists of a short name, a descriptive name, and an IP address. The host also tells Nagios when and how the system should be monitored, as well as who should be contacted with regards to any problems related to this host. It also specifies how often the host should be checked, how retrying the checks should be handled, and how often should a notification about problems be sent out.

A sample definition of a host is as follows:

```
define host
{
  host_name                  linuxbox01
  hostgroups                 linuxservers
  alias                      Linux Server 01
  address                    10.0.2.1
  check_command              check-host-alive
  check_interval             5
  retry_interval             1
  max_check_attempts         5
  check_period               24x7
  contact_groups             linux-admins
  notification_interval      30
  notification_period        24x7
  notification_options       d,u,r
}
```

This defines a Linux box that will use the `check-host-alive` command to make sure the box is up and running. The test will be performed every five minutes, and after five failed tests, it will assume the host is down. If it is down, a notification will be sent out every 30 minutes.

The following is a table of common directives that can be used to describe hosts. Items in bold are required while specifying a host.

Option	Description
host_name	Short, unique name of the host
alias	Descriptive name of the host
address	IP address or fully qualified domain name of the host; it is recommended that you use an IP address as otherwise all tests will fail if the DNS servers are down
parents	List of all parent hosts that this host depends on, separated by commas; this is usually one or more switches and routers that this host is directly connected to
hostgroups	List of all host groups this host should be a member of, separated by commas
check_command	Short name of the command that should be used to test if the host is alive; if the command returns OK, the host is assumed to be UP; otherwise it is assumed to be down

Option	Description
check_interval	Specifies how often a check should be performed, minutes
retry_interval	Specifies how many minutes to wait before re-testing to see if the host is up
max_check_attempts	Specifies how many times a test needs to report that a host is down before it is assumed to be down by Nagios
check_period	Specifies the name of the time period that should be used to determine the times during which tests to see if the host is up should be performed
contacts	List of all contacts that should receive notifications related to host state changes, separated by commas; at least one contact or contact group needs to be specified for each host
contact_groups	List of all contact groups that should receive notifications related to host state changes, separated by comma; at least one contact or contact group needs to be specified for each host
first_notification_delay	Specifies the number of minutes to wait before first notification related to a host being down is sent out
notification_interval	Specifies the number of minutes to wait before each next notification related to a host being down is sent out
notification_period	Specifies the name of the time period during which notifications related to host states should be sent out
notification_options	Specifies which notification types for host states should be sent, separated by comma; there should be one or more of the following: d – host DOWN state u – host UNREACHABLE state r – host recovery (UP state) f – host starts and stops flapping s – notify when scheduled downtime starts or ends

For a complete list of accepted parameters, please consult the Nagios documentation at `http://nagios.sourceforge.net/docs/3_0/objectdefinitions.html#host`.

By default, Nagios assumes all host states to be up. If the `check_command` option is not specified for a host, then it will always be in the up state. When the command to perform host checks is specified, then the regularly-scheduled checks will take place and the host state will be monitored using the value of `check_interval` as the number of minutes between checks.

Nagios uses a soft and hard state logic to handle host states. Therefore, if a host state has changed from UP to DOWN since the last hard state, then Nagios assumes that the host is soft state DOWN and performs retries of the test, waiting `retry_interval` minutes between each test. Once if the result is the same after `max_check_attempts` re-tries, Nagios assumes that the DOWN state is a hard state. The same mechanisms apply for DOWN to UP transitions.

The host object `parents` directive is used to define the topology of the network. Usually, this directive points to a switch, router or any other device that is responsible for forwarding network packets. The host is assumed to be unreachable if the parent host is currently in a hard DOWN state. For example, if a router is down, then all machines accessed through it are considered unreachable and no tests will be performed on them.

If your network consists of servers connected via a switch and routers to a different network, then the parent for all of the servers in the local network, as well as the router, would be the switch. The parent of the router on the other side of the link would be the local router. The following diagram shows the actual network infrastructure and indicates how Nagios hosts should be configured in terms of parents for each element of the network:

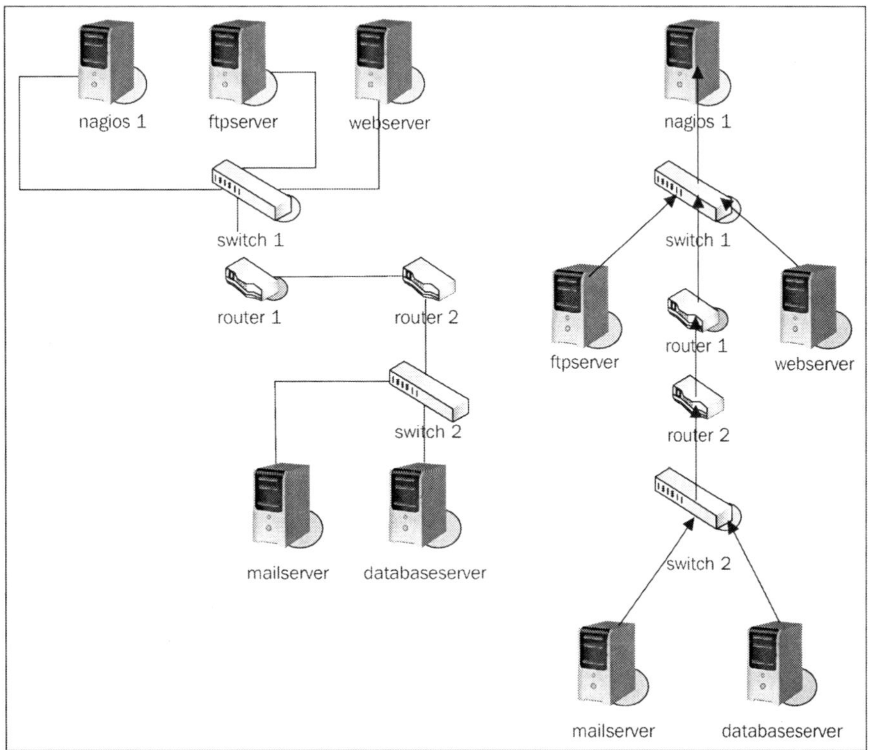

The actual network topology is shown on the left, and the parent hosts setup for the machines is shown on the right. Each arrow represents a mapping from a host to a parent host. There is no need to define a parent for hosts that are directly on the network with your Nagios server. So in this case, `switch1` should not have a parent host defined.

Even though some devices, such as switches, cannot be easily checked to see if they are down, it is still a good idea to describe them as a part of your topology. In this case, you might use a functionality such as scheduled downtime to keep track of when the device is going to be offline, or mark it as DOWN manually. This helps in determining other problems—Nagios will not scan hosts that have the router somewhere along the path that is currently scheduled for downtime. This way, you won't be flooded with notifications on actually unreachable hosts being down.

Check and notification periods specify the time periods during which checks for host state and notifications are to be performed. These can be specified so that different hosts can be monitored at different times.

It is also possible to create a setup where information that a host is down is kept, but nobody is notified about it. This can be done by specifying a `notification_period` that will tell Nagios when a notification should be sent out. No notifications will be sent out outside of this time period.

A typical example is a server that is only required during business hours and has a daily maintenance window between 10 PM and 4 AM. You can set up Nagios so as to not monitor host availability outside of business hours, or you can make Nagios monitor it, but without notifying that it is actually down. If monitoring is not done at all, Nagios will perform fewer operations during this period. In the second case, it is possible to gather statistics on how much of the maintenance window is used—which can be used to see if changes to the window need to be made.

Nagios allows the grouping of multiple hosts in order to effectively manage them. In order to do this, Nagios offers host group objects, which are a group of one or more machines. A host may be a member of more than one host group. Usually, grouping is done either by the type of machines or by the location they are in.

Each host group has a unique short name that specified along with a descriptive name, and one or more hosts that are members of this group.

Example host group definitions that define groups of hosts and a group that combines both groups, are given as follows:

```
define hostgroup
{
  hostgroup_name                linux-servers
  alias                         Linux servers
  members                       linuxbox1,linuxbox2
}

define hostgroup
{
  hostgroup_name                aix-servers
  alias                         AIX servers
  members                       aixbox1,aixbox2
}

define hostgroup
{
  hostgroup_name                unix-servers
  alias                         UNIX servers servers
  hostgroup_members             linux-servers,aix-servers
}
```

The following table shows the directives that can be used to describe host groups. Items in bold are required when specifying a host.

Option	Description
hostgroup_name	Short, unique name of the host group
alias	Descriptive name of the host group
members	List of all hosts that should be a member of this group, separated by commas
hostgroup_members	List of all other host groups whose members should also be members of this group, separated by commas

Host groups can also be used when defining services or dependencies. For example, it is possible to tell Nagios that all Linux servers should have their SSH service monitored and all AIX servers should have a telnet accepting connections.

It is also possible to define dependencies between hosts. They are, in a way, similar to a parent-host relationship, but dependencies offer more complex configuration options. Nagios will only issue host and service checks if all dependant hosts are currently up. More details on dependencies can be found in Chapter 5.

For the purpose of this book, we will define at least one host in our Nagios configuration directory structure.

To be able to monitor the local server that the Nagios installation is running on, we will need to add its definition into the `/etc/nagios/hosts/localhost.cfg` file as follows:

```
define host
{
  host_name                    localhost
  alias                        Localhost
  address                      127.0.0.1
  check_command                check-host-alive
  check_interval               5
  retry_interval               1
  max_check_attempts           5
  check_period                 24x7
  contact_groups               admins
  notification_interval        60
  notification_period          24x7
  notification_options         d,u,r
}
```

If you are planning to monitor other servers as well, you will want to add them—either in a single file, or multiple files.

Configuring Services

Services are objects that describe the functionality a particular host is offering. This can be virtually anything—network servers such as FTP, or resources such as storage space or CPU load.

A service is always tied to a host that it is running on. It is also identified by its description, which needs to be unique within a particular host. A service also defines when and how Nagios should check to see if it is running properly, and how to notify people responsible for this service, if it is not.

A short example of a web server that is defined on the `linuxbox01` machine created earlier is as follows:

```
define service
{
  host_name                    linuxbox01
  service_description          WWW
  check_command                check_http
  check_interval               10
  check_period                 24x7
```

```
    retry_interval                3
    max_check_attempts            3
    notification_interval         30
    notification_period           24x7
    notification_options          w,c,u,r
    contact_groups                linux-admins
}
```

This definition tells Nagios to check that the web server is working correctly every 10 minutes.

The following table shows the common directives that can be used to describe a service. Items in bold are required when specifying a service.

Option	Description
host_name	Short name of the host(s) that the service is running on, separated by comma
hostgroup_name	Short name of the host group(s) that the service is running on, separated by commas
service_description	Description of the service, used to uniquely identify a service running on a host
servicegroups	List of all service groups that this service should be a member of, separated by commas
check_command	Short name of the command that should be used to test if the service is running
check_interval	Specifies how often a check should be performed, in minutes
retry_interval	Specifies how many minutes to wait before re-testing whether the service is working
max_check_attempts	Specifies how many times a test needs to report that a service is down before it is assumed to be down by Nagios
check_period	Specifies the name of the time period that should be used to determine the times during which tests to see if the service is working should be performed
contacts	List of all contacts that should receive notifications related to service state changes, separated by commas; at least one contact or contact group needs to be specified for each service
contact_groups	List of all contacts groups that should receive notifications related to service state changes, separated by commas; at least one contact or contact group needs to be specified for each service

Option	Description
first_notification_ delay	Specifies the number of minutes before the first notification related to a service state change is sent out
notification_interval	Specifies the number of minutes before subsequent notifications related to a service not working correctly should be sent out
notification_period	Specifies the name of the time period during which notifications related to service states should be sent out
notification_options	Specifies which notification types for service states should be sent, separated by commas; these can be one or more of the following: w—service WARNING state u—service UNKNOWN state c—service CRITICAL state r—service recovery (back to OK) state f—host starts and stops flapping s—notify when scheduled downtime starts or ends

For a complete list of accepted parameters, refer to the Nagios documentation at `http://nagios.sourceforge.net/docs/3_0/objectdefinitions.html#host`

Very often, the same service is offered by more than one host. In such cases, it is possible to specify a service that will be provided by multiple machines, or even specify host groups for which all hosts will be checked. It is also possible to specify the hosts for which checks will not be performed—for example, if a service is present on all hosts in a group except for a specific box. To do that, an exclamation mark needs to be added before a host name or a host group name.

For example, to tell Nagios that SSSH should be checked on all Linux servers shown except for `linux01`, as well as on the `aix01` machine, a service definition similar to the one shown here can be created:

```
define service
{
  hostgroup_name              linux-servers
  host_name                   !linux01,aix01
  service_description         SSH
  check_command               check_ssh
  check_interval              10
  check_period                24x7
  retry_interval              2
  max_check_attempts          3
  notification_interval       30
  notification_period         24x7
  notification_options        w,c,r
  contact_groups              linux-admins
}
```

Services can be grouped in a similar way to host objects. This can be done to manage services more conveniently. It also aids in viewing service reports on the Nagios web interface. Service groups are also used to configure dependencies in a more convenient way.

The following table describes the attributes that can be used to define a group. Items in bold are required when specifying a service group.

Option	Description
servicegroup_name	Short, unique name of the service group
alias	Descriptive name of the service group
members	List of all hosts and services that should be a member of this group, separated by commas; see description below
servicegroup_members	List of all other service groups whose members should also be members of this group, separated by commas

The format of the `members` directive of a service group object is one or more `<host>,<service>` pairs.

An example of a service group is shown here:

```
define servicegroup
{
  servicegroup_name  databaseservices
  alias              All services related to databases
  members            linux01,mysql,linux01,pgsql,aix01,db2
}
```

This service group consists of the `mysql` and `pgsql` services on the `linux01` host and `db2` on the `aix01` machine. It is uniquely identified by its name, `databaseservices`.

It is also possible to specify groups that a service should be member of inside the service definition itself. This can be achieved by specifying all groups that this service should be a member of. To do this, add a list of all groups in the `servicegroups` directive in the service definition.

Services may be configured to be dependant on one another, similar to how hosts can. In this case, Nagios will only perform checks on a service if all dependant services are working correctly. More details on dependencies can be found in Chapter 5, *Advanced Configuration*.

Nagios requires that at least one service is defined for every host, and requires that at least one service is defined for it to run. That is why we will now create a sample service in our configuration directory structure. For this purpose, we will monitor the secure shell protocol.

In order to check if the SSH server is running on the Nagios installation, we will need to add its definition into the `/etc/nagios/hosts/localhost.cfg` file:

```
define service
{
  host_name                    localhost
  service_description          ssh
  check_command                check_ssh
  check_interval               5
  retry_interval               1
  max_check_attempts           3
  check_period                 24x7
  contact_groups               admins
  notification_interval        60
  notification_period          24x7
  notification_options         w,c,u,r
}
```

If you are planning on monitoring other services as well, you will want to add them to the same file.

Configuring Commands

Command definitions describe how host/service checks should be done. They can also define how notifications about problems or event handlers should work. A command definition has two parameters—name and command line. The first parameter is a name that is then used for defining checks and notifications. The second parameter is an actual command that will be run, along with all required parameters for the command.

Commands are used by hosts and services. They define what system command to execute when making sure a host or service is working properly. A check command is identified by its unique name.

When used with other object definitions, it can also have additional arguments, and uses an exclamation mark as a delimiter. The commands with parameters have the following syntax: `command_name[!arg1][!arg2][!arg3][...]`.

A command name is often the same as the plugin that it runs, but it can be different. The command line includes macro definitions (such as $HOSTADDRESS$). Check commands also use macros, $ARG1$, $ARG2$ … $ARG32$, if the check command for the host or service pass additional arguments.

The following is an example that defines a command for trying to ping a host to make sure it is working properly. It does not use any arguments.

```
define command
{
  command_name  check-host-alive
  command_line  $USER1$/check_ping -H $HOSTADDRESS$
                -w 3000.0,80% -c 5000.0,100% -p 5
}
```

and a very short host definition that would use this check command, could be similar to the one shown here:

```
define host
{
  host_name     somemachine
  address       10.0.0.1
  check_command check-host-alive
}
```

Such a check is usually done as part of the host checks. This allows Nagios to make sure that a machine is working properly if it responds to ICMP requests.

Commands allow the passing of arguments as it offers a more flexible way of defining checks. Therefore, a definition accepting parameters would be as follows:

```
define command
{
  command_name  check-host-alive-limits
  command_line  $USER1$/check_ping -H $HOSTADDRESS$
                -w $ARG1$ -c $ARG2$ -p 5
}
```

and the corresponding host definition would be:

```
define host
{
  host_name     othermachine
  address       10.0.0.2
  check_command check-host-alive-limits!3000.0,80%!5000.0,100%
}
```

Another example is setting up a check command for a previously-defined service:

```
define command
{
  command_name  check_http
  command_line  $USER1$/check_http -H $HOSTADDRESS$
}
```

This check can then be used when defining a service to be monitored by Nagios. Chapter 4, *Overview of Nagios Plugins*, covers standard Nagios plugins along with sample command definitions. Sample Nagios configurations are also included in sources and installed by the `make-config` target.

Configuring Time Periods

Time periods are definitions of dates and times during which an action should be performed or specified people should be notified. They describe date and time ranges, and can be re-used across various operations.

A time period definition includes a name that uniquely identifies it in Nagios. It also contains a description, and one or more days or dates along with time spans.

A typical example of a time period would be working hours, which defines that a valid time to perform an action is from Monday to Friday during business hours. Another definition of a time period can be weekends, which means Saturday and Sunday, all day long.

The following is a sample time period for working hours:

```
define timeperiod
{
  timeperiod_name  workinghours
  alias            Working Hours, from Monday to Friday
  monday           09:00-17:00
  tuesday          09:00-17:00
  wednesday        09:00-17:00
  thursday         09:00-17:00
  friday           09:00-17:00
}
```

This particular example tells Nagios that the acceptable time to perform something is from Monday to Friday between 9 AM and 5 PM. Each entry in a time period contains information on a date or weekday. It also contains a range of hours. Nagios first checks if the current date matches any of the dates specified. If it does, then it checks if the current time matches the time ranges specified for the date.

There are multiple ways of specifying a date. Depending on what type of date it is, one definition might take precedence over another. For example, a definition for December 24th is more important than a generic definition that every weekday an action should be performed between 9 AM and 5 PM.

Possible date types are mentioned here:

- **Calendar date**: For example, `2009-11-01`, which means November 1st, year 2009, (Nagios accepts dates in the format YYYY-MM-DD)
- **Date recurring every year**: For example, `july 4`, which means 4th of July every year
- **Specific day within a month**: For example, `day 14`, which means the 14 th of every month
- **Specific weekday, along with an offset in a month**: For example, `monday 1 september`, which means the first Monday in September; `monday -1 may` would mean the last Monday in May
- **Specific weekday in all months**: For example, `monday 1`, which means the 1st Monday of every month
- **Weekday**: For example, `monday`, which means every Monday

The above list shows all date types in the order at which Nagios ranks them in terms of importance. This means that a date recurring every year will always be used in preference to an entry describing what should be done every Monday.

In order to be able to correctly configure all objects, we will now create some standard time periods that will be used in configuration. The following example periods will be used in the remaining sections of this chapter, and it is recommended that you put them in the `/etc/nagios/timeperiods/default.cfg` file:

```
define timeperiod
{
  timeperiod_name  workinghours
  alias            Working Hours, from Monday to Friday
  monday           09:00-17:00
  tuesday          09:00-17:00
  wednesday        09:00-17:00
  thursday         09:00-17:00
  friday           09:00-17:00
}

define timeperiod
{
  timeperiod_name  weekends
  alias            Weekends all day long
  saturday         00:00-24:00
  sunday           00:00-24:00
}
```

```
define timeperiod
{
  timeperiod_name  24x7
  alias            24 hours a day 7 days a week
  monday           00:00-24:00
  tuesday          00:00-24:00
  wednesday        00:00-24:00
  thursday         00:00-24:00
  friday           00:00-24:00
  saturday         00:00-24:00
  sunday           00:00-24:00
}
```

The last time period is also used by the `www` service for `linuxbox01` host, defined earlier. This way, the web server will be monitored all the time.

Configuring Contacts

Contacts define people who can either be owners of specific machines, or people who should be contacted in case of problems. Depending on how your organization chooses to contact people in case of problems, the definition of a contact may vary a lot. A contact consists of a unique name, a descriptive name, and one or more email addresses and/or pager numbers. Contact definitions can also contain additional data specific to how a person can be contacted.

A basic contact definition is shown here, and specifies the unique contact name, an alias, and contact information. It also specifies the event types that the person should receive and time periods during which notifications should be sent.

```
define contact
{
  contact_name                   jdoe
  alias                          John Doe
  email                          john.doe@yourcompany.com
  host_notification_period       workinghours
  service_notification_period    workinghours
  host_notification_options      d,u,r
  service_notification_options   w,u,c,r
  host_notification_commands     host-notify-by-email
  service_notification_commands  notify-by-email
}
```

The following table describes all available directives when defining a contact. Items in bold are required when specifying a contact.

Option	Description
contact_name	Short, unique name of the contact
alias	Descriptive name of the contact; usually this is the full name of the person
contactgroups	List of all contact groups this user should be a member of, separated by commas
host_notifications_enabled	Specifies whether this person should receive notifications regarding host state
host_notification_period	Specifies the name of the time period that should be used to determine times during which the person should receive notifications regarding the host state
host_notification_commands	Specifies one or more commands that should be used to notify the person of a host state, separated by commas
host_notification_options	Specifies host states that the user should be notified about, separated by commas; this can be one or more of the following: d - host DOWN state u - host UNREACHABLE state r - host recovery (UP state) f - host starts and stops flapping s - notify when scheduled downtime starts or ends
service_notifications_enabled	Specifies whether this person should receive notifications regarding the service state
service_notification_period	Specifies name of the time period that should be used to determine the times during which a person should receive notifications regarding the service state

Option	Description
service_notification_commands	Specifies one or more commands that should be used to notify the person of a service state, separated by commas
service_notification_options	Specifies the service states that the user should be notified about, separated by commas; this can be one or more of the following: w—service WARNING state u—service UNKNOWN state c—service CRITICAL state r—service recovery (OK state) f—service starts and stops flapping n—person will not receive any service notifications
email	Specifies the email address of the contact
pager	Specifies the pager number of the contact; this can also be an email to the pager gateway
address1 ... address6	An additional six addresses that can be specified for the contact; these can be anything, based on how the notification commands will use these fields
can_submit_commands	Specifies whether the user is allowed to execute commands via the Nagios web interface
retain_status_information	Specifies whether status-related information about this person is retained across restarts
retain_nonstatus_information	Specifies whether non-status information about this person is retained across restarts

Contacts are also mapped to users that log into the Nagios web interface. This means that all operations performed via the interface will be logged as having been executed by that particular user and the web interface will use access granted to particular contact objects when evaluating whether an operation should be allowed or not. The `contact_name` field from a contact object maps to the user name in the Nagios web interface.

Contacts can be grouped. Usually, grouping is used to keep a list of which users are responsible for which tasks, and the group maps to job responsibilities for particular people. It also makes it possible to define people who should be responsible for handling problems at specific time periods, and Nagios will automatically contact the right people depending on the time at which a problem has occurred.

A sample definition of a contact group is as follows:

```
define contactgroup
{
  contactgroup_name              linux-admins
  alias                          Linux Administrators
  members                        jdoe,asmith
}
```

This group is also used when defining the `linuxbox01` and `www` service contacts. This means that both `jdoe` and `asmith` will receive information on the status of this host and service.

The following is a complete list of directives that can be used to describe contact groups. Items in bold are required while specifying a contact group.

Option	Description
contactgroup_name	Short, unique name of the contact group
alias	Descriptive name of the contact group
members	List of all contacts that should be a member of this group, separated by commas
contactgroup_members	List of all other contact groups whose members should also be members of this group, separated by commas

Members of a contact group can be specified either in the contact group definition or by using the `contactgroups` directive in a contact definition. It is also possible to combine both methods—some of the members can be specified in the contact group definition, and others can be specified in their contact object definition z`.

Contacts are used to specify who should be contacted if the status of one or more hosts or services changes. Nagios accepts both contacts and contact groups in its object definitions. This allows making either specific people or entire groups responsible for particular machines or services.

It is also possible to specify different people or groups for handling host-related and service-related problems—for example, hardware administrators for handling host problems and system administrators for handling service issues.

In order to function properly, we need to create at least one contact that will be used by Nagios, and put this definition in the `/etc/nagios/contacts/nagiosadmin.cfg` file:

```
define contact
{
  contact_name                   nagiosadmin
  contactgroups                  admins
  alias                          Nagios administrator
  email                          administrator@yourcompany.com
  host_notification_period       workinghours
  service_notification_period    workinghours
  host_notification_options      d,u,r
  service_notification_options   w,u,c,r
  host_notification_commands     host-notify-by-email
  service_notification_commands  notify-by-email
}
```

We also need to define the `admins` group in the `/etc/nagios/contacts/groups.cfg` file:

```
define contactgroup
{
  contactgroup_name              admins
  alias                          System administrators
}
```

If you are not very familiar with Nagios, it is recommended that you leave the contact's name as `nagiosadmin`, as this will also be the user for all web interface operations.

Templates and Object Inheritance

In order to allow the flexible configuration of machines, Nagios offers a powerful inheritance engine. The main concept is that administrators can set up templates that define common parameters, and re-use these templates in actual host or service definitions. The mechanism even offers the possibility to create templates that inherit parameters from other templates.

This mechanism works in a way where templates are plain Nagios objects that specify the `register` directive and set it to `0`. This means that they will not be registered as an actual host or service to monitor. Objects that inherit parameters from a template or another host should have a `use` directive pointing to the short name of the template object they are using.

When defining a template, its name is always specified using the `name` directive. This is slightly different to how typical hosts and services are registered, as they require the `host_name` and/or `service_description` parameters.

Inheritance can be used to define a template for basic host checks, with only basic parameters such as IP address being defined for each particular host. For example:

```
define host
{
  name                          generic-server
  check_command                 check-host-alive
  check_interval                5
  retry_interval                1
  max_check_attempts            5
  check_period                  24x7
  notification_interval         30
  notification_period           24x7
  notification_options          d,u,r
  register                      0
}

define host
{
  use                           generic-server
  name                          linuxbox01
  alias                         Linux Server 01
  address                       10.0.2.1
  contact_groups                linux-admins
}
```

Version 3 of Nagios also introduces inheriting from multiple templates. To do this, simply put multiple names in the `use` directive, separated by commas. This allows the host to use several templates, which define parts or all directives. In case multiple templates specify the same parameters, the value from the first template specifying it will be used. For example:

```
define service
{
  name                          generic-service
  check_interval                10
  retry_interval                2
  max_check_attempts            3
  check_period                  24x7
  register                      0
}
```

```
define service
{
  host_name                 workinghours-service
  check_period              workinghours
  notification_interval     30
  notification_period       workinghours
  notification_options      w,c,u,r
  register                  0
}

define service
{
  use                       workinghours-service,generic-service
  contact_groups            linux-admins
  host_name                 linuxbox01
  service_description       SSH
  check_command             check_ssh
}
```

In this case, values from both templates will be used. The value of `workinghours` will be used for the `check_period` directive as this directive was first specified in the `workinghours-service` template. Changing the order in the use directive to `generic-service,workinghours-service` would cause value of the `check_period` parameter to be `24x7`.

Nagios also accepts creating multiple levels of templates. For example, you can set up a generic service template, and inherit it to create additional templates for various types of checks such as local services, resource sensitive checks, and templates for passive-only checks.

Let's consider the following objects and template structures:

```
define host
{
    host_name       linuxserver1
    use             generic-linux,template-chicago
    .....
}

define host
{
    register        0
    name            generic-linux
    use             generic-server
    .....
}
```

```
define host
{
    register        0
    name            generic-server
    use             generic-host
    .....
}

define host
{
    register        0
    name            template-chicago
    use             contacts-chicago,misc-chicago
    .....
}
```

The following illustration shows how Nagios will search for values for all directives.

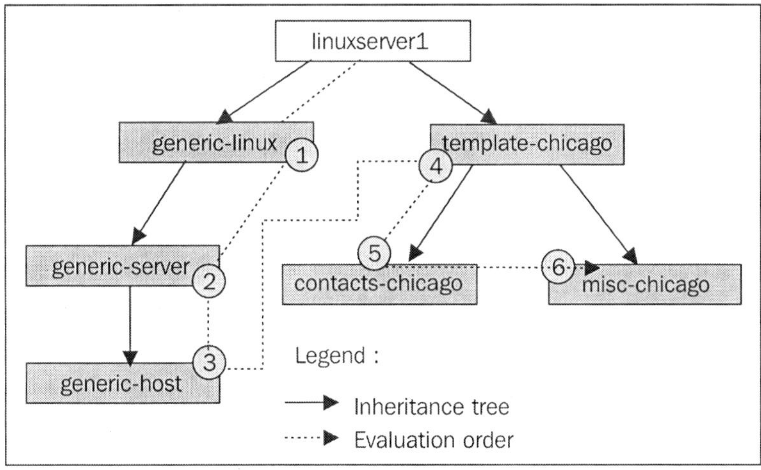

When looking for parameters, Nagios will first look for the value in the `linuxserver1` object definition. Next, it will use the following templates, in this order: `generic-linux`, `generic-server`, `generic-host`, `template-chicago`, `contacts-chicago`, and `misc-chicago` in the end.

It is also possible to set up host or service dependencies that will be inherited from a template. In this case, the dependant hosts or services can't be templates themselves, and need to be registered as objects that will be monitored by the Nagios daemon.

Introduction to Notifications

Notifications are the way by which Nagios lets people know that something is either wrong or has returned to the normal way of operations. They are not objects on their own, but provide very important functionality in Nagios. Configuring notifications correctly might seem a bit tricky in the beginning.

When and how notifications are sent out is configured as part of contact configuration. Each contact has configuration directives on when notifications can be sent out, and how he or she should be contacted. Contacts also contain information about contact details—telephone number, email address, Jabber/MSN address, and so on. Each host and service is configured for when the information about it should be sent, and who should be contacted. Nagios then combines all of this information in order to notify people of the changes in status.

Notifications may be sent out in one of the following situations:

1. The host has changed its state to `DOWN` or `UNREACHABLE` state; notification is sent out after `first_notification_delay` number of minutes specified in the corresponding host object
2. The host remains in `DOWN` or `UNREACHABLE` state; notification is sent out every `notification_interval` number of minutes specified in the corresponding host object
3. Host recovers to an `UP` state; notification is sent out immediately and only once
4. Host starts or stops flapping; notification is sent out immediately
5. Host remains flapping; notification is sent out every `notification_interval` number of minutes specified in the corresponding host object
6. Service has changed its state to `WARNING`, `CRITICAL` or `UNKNOWN` state; notification is sent out after `first_notification_delay` number of minutes specified in the corresponding service object
7. Service remains in `WARNING`, `CRITICAL` or `UNKNOWN` state; notification is sent out every `notification_interval` number of minutes specified in the corresponding service object
8. Service recovers to an `OK` state; notification is sent out immediately and only once
9. Service starts or stops flapping; notification is sent out immediately
10. Service remains flapping; notification is sent out every `notification_interval` number of minutes specified in the corresponding service object

If one of these conditions occurs, Nagios starts evaluating whether information about it should be sent out and to whom.

First of all, the current date and time is checked against the notification time period. The time period is taken from the `notification_timeperiod` field from the current host or service definition. Only if the time period includes current time, will the notification be sent out.

Next, a list of users based on the `contacts` and `contact_groups` fields is created. A complete list of users is made based on all members of all groups, and included groups, as well as all the contacts directly bound to the current host or service.

Each of the matched users is checked to see whether he or she should be notified about the current event. In this case, each user's time period is also checked to see if it includes the current date and time. The directive `host_notification_period` or `service_notification_period` is used depending on whether the notification is for the host or the service.

For host notifications,the `host_notification_options` directive for each contact is also used to determine whether that particular person should be contacted—for example, different users might be contacted about an unreachable host than those contacted if the host is actually down. For service notifications, the `service_notification_options` parameter is used to check every user if he or she should be notified about this issue. The section on hosts and services configuration describes what values these directives take.

If all of these criteria have been met, Nagios will send a notification to this user. It will now use commands specified in the `host_notification_commands` and `service_notification_commands` directives.

It is possible to specify multiple commands that will be used for notifications. So it is possible to set up Nagios such that it sends both an email as well as a message on an instant messaging system.

Nagios also offers escalations that allow emails to be sent to other people when a problem remains unresolved for too long. This can be used to propagate problems to higher management, or to teams that might be affected by unresolved problems. It is a very powerful mechanism and is split between host- and service-based escalations. This functionality is described in more detail in Chapter 6, *Notifications and Events*.

Summary

Our Nagios setup is now complete and is ready to be started! We took the road from source code into a working application. We have also configured it so that it monitors the machine it is running on from scratch, and it took very little time and effort to do so.

Our Nagios installation now uses three directories—`/opt/nagios` for binaries, `/etc/nagios` for configuration, and `/var/nagios` for storing data. All object definitions are stored in a categorized way as the subdirectories `/etc/nagios`. This allows much easier management of Nagios objects.

We have configured the server that Nagios is running on, to be monitored. You might want to add more servers just to see how they works.

We told Nagios to monitor only the SSH server. But in all proability, you will also want to monitor other things such as a web server or email.

Chapter 4, *Overview of Nagios Plugins*, will help when it comes to setting up various types of checks. Make sure to read the `/etc/nagios/commands/default.cfg` file to see what commands Nagios already came configured with. Sometimes, it will also be needed to set up your own check commands—either custom scripts, or using Nagios plugins in a different way from the default command set.

You would also want to set up other users if you are working as part of a larger team. It will definitely help everyone in your team if you tell Nagios who is taking care of which parts of the infrastructure!

All that should be a good start for making sure everything works fine in your company. Of course, configuring Nagios for your needs might take a lot of time, but starting with monitoring just the essentials is a good thing. You will learn how it works and increase the number of monitorables over time.

The next step is to set up the web interface so that you will be able to see things from your favorite browser or even put on your desktop. The next chapter provides the essential information on how to install, configure, and use it.

3
Using the Nagios Web Interface

Your Nagios system is now up and running. It will also send out notifications to people if something goes wrong. What we need now, is a way to be able to view current and historical information on which hosts and services are failing. Nagios offers just that! It comes with a web interface that can be used to view the status of all hosts and services, read logs, and generate reports. And that is just a small part of its functionality.

Using any browser, you can access almost any information Nagios keeps—statuses, performance data, history, and logs. With just a few clicks, you can check if all of your hosts and services are working correctly. The interface also offers the ability to change parts of a configuration on the fly. This means that you can, for example, disable host or service checks in just a few clicks. Nagios web pages are usually password protected. In many cases, they are also only accessible from within a trusted IP address—for example, only from the Intranet or a company VPN.

The ability to check the status of all hosts and services is a very valuable functionality. Usually, a notification that something is wrong should just be a trigger to investigate the problem. Being able to see the big picture via various views of the web interface is very useful. You can use different detailed views and see what is not working properly. Quick access to such information from all monitored machines in your network is a blessing in case of any problems. You can clearly see which hosts and services are working as they should, and which ones aren't.

Nagios can also show you a tree of your infrastructure that includes parent host mappings. This is a great way to see which machines are down, and which are assumed to be unreachable. In larger systems, where there are a lot of dependencies, being able to see this clearly is very useful.

The web interface also uses Nagios object structure to handle access rights. Nagios web interface is commonly configured in such a way that there is a single user who has access to all information. It is also possible to set up additional users based on actual contact names. These users will have access to only the hosts and services for which they are the people to be contacted. This way, the administrator of specific machines or host groups can log into the site and see only what he or she is authorized to see.

Setting up the Web Interface

The Nagios web interface is part of the main Nagios sources and binary distributions. Therefore, if you installed Nagios, you also have the web interface files.
The only thing you need now is a web server—in our case, it will be Apache 2 (visit `http://httpd.apache.org/`).

The web interface uses CGI mechanisms to work, as this is the most-commonly offered way to run applications. It also allows a more flexible set-up in terms of security as CGI binaries can be run as a different user than the one the web server is running as. It also uses additional files such as many static HTML pages, CSS, and images.

As described in the previous chapter, Nagios CGI scripts need to be able to write to the Nagios external command pipe. If you have followed the installation instructions provided in Chapter 2, *Installation and Configuration*, your Apache server already has the correct access rights. If you set up Nagios on your own, you need to make sure your web server can write to the Nagios pipe. Please check your external command pipe permissions and make sure—for our installation parameters—that the file is called `/var/nagios/rw/nagios.cmd`, and it is writable by the `nagioscmd` group. It needs to be writable by the user your web server is running as; so, it is best to add your web server user to a group owning the file.

Configuring the Web Server

By default, all Nagios HTML and other static files that are used by the web interface are copied into the `share` subdirectory of the Nagios installation, and all CGI binaries go into the `sbin` subdirectory. Assuming that Nagios has been configured using the default directories used in the previous chapter, these would be `/opt/nagios/share` and `/opt/nagios/sbin` respectively.

If you installed Nagios from a binary distribution, it might have configured the web server so that it is accessible. In that case, the package management should have asked you for a password to access the Nagios Web interface. You should start by trying to access `http://127.0.0.1/nagios/` from the machine that has Nagios installed. It should prompt you for a username and password. The main Nagios administrator is called `nagiosadmin`, and the password will be the one you supplied during the package installation. In such a case, you should skip this section and proceed to the next ones that describe how Nagios's web interface works.

If you have followed the steps in the previous chapter to install Nagios, then all that's needed is to configure Apache to use proper aliasing and to create a valid user that will be able to access Nagios.

The following instructions assume that your Apache configuration is under `/etc/apache2`, and that your web server will read all configuration files under `/etc/apache2/conf.d`. If your paths are different, please modify them in the following examples, accordingly.

The first thing that we will do is create a configuration file called `/etc/apache2/conf.d/nagios`.

We will need to add an alias to the `/nagios` URL that will point to `/opt/nagios/share` and the CGI scripts under `/nagios/cgi-bin` URL to `/opt/nagios/sbin`, as follows:

```
ScriptAlias /nagios/cgi-bin /opt/nagios/sbin
Alias /nagios /opt/nagios/share
```

Next, we need to set up password protection for the Nagios web interface. We can also limit IP addresses from being able to access the site. To do this, add the following directives to the `/etc/apache2/conf.d/nagios` file:

```
<DirectoryMatch /opt/nagios/share>
        Options FollowSymLinks
        AllowOverride AuthConfig
        Order Allow,Deny
        Allow From All
        AuthName "Nagios Access"
        AuthType Basic
        AuthUserFile /etc/nagios/htpasswd.users
        AuthGroupFile /etc/nagios/htpasswd.groups
        require valid-user
</DirectoryMatch>
```

```
<DirectoryMatch /opt/nagios/sbin>
        Options ExecCGI
        AllowOverride AuthConfig
        Order Allow,Deny
        Allow From All
        AuthName "Nagios Access"
        AuthType Basic
        AuthUserFile /etc/nagios/htpasswd.users
        AuthGroupFile /etc/nagios/htpasswd.groups
        require valid-user
</DirectoryMatch>
```

If you want to limit the hosts that will be able to access the Nagios web interface, you can replace the `Order` and `Allow` directives in both of the `DirectoryMatch` definitions as follows:

```
Order Deny,Allow
Deny From All
Allow From 192.168.0.0/16
```

This will only allow access to the Nagios web site from IP addresses starting with `192.168`.

The final step is to create the files that will be used for authorization.

We will need to run the following commands to set these up:

```
# cp /dev/null /etc/nagios/htpasswd.groups
# htpasswd -bc /etc/nagios/htpasswd.users nagiosadmin yourpassword
Adding password for user nagiosadmin
```

Make sure you replace `yourpassword` with the actual password you want to use.

The last thing that needs to be done is to restart Apache by invoking:

```
/etc/init.d/apache restart
```

On some operating systems, such as RedHat Linux, this script might be called `/etc/rc.d/init.d/httpd` or `/etc/init.d/httpd`.

Accessing the Web Interface

After restarting the web server, we can now access Nagios Web interface by going to URL `http://127.0.0.1/nagios/` from that machine. This will prompt for a username and password—these are the ones used in the example above. After a successful login, you should see a welcome screen similar to the following one:

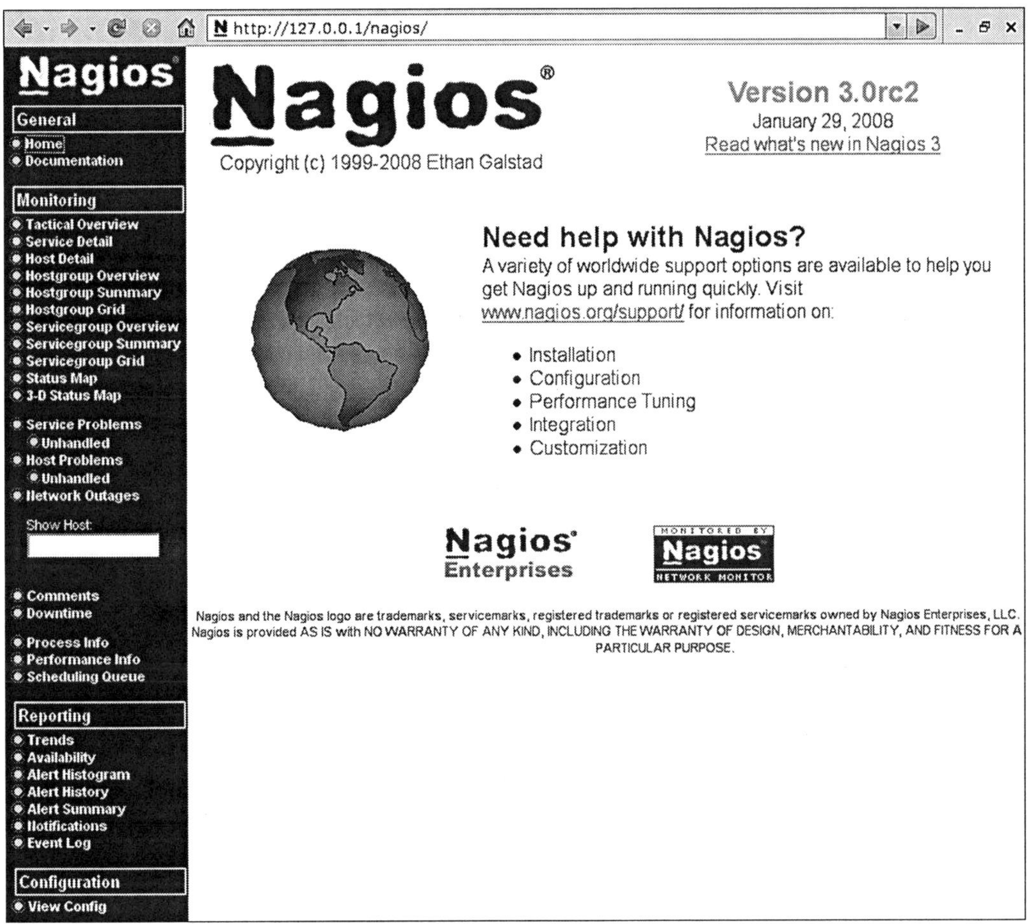

Troubleshooting

There might be cases where accessing the Nagios URL shows an error instead of the welcome screen. If this happens, it can be due to various reasons, for example, because the web server has not started, or the Nagios related configuration setup is incorrect, or permissions on the Nagios directories are incorrect.

The first thing that we should check is whether Apache is working properly. We can manually run the `check_http` plugin from Nagios. If the web server is up and running, we should see something similar to what is shown here:

```
# /opt/nagios/plugins/check_http -H 127.0.0.1
HTTP OK HTTP/1.1 200 OK - 296 bytes in 0.006 seconds
```

and if Apache is not running currently, the plugin will report an error similar to the following one:

```
# /opt/nagios/plugins/check_http -H 127.0.0.1
HTTP CRITICAL - Unable to open TCP socket
```

If it was stopped, start it by running `/etc/init.d/apache2 start`.

The next step is to check whether the `http://127.0.0.1/nagios/` URL is working properly. We can also use the same plugin for this. The `-u` argument can specify the exact link to access, and `-a` allows you to specify the username and password to be authorized. It is passed in the form of `<username>:<password>`.

```
# /opt/nagios/plugins/check_http -H 127.0.0.1 \
    -u /nagios/ -a nagiosadmin:<yourpassword>
HTTP OK HTTP/1.1 200 OK - 979 bytes in 0.019 seconds
```

We can also check the actual CGI scripts by passing a URL to one of the scripts:

```
# /opt/nagios/plugins/check_http -H 127.0.0.1 \
    -u /nagios/cgi-bin/tac.cgi -a nagiosadmin:<yourpassword>
HTTP OK HTTP/1.1 200 OK - 979 bytes in 0.019 seconds
```

If any of these checks return any HTTP code other than 200, it means that this is the problem.

If the code is 500, it means that Apache is not configured correctly. In such cases, the Apache error log contains useful information about any potential problems. On most systems, including Ubuntu Linux, the file name of the log is `/var/log/apache2/error.log`. An example entry in the error log could be:

```
[error] [client 127.0.0.1] need AuthName: /nagios/cgi-bin/tac.cgi
```

In this particular case, the problem is the missing `AuthName` directive for CGI scripts.

Internal errors can usually be resolved by making sure that the Nagios-related Apache configuration is correct. If you followed the installation steps from this chapter and the previous one, Apache configuration should be exactly the same as in the examples above.

If this does not help, it is worth checking other parts of the configuration, especially the ones related to virtual hosts and CGI configuration. Commenting out parts of the configuration can help in determining which parts of the configuration are causing problems.

Another possibility is that either the check for /nagios/ or the check for the /nagios/cgi-bin/tac.cgi URL returned code 404. This code means that the page was not found. In this case, please make sure that Apache is configured according to the previous steps.

If it is, then it's a good idea to enable more verbose debugging to a custom file. The following Apache 2 directives can be added either to /etc/apache2/conf.d/nagios or to any other file in Apache configuration:

```
LogFormat "%h %l %u \"%r\" %>s %b %{Host}e %f" debuglog
CustomLog /var/log/apache2/access-debug.log debuglog
```

The first entry defines a custom logging format that also logs exact paths to files. The second one enables logging with this format to a dedicated file. An example entry in such a log would be:

```
127.0.0.1 - - "GET /nagios/ HTTP/1.1" 404 481 127.0.0.1 /var/www/
nagios
```

This log entry tells us that http://127.0.0.1/nagios/ was incorrectly expanded to the /var/www/nagios directory. In this case, the Alias directive describing the /nagios/ prefix is missing. Making sure that actual configuration matches the one provided in the previous section will also resolve this issue.

Another error that you can get is 403, which indicates that Apache was unable to access either CGI scripts in /opt/nagios/sbin, or Nagios static pages in /opt/nagios/share. In this case, you need to make sure that these directories are readable by the user Apache is running as.

The error might also be related to the directories above— /opt/nagios or /opt. One of these might also be inaccessible to the user Apache is running as, which will also cause the same error to occur.

If you run into any other problems, it is best to start with making sure that Nagios related configuration matches the examples from the previous section. It is also a good idea to reduce the number of enabled features and virtual hosts in your Apache configuration.

Using the Web Interface

Nagios Web interface always offers a menu in the left frame, while current information is shown in the remaining area. You can easily access all views from the left-side menu.

In case you want to replace the standard Nagios welcome screen with your own, all you need to do is change the `/opt/nagios/share/main.html` file. As this page is shown to everyone after they log in correctly, it can be used to provide administrators with some guidelines on how Nagios monitoring is used within your company, and what should be done in certain circumstances. It can also be used to define links to commonly-checked hosts and commonly-accessed services.

It is also possible to extend the left side menu, which is defined in the `/opt/nagios/share/side.html` file. This way, quick links can be added to the menu and/or unused functionality can be removed from it.

Henceforth in this chapter, we will use configuration that is far more complex than the one we created in the previous chapter. This will allow us to see more functionality in Nagios and its web interface.

Tactical Overview

Nagios offers a panel that shows the overall status of all of the hosts, services and other features. It can be accessed by clicking on the **Tactical Overview** link in the left-side menu. You can use this page to assess number of hosts and services failing, flapping and pending checks. It also shows how many hosts are unreachable due to other hosts being down.

The following is a screenshot of the **Tactical Overview** page:

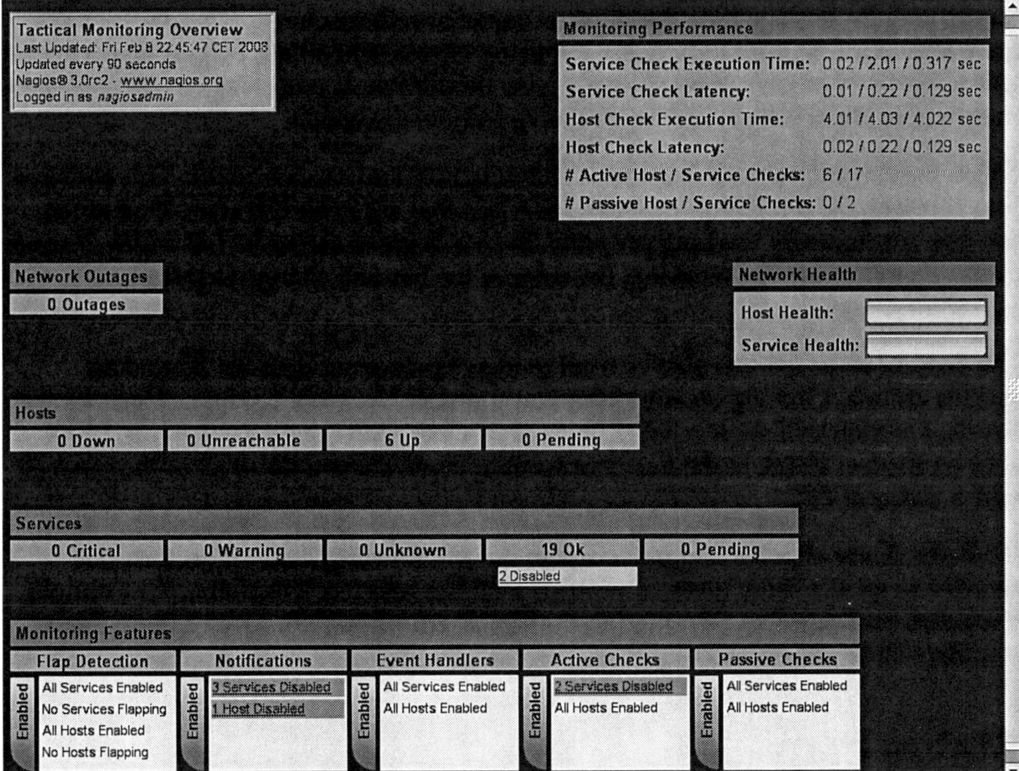

The tactical Overview presents overall information on Nagios and its monitoring. The page provides information about host and service conditions. It shows how many hosts and services are in which status. It also shows if any hosts or services have their checks, notifications, or event handlers disabled.

Performance information is shown in the top right-hand corner. This shows details of the checks that have been performed. It also reports latency while performing the checks and the average time that it takes to perform these checks. These values are quite important because if there are too many checks scheduled, Nagios might not be able to perform some of them. Usually, you should tweak your Nagios installation in cases where latency is getting larger than a couple of seconds.

Following this information is a status showing host and service health. This contains bars showing the number of hosts and services that are in an **OK** state. If all of the services are currently working properly, the bar is green across its full width. If some hosts or services are not working, the color of the bar will change to yellow or red, accordingly.

The Tactical overview can also be used to view hosts or services list filtered on specific criteria. Clicking on any status count text in **Network Outages**, **Hosts** or the **Services** section will show a list of hosts or services with the selected status. If we click on the text **19 Ok** in the **Services** section, it will show a list of all of the services with a status of OK.

Similarly, if any object is flagged as red in the **Monitoring Features** section, it is possible to go to a list of hosts or services with the selected symptoms. For example, if we click on **3 Services Disabled** in the **Notifications** section, a list of these three services will be displayed.

Status map

Nagios allows the display of a graphical map of host parent-child relations, along with their statuses. This can be accessed by clicking on the **Status Map** link on the left-side menu. This information can be used to keep track of hosts and their statuses. In this way, you can see how a host being down causes other parts of your network to be unreachable.

The following is a screenshot of a status page:

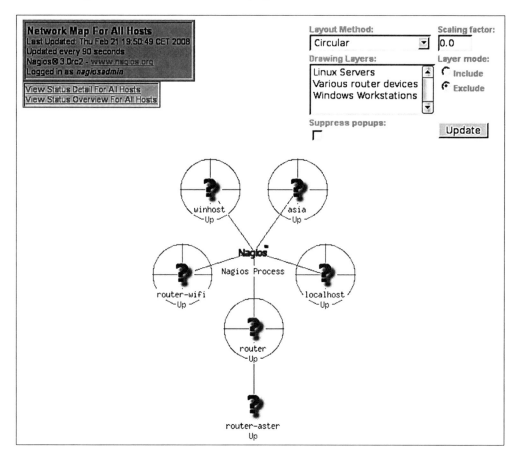

The status page can be shown in many ways. The preceding image shows a circular tree of all hosts. It is also possible to show a top-down tree of all hosts.

Further, it is possible to show all your machines in a 3D environment using **Virtual Reality Modeling Language** (**VRML**). This can be accessed by clicking on the **3-D Status Map** link on the left-side menu.

Managing Hosts

Nagios offers several pages that can be used to view and modify host information. The Nagios web interface offers a view of all defined hosts, their statuses, and basic information. These can be used to determine the status of hosts. Hostgroup-related views also show the status of services bound to hosts. Host information pages also allows the modification of several parameters related to host configuration.

Status

Nagios offers a panel that shows all hosts along with their statuses. It can be accessed by clicking on the **Host Detail** link on the left-side menu.

The following is a screenshot reporting six hosts, all of which are currently **UP**:

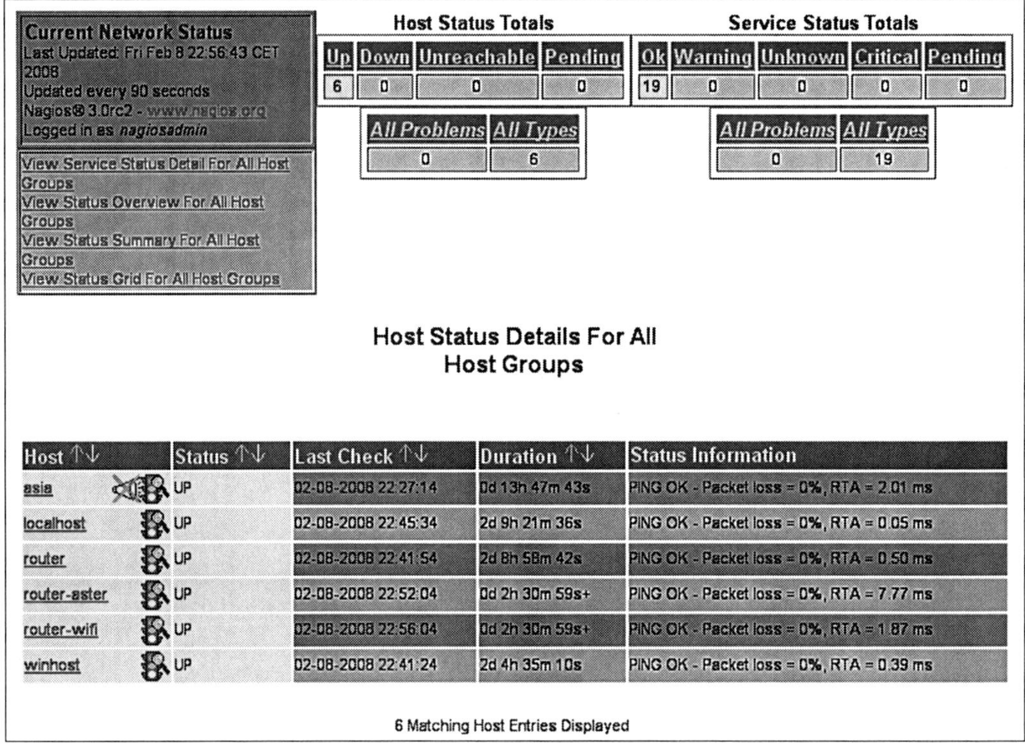

The page shows a list of all hosts, their statuses, and basic information on when the host was last checked and when the status was last changed. It also shows the information text response from the check. The sort order of the table can be changed by using the arrow buttons next to each column's header.

Similar to the Tactical Overview page, the totals on the top of the page can be used to filter hosts or services to only the ones with a specific status. After clicking on any status type in the **Host Status Totals** table, the list of hosts is filtered to the show only the ones that currently have the selected status. Clicking on any status type in **Service Status Totals** will show a list of services filtered to the ones that currently have the specified status.

There is also a quick jump menu on the left that allows you to move to a list of all of the services and views related to the host groups.

Nagios also offers three views that show the status of all of the host groups. One such view is the status grid, which shows host groups along with the hosts in them and each service for that host, along with its status. This view can be accessed by clicking on the **Hostgroup Grid** link on the left-side menu.

The following is a screenshot of such a status grid view:

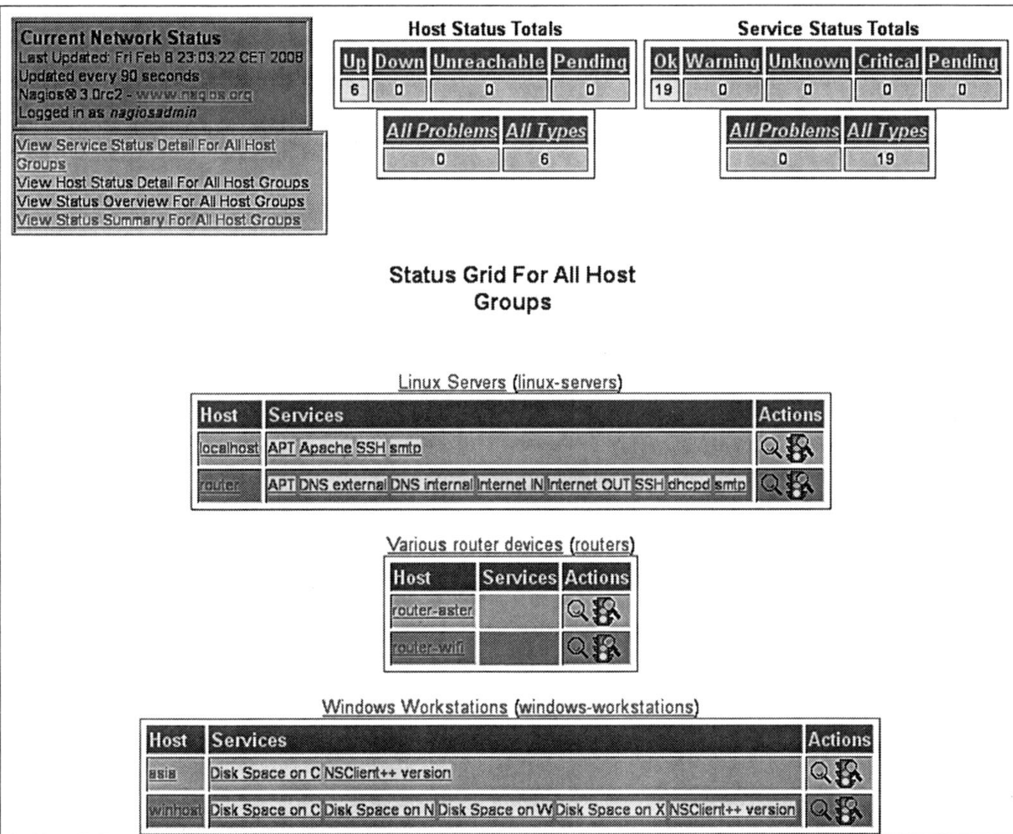

As with the previous view, clicking on the **Host Status Totals** or **Service Status Totals** will cause Nagios to filter the results according to the selected criteria. The page also contains a quick jump menu on the left that can be used to change the currently-selected view.

Clicking on any host group description will show a list of all of the services on all hosts within that group.

Clicking on a host group name, which is specified in brackets, will display a host group menu that allows you to modify attributes for all hosts or services related to that host group.

Clicking on a host name in any host or service related view will cause Nagios to show detailed information about the chosen host.

Host Information

Clicking on a host in any view of the web interface will take you to the host information page. This page contains the details of the current host status, a list of comments, and a command panel that allows you to modify the host configuration, schedule checks, or send custom notifications.

The following is a screenshot of the host information page:

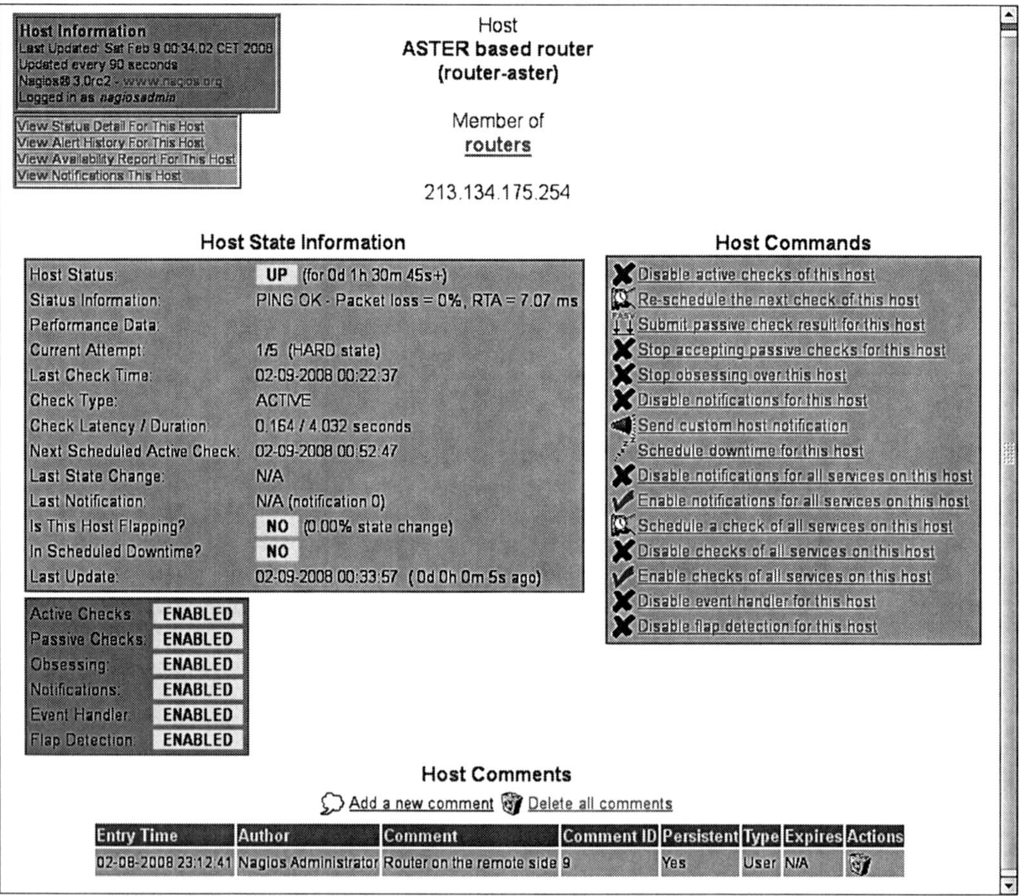

This page contains detailed information of the selected host. It shows the current status and the host checks that have been, or will be, performed. It also contains information on which functionality is enabled or disabled for specified host, whether the host is flapping along with flapping threshold value.

The menu on the right can be used to perform operations related to this host. It allows you to toggle whether active checks should be performed, whether Nagios should accept passive check results, and whether it should detect flapping. You can also configure Nagios to obsess over a host or send notifications and events. It is also possible to create options for all of the services bound to this host. There is also an option to schedule checks for a host or all services bound to this host. You can also submit passive check results over the web interface.

The host information page also allows the reading and modification of all of the comments related to this host. All current comments are listed under the **Host Comments** section. Clicking on **trash** icon in the **Actions** column will delete a comment. You can also delete all comments and add a new comment bound to this host.

Managing Services

Similar to host-related information and operations, Nagios has panels for working with services. This consists of several service and service group views, in addition to being able to view detailed information on each service and modify the parameters of the service.

Status

The Nagios web interface offers a view of all defined services, their statuses, and basic information about the services. This information can be accessed by clicking on the **Service Detail** link on the left-side menu.

The following screenshot reports 19 services, all of which are currently working correctly:

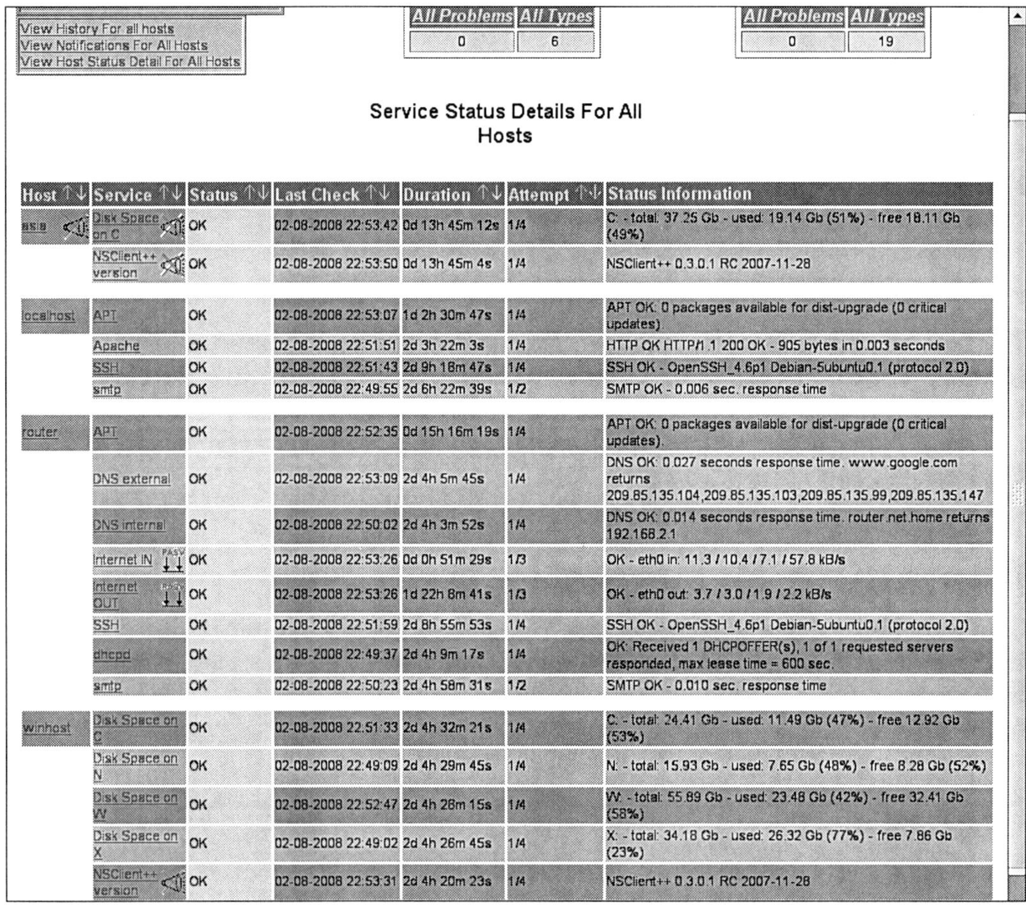

The main part of the page is a table showing all services, along with their statuses and detailed information on the output from the checks carried out against these services.

Services are grouped by the hosts they are configured for, and they are sorted by service description. This is the default order by which the table is sorted. It is possible to sort the table according to your needs by clicking on the arrows in any column in the header of the table.

Above the table, there are total values for each host and service status. These totals can also be used to filter the service table to show only specific statuses or services for a host with a specific status.

The page also contains a quick menu that allows navigation to commonly-used views. This allows you to jump to the history and notification logs, as well as navigate to a list of all hosts along with their detailed statuses.

Clicking on any host will take you to a host information page for the selected object. Similarly, clicking on any service will show a detailed information page for that object.

Another interesting view is the summary of all of the services specified for each service group. The following is a screenshot of this page:

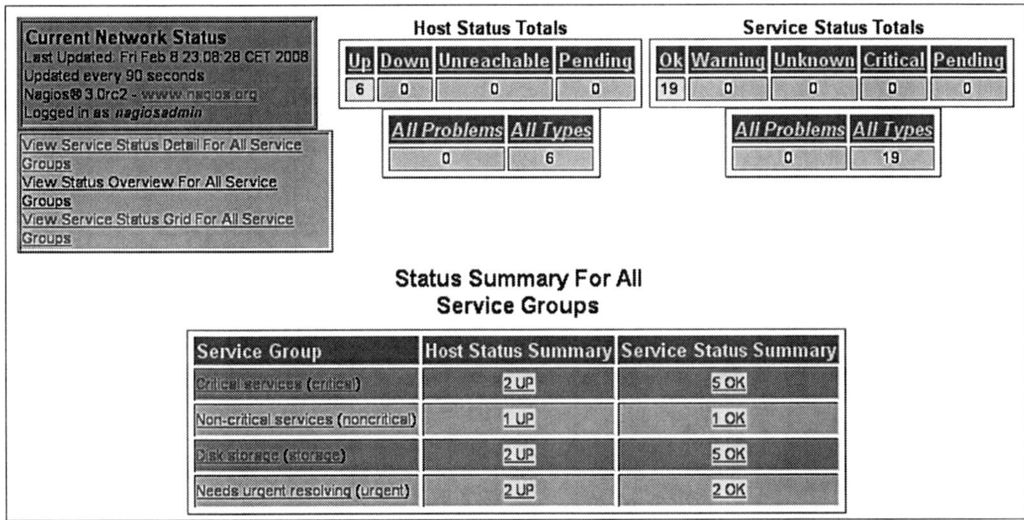

This page shows each **Service Group**, along with the count of all services for each status. The page contains a **Service Status Summary,** which is the summary of all of the services that are members of a specific service group. It also shows a **Host Status Summary,** which is the summary of all the hosts that have at least one service configured.

Clicking on any status summary column will show a list of all of the services in that group, along with detailed information about these sevices. Clicking on a service group will show an overview of the services split into individual hosts.

Service Information

Clicking on a service in any view of the web interface will take you to the service information page. This page contains details on the current service status, a list of comments, and a command panel that allows you to modify the service configuration, schedule checks, or send custom notifications.

The following is a screenshot of this page:

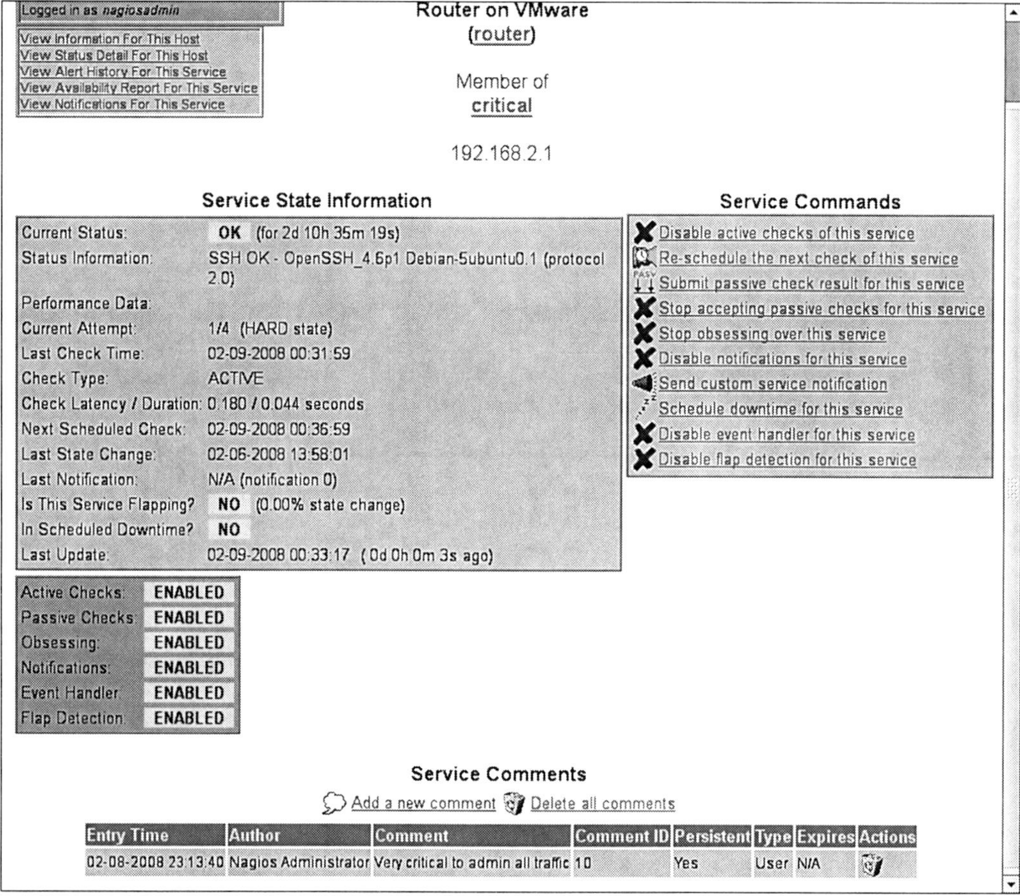

The main table on the left shows the detailed information for the service—its current status, output from the checks carried out against the service, and detailed information on the last and next planned check. The page also shows whether the service is flapping along with the flapping, threshold, and when the last notification was sent out.

The menu on the right allows you to change whether checks should be performed, notifications and events should be done, and whether Nagios should obsess over this service. There is also an option to schedule when the next check is to be performed.

At the bottom of the page there is a **Service Comments** section that contains a table that shows all existing comments related to this service, similar to host information page. It is possible to add or delete a single comment or all comments related to this service, as you can with host comments.

Managing Downtimes

Nagios allows you to use the web interface to manage scheduled downtimes for hosts and services. This includes listing, adding, and deleting downtimes for both hosts and services.

Downtimes Status

Nagios's web interface allows you to list all scheduled downtimes. This page can be accessed by clicking on the **Downtime** link on the left-side menu. The following is an example of this page:

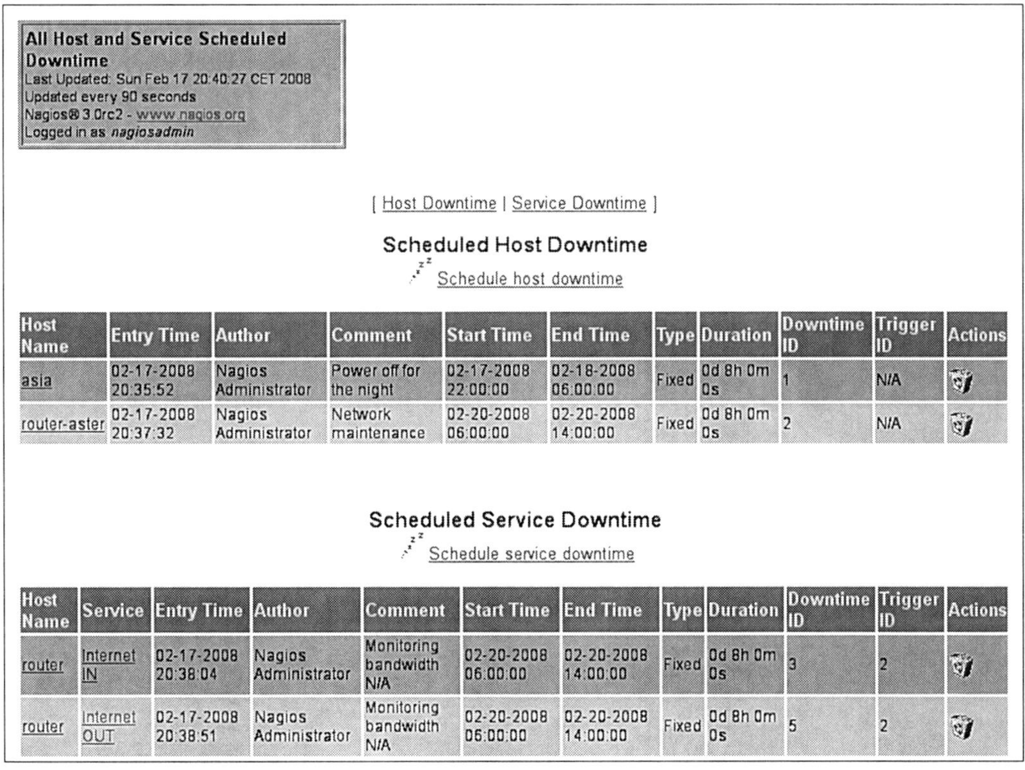

All Host and Service Scheduled Downtime
Last Updated: Sun Feb 17 20:40:27 CET 2008
Updated every 90 seconds
Nagios® 3.0rc2 - www.nagios.org
Logged in as *nagiosadmin*

[Host Downtime | Service Downtime]

Scheduled Host Downtime

Schedule host downtime

Host Name	Entry Time	Author	Comment	Start Time	End Time	Type	Duration	Downtime ID	Trigger ID	Actions
asia	02-17-2008 20:35:52	Nagios Administrator	Power off for the night	02-17-2008 22:00:00	02-18-2008 06:00:00	Fixed	0d 8h 0m 0s	1	N/A	
router-aster	02-17-2008 20:37:32	Nagios Administrator	Network maintenance	02-20-2008 06:00:00	02-20-2008 14:00:00	Fixed	0d 8h 0m 0s	2	N/A	

Scheduled Service Downtime

Schedule service downtime

Host Name	Service	Entry Time	Author	Comment	Start Time	End Time	Type	Duration	Downtime ID	Trigger ID	Actions
router	Internet IN	02-17-2008 20:38:04	Nagios Administrator	Monitoring bandwidth N/A	02-20-2008 06:00:00	02-20-2008 14:00:00	Fixed	0d 8h 0m 0s	3	2	
router	Internet OUT	02-17-2008 20:38:51	Nagios Administrator	Monitoring bandwidth N/A	02-20-2008 06:00:00	02-20-2008 14:00:00	Fixed	0d 8h 0m 0s	5	2	

The page consists of two pages, which all scheduled downtimes, separately for hosts and services. You can delete a downtime by clicking the 'trash' icon on the right in the row that describes that particular downtime entry.

Downtimes can be triggered by other downtimes. When a host downtime is scheduled, Nagios automatically adds downtimes for all child hosts. For example, in the current configuration, if host `router` has a downtime scheduled, then `router-aster` will also have the same downtime as it will be unreachable during this period. Such downtimes are indicated by the Downtime ID and Trigger ID columns. In the example above, the `Internet IN` and `Internet OUT` services are scheduled to be down as the `router-aster` host will also be down. We can see that the `router-aster` host downtime has its **Downtime ID** set to **2**, and both service downtimes have **Trigger ID** also set to **2**.

Scheduling Downtimes

In order to schedule a downtime, open a host or service information page and use the **Schedule downtime for this host** option or the **Schedule downtime for this service** option. It is also possible to use the Downtime page to schedule downtimes directly. In this case, you will need to know the host name and service description of the service you want to disable, as Nagios will not fill these in automatically.

The following is a screenshot of scheduling downtime for a service:

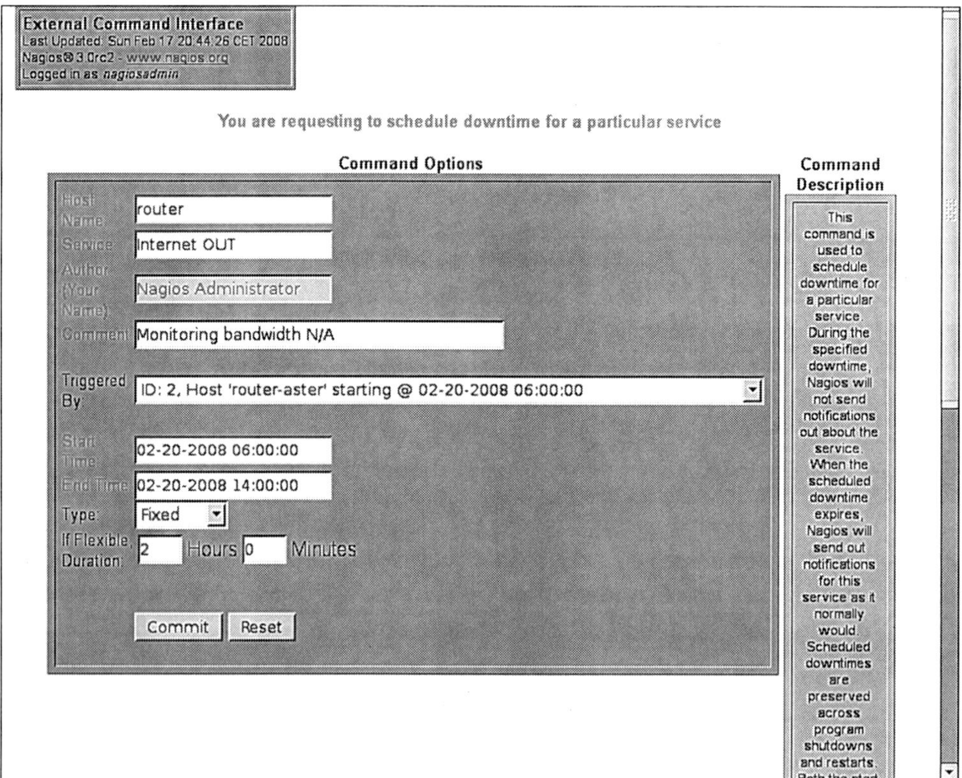

The form consists of **Host** and **Service Name**, **Comment**, and an option list to choose a downtime that triggered this host/service to also be down. When specifying the period during which the downtime should be scheduled, it is possible to enter **Start Time** and **End Time** or use the **Duration** field. If you want to specify how long the service will be offline, choose **Flexible** in the **Type** field. Otherwise, choose **Fixed** to specify the start and end time.

Scheduling downtime for a host is very similar—the only difference being that the **Service** field is missing, and the **Child Hosts** option list is added to specify how child hosts should be handled.

Nagios can automatically schedule downtimes for child hosts. When scheduling a host downtime, an additional option is present to indicate whether child hosts should also be scheduled for downtime and be triggered by this downtime.

Managing Comments

Nagios allows you to enter one or more comments for a host or a service. These can be anything from 'Third machine from top on the left shelf' to 'Reset button not working'. Nagios also adds comments automatically in several cases. For example, when an object is scheduled for downtime, a comment is created stating this.

Comments associated with a specific object are shown on the host or service detail information pages(as appropriate). Comments can also be added and removed via these pages.

Nagios also offers a page that allows you to manage comments for all hosts and services, similar to how you manage scheduled downtimes. This page allows you to add or delete comments for all hosts. You can also navigate to the detailed information page for a host or service by clicking on the object's name. This page can be accessed via the **Comments** link on the left-side menu.

The following is a screenshot of the comments page:

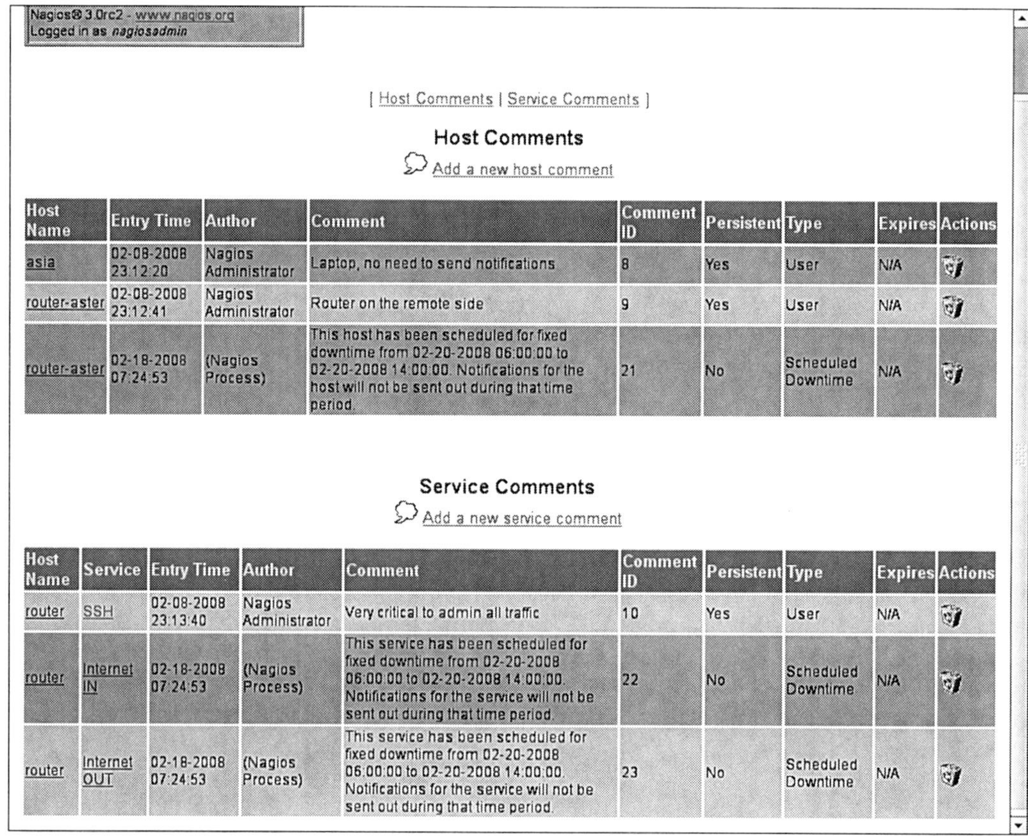

Nagios® 3.0rc2 - www.nagios.org
Logged in as nagiosadmin

[Host Comments | Service Comments]

Host Comments

Add a new host comment

Host Name	Entry Time	Author	Comment	Comment ID	Persistent	Type	Expires	Actions
asia	02-08-2008 23:12:20	Nagios Administrator	Laptop, no need to send notifications	8	Yes	User	N/A	
router-aster	02-08-2008 23:12:41	Nagios Administrator	Router on the remote side	9	Yes	User	N/A	
router-aster	02-18-2008 07:24:53	(Nagios Process)	This host has been scheduled for fixed downtime from 02-20-2008 06:00:00 to 02-20-2008 14:00:00. Notifications for the host will not be sent out during that time period.	21	No	Scheduled Downtime	N/A	

Service Comments

Add a new service comment

Host Name	Service	Entry Time	Author	Comment	Comment ID	Persistent	Type	Expires	Actions
router	SSH	02-08-2008 23:13:40	Nagios Administrator	Very critical to admin all traffic	10	Yes	User	N/A	
router	Internet IN	02-18-2008 07:24:53	(Nagios Process)	This service has been scheduled for fixed downtime from 02-20-2008 06:00:00 to 02-20-2008 14:00:00. Notifications for the service will not be sent out during that time period.	22	No	Scheduled Downtime	N/A	
router	Internet OUT	02-18-2008 07:24:53	(Nagios Process)	This service has been scheduled for fixed downtime from 02-20-2008 06:00:00 to 02-20-2008 14:00:00. Notifications for the service will not be sent out during that time period.	23	No	Scheduled Downtime	N/A	

Clicking on the 'trash' icon next to any comment will delete it. Adding a comment can be done by clicking on a host or a service name from the detailed information page, or by clicking on the comments table. In the latter case, you will need to specify the host name and the service description yourself in the Add Comment form.

Nagios Information

The web interface allows you to check the Nagios daemon status along with general information on the enabled and disabled features. It also allows you to check performance information related to Nagios. This can be used to make sure that Nagios is not overloaded with checks to perform, and see how much time checks take, and how often they're performed.

Process Information

The Nagios **Process Information** page shows generic information on Nagios processes. It also allows you to perform several actions via the **Process Commands** panel. This page can be accessed via the **Process Info** link on the left-side menu.

The following is a screenshot of this page:

Nagios Process Information
Last Updated: Sat Feb 9 00:35:02 CET 2008
Updated every 90 seconds
Nagios® 3.0rc2 - www.nagios.org
Logged in as *nagiosadmin*

Process Information

Program Version:	3.0rc2
Program Start Time:	02-08-2008 23:03:17
Total Running Time:	0d 1h 31m 45s
Last External Command Check:	02-09-2008 00:34:56
Last Log File Rotation:	02-09-2008 00:00:00
Nagios PID	395
Notifications Enabled?	YES
Service Checks Being Executed?	YES
Passive Service Checks Being Accepted?	YES
Host Checks Being Executed?	YES
Passive Host Checks Being Accepted?	YES
Event Handlers Enabled?	Yes
Obsessing Over Services?	No
Obsessing Over Hosts?	No
Flap Detection Enabled?	Yes
Performance Data Being Processed?	No

Process Commands

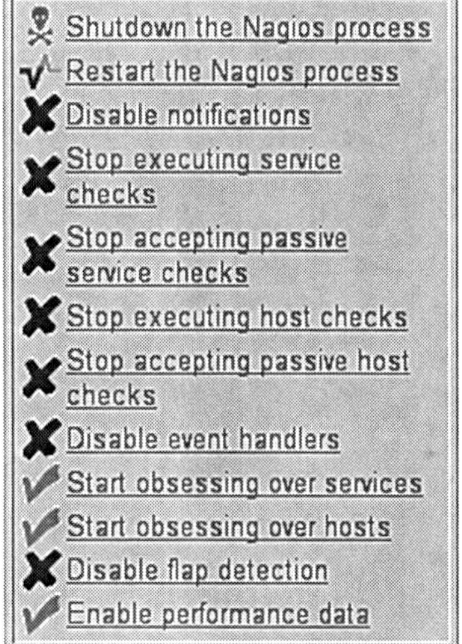

This page contains information on the Nagios version, its process ID, status, and log rotation. It also shows whether the checks, notifications, and other functions are enabled.

The menu on the right also allows you to stop and restart the Nagios daemon. It also allows you to enable or disable the performance of checks and sending notifications. Flap detection and performance data processing can also be turned on or off from this page.

Performance Information

The **Program-Wide Performance Information** page shows information about the performance and load of Nagios process. This page can be accessed via the **Process Info** link on the left-side menu.

The following is a screenshot of this page:

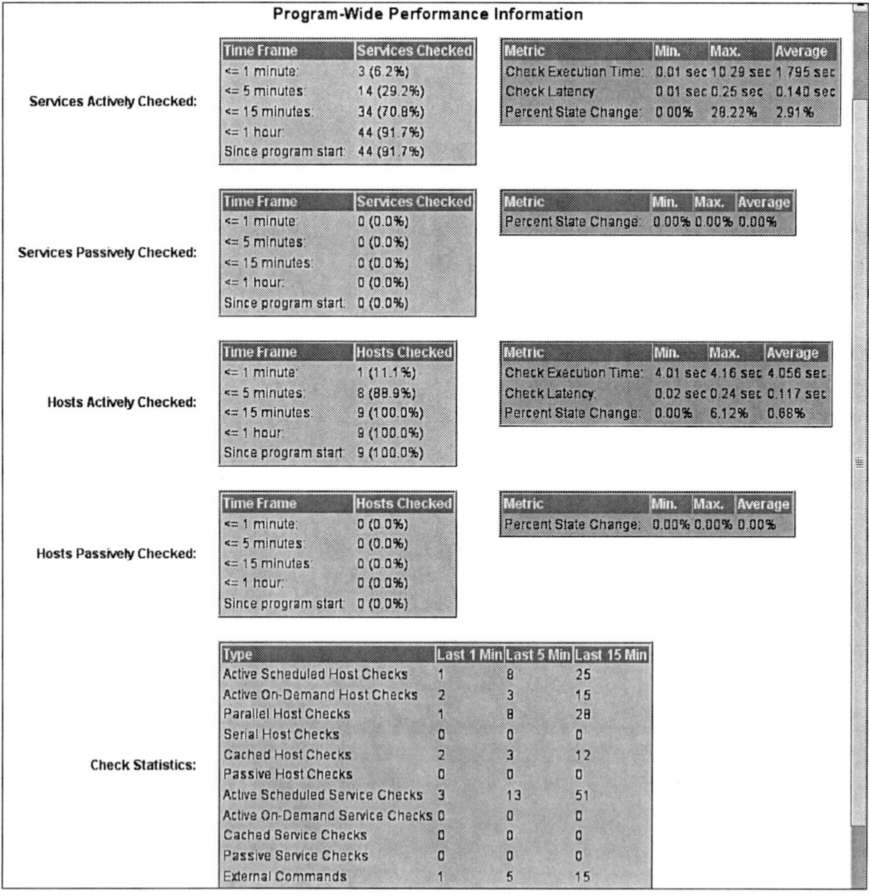

This page contains information on a number of host and service checks performed within various periods of time, as well as the number of reports received from external applications. It also shows the number of commands received from external applications, which is usually the web interface.

This page also contains information on average check execution times, as well as latencies. This information is useful in determining whether the Nagios process is overloaded or not. If the average latency is above 60 seconds, or is constantly increasing, then this means Nagios is not able to perform all of the specified checks. In such cases, it is a good idea to increase the check or notification intervals, so that the number of commands Nagios runs in any given period of time is lower.

Reports

One of the most important features of the Web interface is the ability to create reports. Many larger companies need reports to allow them to take decisions at a higher management level. Reporting functionality can also be used to browse historical notifications to alerts, and to see complete logs for a specified period.

Nagios offers the following types of reports:

- **Trend reporting for host or service**: Shows the state changes history for a single object along with the status information from performed checks
- **Availability report for hosts or services**: Shows how much time an object has spent in a particular status; can report on all objects or a single object; can also generate reports for host groups and service groups
- **Alert histogram**: Shows the number of alerts that have occurred over a period of time for a particular host or service

In addition, Nagios can report a history of alerts, notifications, or all events. This can be considered as reading Nagios logs in a more convenient way. It allows you to read the history either for all hosts and/or services, or for a specific object. The reports are also formatted in a more readable way than the raw logs.

Generating most reports begins with choosing the report type, then the object type—host, host group, service, or service group. Then either all objects, or a specific object, is chosen for which a report is generated.

Next, you need to specify the period for which a report, should be generated, along with additional options that can depend on the type of report being be generated. Additionally, a time period can be specified, so that the report only includes specific time periods, such as working hours.

The following is a screenshot of a sample form for specifying the parameters for a report. The actual fields may vary depending on the type of report that you want to generate.

Host Availability Report
Last Updated: Sat Feb 9 00:35:55 CET 2008
Nagios® 3.0rc2 - www.nagios.org
Logged in as *nagiosadmin*

Step 3: Select Report Options

Report Period: Last 24 Hours
If Custom Report Period...
Start Date (Inclusive): February 1 2008
End Date (Inclusive): February 9 2008
Report time Period: None
Assume Initial States: Yes
Assume State Retention: Yes
Assume States During Program Downtime: Yes
Include Soft States: No
First Assumed Host State: Unspecified
First Assumed Service State: Unspecified
Backtracked Archives (To Scan For Initial States): 4
Output in CSV Format:
Create Availability Report!

After specifying the parameters in the form, and submitting it, the web interface will generate a report matching your criteria. Some types of reports also allow you to export the information in CSV format for further analysis. For a trend history report, it is also possible to zoom in or out in order to customize the period for which the report is generated.

The following screenshot shows the availability report for all hosts. It shows how much time each host has been up, down, or unreachable due to the parent machines not being up.

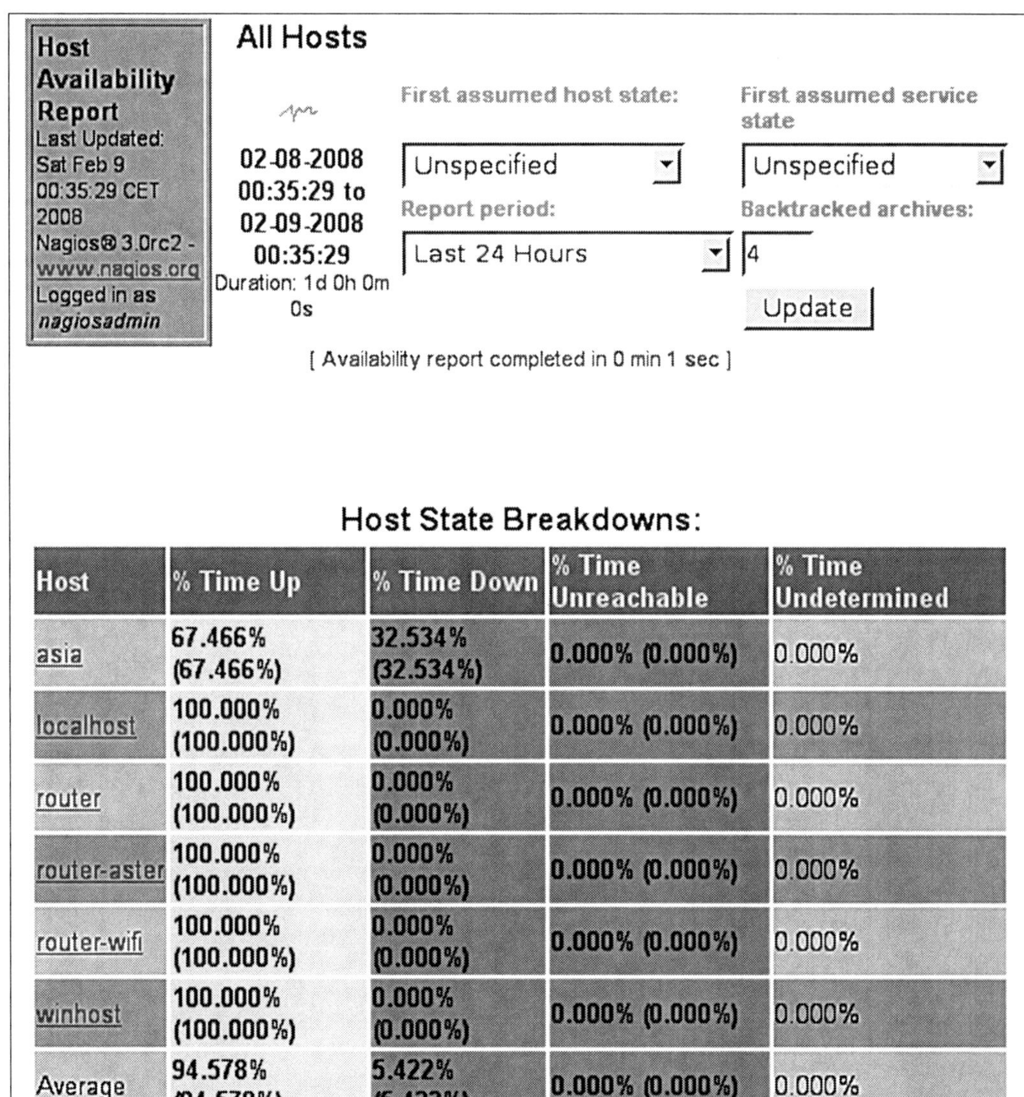

Host	% Time Up	% Time Down	% Time Unreachable	% Time Undetermined
asia	67.466% (67.466%)	32.534% (32.534%)	0.000% (0.000%)	0.000%
localhost	100.000% (100.000%)	0.000% (0.000%)	0.000% (0.000%)	0.000%
router	100.000% (100.000%)	0.000% (0.000%)	0.000% (0.000%)	0.000%
router-aster	100.000% (100.000%)	0.000% (0.000%)	0.000% (0.000%)	0.000%
router-wifi	100.000% (100.000%)	0.000% (0.000%)	0.000% (0.000%)	0.000%
winhost	100.000% (100.000%)	0.000% (0.000%)	0.000% (0.000%)	0.000%
Average	94.578% (94.578%)	5.422% (5.422%)	0.000% (0.000%)	0.000%

The report shows information for all hosts, in a table, along with a summary of the overall availability.

It is possible to change the parameters of a report after it first has been generated, to modify the reported period or the information included on the report.

Summary

Being able to view the status of your infrastructure from a web browser is a great very useful. Combined with an SSL-enabled web server, or by using a VPN, this functionality can allow people in your company to check the status of the entire network from any location in the world.

A large number of views can assist you in finding out what the root cause of a problem is. You can view objects by their groups, as well as by individual host or service.

If one or more hosts is down, then checking the network status on a 2D or 3D status map should be the first step you perform. There are also views for problems related to hosts and services that only show the direct causes of the problems, and skip issues that arise due to problems with other hosts or services.

The web interface also allows you to modify Nagio's behavior. It can also be used to configure individual hosts and services. You can also schedule host and service checks for a specified time. You can use this, for example, if you want to check whether the changes your team has performed will resolve current problems.

The web interface also allows you to schedule and manage host and service downtimes. You can also read, create, and manage comments associated with all objects.

Getting to know the web interface is really essential in order to use Nagios effectively.

4

Overview of Nagios Plugins

Nagios' strength comes from its ability to monitor servers and the services they offer in a large number of ways. What's more interesting is that all of these ways make sure that your services are provided as functional, are external plugins, and work in quite an easy way. Many of these are even shipped with Nagios, as we mentioned in Chapter 2, Installation and Configuration. Therefore, it is possible to either use existing plugins or write your own.

The previous chapter discussed basic configuration of host and service checking. Nagios can be set up to check if your services are up and running. This chapter describes how these checks work in more detail. It also introduces some of the Nagios plugins that are developed as a part of Nagios, and as a part of the **Nagios Plugins** project.

Nagios performs checks by running an external command, and uses the return code, along with output from the command, as information on whether the check worked or not. It is the command's responsibility to verify if a host or service is working at the time the command is invoked.

Nagios itself handles all of the internals, such as scheduling the commands to be run, storing their results, and determining what the status is for each host and service.

Nagios requires that all plugins follow a specific, easy-to-follow behavior in order for them to work smoothly. These rules are common for both host checks and service checks. It requires that each command returns specific result codes, which are:

Exit code	Status	Description
0	OK	Working correctly
1	WARNING	Working, but needs attention (for example, low resources)
2	CRITICAL	Not working correctly or requires attention
3	UNKNOWN	Plugin was unable to determine the status for the host or service

Standard output from the command is not parsed in any way by Nagios. It is usually formatted in the following way:

```
PLUGIN STATUS - status description
```

Usually, the status description contains human-readable information that is visible using the web interface. Some sample outputs from various plugins and states are:

```
PING OK - Packet loss = 0%, RTA = 0.18 ms
DNS WARNING: 0.015 seconds response time
DISK CRITICAL - free space: /boot 18 MB (8% inode=99%)
```

Nagios plugins use options for their configuration. It is up to the plugin author's host to parse these options. However, most commands that come as part of the Nagios Plugins package use standard options and support the `-h` or `--help` options to provide a full description of all the arguments they accept.

Standard Nagios plugins usually accept the following parameters:

Option	Description
-h, --help	Provide help
-V, --version	Print the exact version of the plugin
-v, --verbose	Make the plugin report more detailed information on what it is doing
-t, --timeout	Timeout (seconds); after this time plugin will report CRITICAL status
-w, --warning	Plugin-specific limits for the WARNING status
-c, --critical	Plugin-specific limits for the CRITICAL status
-H, --hostname	Host name, IP address or unix socket to communicate with
-4, --use-ipv4	Use IPv4 for network connectivity
-6, --use-ipv6	Use IPv6 for network connectivity

Commands that verify various daemons also have a common set of options. Many of the networking-related plugins use the following options in addition to the preceding standard ones

Option	Description
-p, --port	TCP or UDP port to connect to
-w, --warning	Response time that will issue a WARNING status (seconds)
-c, --critical	Response time that will issue a CRITICAL status (seconds)
-s, --send	String that will be sent to the server
-e, --expect	String that should be sent back from the server (option might be passed several times; see `--all` for details)

Option	Description
-q, --quit	String to send to the server to close the connection
-A, --all	In case multiple --expect parameters are passed, this option indicates that all responses need to be received; if this option is not present, at least one matching result indicates a success
-m, --maxbytes	The maximum number of bytes to read when expecting a string to be sent back from the server; after this number of bytes, a mismatch is assumed
-d, --delay	Delay in seconds between sending a string to server and expecting a response
-r, --refuse	Status that should be indicated in case the connection is refused (ok, warn, crit; defaults to crit)
-M	Status in case the expected answer is not returned by the server (ok, warn, crit; defaults to warn)
-j, --jail	Do not return output from the server in plugin output text
-D, --certificate	The number of days that the SSL certificate must still be valid; requires -ssl
-S, --ssl	Connect using SSL encryption
-E, --escape	Allows using \n, \r, \t or \\ in send or quit string; must be passed before --send or --quit option

This chapter describes the commands provided by a standard distribution Nagios Plugins and is based on version 1.4.10. Before using specific options for a command, it is recommended that you use the `--help` option and familiarize yourself with the functionality available on your Nagios installation.

All plugins have their nonstandard options, described in more detail in this chapter. All commands described in this chapter also have a sample configuration for the Nagios `check` command. Even though some longer definitions might span multiple lines, please make sure that you put it on a single line in your configuration. Some of the plugins already have their command counterparts configured with the sample Nagios configuration that is installed along with Nagios. Therefore, it is also worth checking if your `commands.cfg` file contains a definition for a particular command.

Standard Network Plugins

One of the basic roles of a plugin is to monitor local or remote hosts and verify if they are working correctly. There is a choice of generic plugins to accomplish this task.

Standard networking plugins allow hosts to be monitored using ICMP ECHO (ping: refer to `http://en.wikipedia.org/wiki/Ping`). This is used to determine whether a computer is responding to IP requests. It is also used to measure the time that a machine takes to respond, and how many packages are lost during the communication. These plugins also try to connect to certain TCP/UDP ports. This is used to communicate with various network based services to make sure that they are working properly, and respond within a defined amount of time.

Checking If a Host is Alive

Checking if a host is alive is a basic test that should be performed for all remote machines. Nagios offers a command that is commonly used for checking if a host is alive and plugged into the network. The syntax of the plugin is as follows:

```
check_ping -H <host_address> -w <wrta>,<wpl>% -c <crta>,<cpl>%
           [-p packets] [-t timeout] [-4|-6]
```

This command accepts the standard options described above, as well as the following nonstandard options:

Option	Description
-p,--packets	Number of packets to send; defaults to 5
-w, --warning	WARNING status limit in form of RTA,PKTLOSS%
-c, --critical	CRITICAL status limit in form of RTA,PKTLOSS%

RTA means **Round Trip Average**, and is the average time taken in milliseconds for the package to return. **PKTLOSS** is **Packet Loss**, which is the maximum percentage of packages that can be lost during communication. For example, a value of 100, 20% means that a ping must return within 0.1 seconds on average, and at least 4 out of 5 packages have to come back.

A sample command definition for checking if a host is alive is:

```
define command
{
  command_name  check-host-alive
  command_line  $USER1$/check_ping -H $HOSTADDRESS$ -w 3000.0,80%
                -c 5000.0,100% -p 5
}
```

Testing Connectivity over TCP and UDP

In many cases, Nagios is used to monitor services that work over the network. For checking if a service is working properly, it is necessary to make sure that a certain TCP or UDP port is accessible over the network. For example, Microsoft SQL Server listens on TCP port 1433. In many cases, it is enough to simply run generic plugins that check whether a service is available on a specified TCP or UDP port. However, it is recommended that you run specialized plugins for various services such as web or email servers, as these commands also try basic communication with the server and/or measure response time.

Internally, as this command is also handling many other checks, the syntax is almost the same. It is designed so that, it behaves slightly differently based on the name it is called with. Many other plugins are symbolic links to `check_tcp`. The `check_tcp` plugin is mainly intended to test services that do not have a corresponding Nagios `check` command. The second command, `check_udp` is also a symbolic link to `check_tcp` and differs only by communicating over UDP instead of TCP. Its syntax is as follows:

```
check_tcp|check_udp -H host -p port [-w <warning >] [-c <critical >]
          [-s <send string>] [-e <expect string>] [-q <quit string>]
          [-A] [-m <maximum bytes>] [-d <delay>] [-t <timeout>]
          [-r <refuse state>] [-M <mismatch state>] [-v] [-4|-6]
          [-j] [-D <days to cert expiry>] [-S] [-E]
```

These commands accept several nonstandard options as follows:

Option	Description
-p, --port	TCP or UDP Port to connect to
-w, --warning	Response time that will issue a WARNING status (in seconds)
-c, --critical	Response time that will issue a CRITICAL status (in seconds)

An example, to verify whether VMware server 1.x is listening for connections, is as follows:

```
define command
{
  command_name  check_vmware
  command_line  $USER1$/check_tcp -H $HOSTADDRESS$ -p 902
                -e "220 VMware"
}
```

For UDP, the following is an example command definition to verify if the OpenVPN server is listening on UDP port 1142:

```
define command
{
  command_name  check_openvpn
  command_line  $USER1$/check_udp -H $HOSTADDRESS$ -p 1142
}
```

Monitoring Email Servers

Making sure that all email-related services are working correctly is something that each hosting company and intranet administrator needs to perform on a daily basis. In order to do this, Nagios can watch these servers and make sure things are working as expected. This can be done by a remote machine to make sure that the services are accessible, or can be monitored by the same server that offers these services.

Nagios can make sure that the processes are running and waiting for connections. It is also easy to verify whether a predefined user/password pair is working properly to make sure that a custom authorization system is working properly.

This section describes the commands that check email servers using network connectivity. Plugins that verify specific processes on a server can be used to make sure a particular daemon is up and running as well.

POP3 and IMAP Checks

POP3 is the most popular protocol for retrieving email messages from an email client application. It uses TCP port 110 for unencrypted connections and port 995 for SSL encrypted connections. Nagios offers means to verify both unencrypted and encrypted POP3 connections that can be made. Even though POP3 is the most popular email retrieving protocol, another protocol is also very common. IMAP is a protocol that is used to access emails on remote servers rather than download them to the user's computer. It uses TCP port 143 for standard connections and port 993 for encrypted connections over SSL. The following plugins are based on `check_tcp` (and are actually symbolic links to `check_tcp`). The syntax is identical to the original plugin:

```
check_pop|check_imap -H host [-p port] [-w <warning>] [-c <critical >]
        [-s <send string>] [-e <expect string>] [-q <quit string>]
        [-A] [-m <maximum bytes>] [-d <delay>]
        [-t <timeout seconds>] [-r <refuse state>]
        [-M <mismatch state>] [-v] [-4|-6] [-j]
        [-D <days to cert expiry>] [-S] [-E]
```

The only difference between this plugin and the standard command is that the port parameter can be omitted for this plugin, and in this case, a default value for both non-SSL and SSL variants is chosen. In order to enable connection over SSL, either pass the `--ssl` option, or invoke the command as `check_spop` instead of `check_pop` and `check_simap` instead of `check_imap`.

The following are sample command definitions that check for a daemon listening on a specified host and verify that a valid POP3 and IMAP welcome message can be retrieved:

```
define command
{
  command_name  check_pop
  command_line  $USER1$/check_pop -H $HOSTADDRESS$
}

define command
{
  command_name  check_imap
  command_line  $USER1$/check_imap -H $HOSTADDRESS$
}
```

However, it seems more useful to verify the actual functionality of the server. It is, therefore, reasonable to also verify that a predefined username and password is accepted by our POP3 daemon. In order to do that, the example uses `-E` to escape newline characters, `-s` to send commands that authenticate, and `-e` to verify that the user has actually been logged in. In addition, the `-d` option is passed to indicate that the command should wait a couple of seconds before analyzing the output. If this option is not passed, the command will return after the first line. The following examples should work with any POP3/IMAP server, but it may be necessary to customize the response for your particular environment.

```
define command
{
  command_name  check_pop3login
  command_line  $USER1$/check_pop -H $HOSTADDRESS$ -E
                -s "USER $ARG1$\r\nPASS $ARG2$\r\n" -d 5
                -e "ogged in"
}

define command
{
  command_name  check_imaplogin
  command_line  $USER1$/check_imap -H $HOSTADDRESS$ -E
                -s "pr01 LOGIN $ARG1 $ARG2$\r\n" -d 5
                -e "pr01 OK"
}
```

The value that is passed in the -s option is a string with two lines for POP3 and one line for POP4. Each line ends with a newline character (\r\n) that are sent as newline characters due to using the -E option.

For POP3, these lines are standard protocol commands to log into an account. The POP3 server should then issue a response stating that the user is authenticated, and this is what the command is expecting to receive—because of the -e option. In addition, $ARG1$ and $ARG2$ will be replaced with a username and a password that is supplied in a service check definition, which allows different usernames and passwords to be specified for different checks.

With IMAP4, there is only a slight difference in the protocol dialect. IMAP requires the sending of only a single LOGIN command in order to authenticate. As for POP3, $ARG1$ and $ARG2$ will be replaced with a username and password. In this way it is possible to set up checks for different users and passwords with a single command definition. The pr01 string can be replaced by any other text without spaces. It is necessary with the IMAP protocol to bind requests with answers provided by the server.

To be able to determine exactly what is sent to and received from the server, the -v option can be used.

SMTP Daemon Testing

SMTP is a protocol for sending emails—both from a client application as well as between email servers. Therefore, monitoring it is also very important from the point of view of availability.

Nagios standard plugins offer a command to check whether an SMTP server is listening. Unlike checks for POP3 and IMAP, the command is available only for this particular protocol and therefore, the options are a bit different:

```
check_smtp -H host [-p port] [-C command] [-R response] [-f from addr]
           [-F hostname] [-A authtype -U authuser -P authpass]
           [-w <warning time>] [-c <critical time>] [-t timeout]
           [-S] [-D days] [-n] [-4|-6]
```

The plugin accepts most of the standard options. Additional ones are as follows:

Option	Description
-C, --command	SMTP command to execute on the server (option might be repeated)
-R, --response	Response to expect from the server (option might be repeated)
-f, --from	Attempt to set from where the email is originating

Option	Description
-F, --fqdn	Fully-qualified domain name to send during SMTP greeting (defaults to the local hostname if not specified)
-S, --starttls	Use STARTTLS to initialize connection over SMTP

The port can be omitted and defaults to 25. In this case,the `-S` option also behaves a bit differently and uses the STARTTLS function of SMTP servers instead of connecting directly over SSL. A basic SMTP check command definition looks like this:

```
define command
{
  command_name  check_smtp
  command_line  $USER1$/check_smtp -H $HOSTADDRESS$
}
```

Most of these options are similar to the standard send/expect parameters in the way they work. Therefore, it is quite easy to create a more complex definition that verifies the sending of emails to a specific address:

```
define command
{
  command_name  check_smtpsend
  command_line  $USER1$/check_smtp -H $HOSTADDRESS$
                -f "$ARG1$" -C "RCPT TO:<$ARG2$>" -R "250"
}
```

This check will attempt to send an email from `$ARG1$` to `$ARG2$`, which will be passed from a check definition, and expects to receive a return code 250, which indicates that no error has occurred.

Monitoring Network Services

Nagios also offers plugins that monitor different network services. These include commands for checking FTP, DHCP protocol, and WWW servers. It is also possible for Nagios to monitor itself.

FTP Server

Nagios allows you to verify whether an FTP server is listening for connections by using the check_tcp command. This plugin is identical to `check_tcp`, with the difference that the port is optional, and by default a valid FTP welcome message is expected.

```
check_ftp -H host [-p port] [-w <warning time>] [-c <critical time>]
          [-s <send string>] [-e <expect string>] [-q <quit string>]
          [-A] [-m <maximum bytes>] [-d <delay>]
```

```
          [-t <timeout seconds>] [-r <refuse state>]
          [-M <mismatch state>] [-v] [-4|-6] [-j]
          [-D <days to cert expiry>] [-S] [-E]
```

The port argument can be omitted and defaults to 21, or 990 for SSL based connections. A sample command definition for checking FTP accepting connections is as follows:

```
define command
{
  command_name  check_ftp
  command_line  $USER1$/check_ftp -H $HOSTADDRESS$
}
```

By using the `-s` and `-e` flags, it is also possible to verify if a specified username and password is allowed to log in:

```
define command
{
  command_name  check_ftplogin
  command_line  $USER1$/check_ftp -H $HOSTADDRESS$ -E
                -s "USER $ARG1\r\nPASS $ARG2$\r\n" -d 5
                -e "230"
}
```

This example is quite similar to POP3 authentication as the commands are the same. The only difference is that the requested response is `230` as this is a code for a successful response to the PASS command. In order to preview what is sent to and received from the server, the `-v` option can be used.

DHCP Tests

If your network has a server or a router that provides the users with IP addresses via DHCP, it would be wise to make sure that this server is also working correctly. Nagios offers a plugin that attempts to request an IP address via a DHCP protocol, which can be used for this purpose. The syntax is a bit different from other plugins:

```
check_dhcp [-v] [-u] [-s serverip] [-r requestedip] [-t timeout]
           [-i interface] [-m mac]
```

This command accepts the options described in the following table:

Option	Description
-s, --serverip	The IP of the server that needs to reply with an IP (option might be repeated)
-r, --requestedip	Indicates that at least one DHCP server needs to offer the specified IP address
-m, --mac	The MAC address that should be used in the DHCP request
-i, --interface	The name of the interface that is to be used for checking (for example `eth0`)
-u, --unicast	Unicast - for testing a DHCP relay request; requires `-s`

Options for DHCP checking are very powerful—they can be used to check if any server is responding to the DHCP requests, for example:

```
define command
{
  command_name  check_dhcp
  command_line  $USER1$/check_dhcp
}
```

This plugin can also be used to verify if specific servers work, if a specified MAC address will receive an IP address, if a specific IP address is returned, or a combination of these check, as shown below:

```
define command
{
  command_name  check_dhcp_mac
  command_line  $USER1$/check_dhcp -s $HOSTADDRESS$
                -m $ARG1$ -r $ARG2$
}
```

This check will ensure that a specific machine provides a specific IP for requesting a specific MAC address. This allows checks to be created for specific DHCP rules, which is crucial in the case of networks that need to provide specific devices with IP addresses, which other services depend upon.

It is also worth noting that such tests are safe from a network's perspective as the IP received from the server is not acknowledged by the Nagios plugin. Therefore, a check for a specific MAC address can be done even if a network card with the same address is currently connected. DHCP works over broadcast IP requests and therefore it is not recommended that you set up testing of this service often as it might cause excessive traffic for larger networks.

Verifying the Nagios Daemon

It is possible for Nagios to monitor whether or not it is running on the local machine. This works by checking the Nagios log file for recent entries, as well as reading the output from the `ps` system command to ensure that the Nagios daemon is currently running. This plugin is mainly used in combination with NRPE or SSH, which are described in more detail in Chapter 8 *Monitoring Remote Hosts*. However, it can also be deployed to check the same Nagios that is scheduling the command - mainly to make sure that the log files contain recent entries. The syntax and options are as follows:

```
check_nagios -F <status log file> -e <expire_minutes>
             -C <process_string>
```

Option	Description
-F, --filename	IP of the server that needs to reply with an IP (option might be repeated)
-e, --expires	The number of minutes after which the log file is assumed to be stale
-C, --command	Command or partial command to search for in the process list

All of the arguments listed above are required. The check for the `--expires` option is done by comparing the date and time of the latest entry in the log with the current date and time. The log file is usually called `nagios.log` and is stored in the directory that was passed in the `--localstatedir` option during Nagios compilation. For an installation performed according to the steps given in Chapter 2, the path will be `/var/nagios/nagios.log`. The Nagios process for such a setup would be `/opt/nagios/bin/nagios`. An example definition of a command receiving all of the information as arguments is as follows:

```
define command
{
  command_name  check_nagios
  command_line  $USER1$/check_nagios -F $ARG1$ -C $ARG2$ -e $ARG3$
}
```

The first argument is the path to the log file, the second is the path to the Nagios daemon binary, and the last one is the maximum acceptable number of minutes since the last log updated.

Testing Web Sites

Making sure that the web sites are up and running 24/7 is vital to many large companies. Verifying that the returned pages contain correct data may be even more important for companies conducting e-commerce. Nagios offers plugins to verify that a web server works. It can also make sure that your SSL certificate is still valid, and can also verify the contents of specific pages to check that they contain specific text. This command accepts various parameters, as follows:

```
check_http -H <vhost> | -I <IP-address> [-u <uri>] [-p <port>]
           [-w <warning time>] [-c <critical time>] [-t <timeout>]
           [-L] [-a auth] [-f <ok | warn | critcal | follow>]
           [-e <expect>] [-s string] [-l]
           [-r <regex> | -R <regex>] [-P string]
           [-m <min_pg_size>:<max_pg_size>]
           [-4|-6] [-N] [-M <age>] [-A string] [-k string] [-S]
           [-C <age>] [-T <content-type>]
```

The following table lists the options that differ from their usual behavior, or are not common in other commands:

Option	Description
-H, --hostname	The host name that should be used for the `Host` http header; The port might be appended, so it is also present in the http header
-I, --IP-address	The IP address to connect to; if not specified, `--hostname` is used
-u, --url	The URL to GET or POST (defaults to /)
-P, --post	Post the encoded http via POST; content is specified as argument
-N, --no-body	Do not wait for the document, only parse the http headers
-M, --max-age	Warn if the document is older than the number of seconds provided; this parameter can also be specified as (for example) "15m" for minutes, "8h" for hours or "7d" for days
-T,--content-type	Specify the http `Content-Type` header
-e, --expect	The text to expect in the first line of the http response; If specified, the plugin will not handle status code logic (i.e. won't warn about 404)
-s, --string	Search for the specified text in `result html`
-r, --ereg	Search for a specified regular expression in html (case sensitive)
-R, --eregi	Search for a specified regular expression in html (case insensitive)
-l, --linespan	Allow the regular expression to span across new lines
--invert-regex	return a state of CRITICAL if the text is found, and OK if it is not found
-a, --authorization	Authorize on the page using the basic authentication type. Must be passed in the form of `<username>:<password>`

Option	Description
-A, --useragent	Pass the specified value as the `User-Agent` http header
-k, --header	Add other parameters to be sent in http header (might be repeated)
-f, --onredirect	How to handle redirects; can be one of: ok, warning, critical, follow
-m, --pagesize	The minimum and maximum html page sizes in bytes, as `<min>:<max>`

For example, to verify if a main page has at least the specified number of bytes, and is returned promptly, the following check can be done:

```
define command
{
  command_name  check_http_basic
  command_line  $USER1$/check_http -H $HOSTADDRESS$ -f follow
                -m $ARG1$:1000000 -w $ARG2$ -c $ARG3$
}
```

More complex tests of the WWW infrastructure should be carried out frequently. For example, to verify if an SSL-enabled page works correctly and quickly, a more complex test might be required. The following command will verify the SSL certificate and the page size, and will look for a specific string in the page body.

```
define command
{
  command_name  check_https
  command_line  $USER1$/check_http -H $HOSTADDRESS$ -S -C 14 -u
                $ARG1$
                -f follow -m $ARG1$:$ARG2$ -R $ARG3$
}
```

Checking web pages at a higher level is described in more detail in Chapter 11, *Extending Nagios*, and uses plugins custom-written for this purposes.

Monitoring Database Systems

Databases allow the storage of information that is used often by entire departments or whole companies. Because most systems usually depend on one or more databases, a failure in these databases can cause all of the underlying systems to go down as well. Imagine a business-critical database failure that went unnoticed over a weekend, making both the company's web site, as well as email, unavailable. That would be a disaster! A series of scheduled reports that was supposed to be sent out, would fail to be generated because of this.

This is why, making sure databases are working correctly and have enough resources to operate, might be essential for many companies. Many enterprise-class databases also have table space capacity management which should also be monitored—even though a valid user may be able to log in, this does not necessarily mean that a database is up and running correctly.

MySQL

One of the most commonly-used database types is MySQL. MySQL is, very often, used to provide a basic database for PHP-based web applications. It is also commonly used as a database systems for client-server applications. Nagios offers two plugins to verify if MySQL is working properly. One of the plugins allows checking of connectivity to the database and checking master-slave replication status. The other one allows the measurement of the time taken to execute an SQL query. The syntax of both the commands, and the definition of their options is as follows:

```
check_mysql [-H host] [-d database] [-P port]
            [-u user] [-p password] [-S]

check_mysql_query -q SQL_query [-w <warn>] [-c <crit>] [-d database]
                  [-H host] [-P port] [-u user] [-p password]
```

Option	Description
-P, --port	The port to use for connections (defaults to 3306)
-d, --database	The database to which an attempt to connect is to be made
-u, --username	Username to log in with
-p, --password	Password to log in with
-S, --check-slave	(`check_mysql` only) Verify that the slave thread is running; this is used for monitoring replicated databases
-w, --warning	Specifies the warning threshold; dependant on the plugin used
-c, --critical	Specifies the critical threshold; dependant on the plugin used
-q, --query	(`check_mysql_query` only) Query to perform

For the `check_mysql` command, the `-w` and `-c` options allow us to verify if the slave server is in sync with the master server. If the slave is more than the specified number of seconds behind the master server, a `warning` or `critical` status (as appropriate) is returned.

If the -S option is specified, the plugin will also check whether the replication of MySQL databases is working correctly. This check should be run on MySQL slave servers to make sure that the replication with the master server is in place. Monitoring the number of seconds by which the slave server is behind the master server can be done using the -w and -c flags. In this case, if the slave server is more than the specified number of seconds behind the master server in the replication process, a warning or critical status is issued. More information about checking the replication status can be found under the MySQL documentation for the SHOW SLAVE STATUS command (visit http://dev.mysql.com/doc/refman/5.0/en/show-slave-status.html).

For the check_mysql_query command, the -w and -c options specify the limits for the execution time of the specified SQL query. This allows us to make sure that database performance is within acceptable limits.

The definitions of the check commands for both a simple test and running an SQL query within a specified time are as follows.

```
define command
{
  command_name  check_mysql
  command_line  $USER1$/check_mysql -H $HOSTADDRESS$ -u $ARG1$
                -p $ARG2$ -d $ARG3$ -S -w 10 -c 30
}

define command
{
  command_name  check_mysql_query
  command_line  $USER1$/check_mysql_query -H $HOSTADDRESS$ -u
  $ARG1$
                -p $ARG2$ -d $ARG3$ -q $ARG4$ -w $ARG5$ -c $ARG6$
}
```

Both the examples need the username, password, and dbname as arguments. The second example also requires an SQL query, and warning, and critical time limits.

PostgreSQL

PostgreSQL is another open source database which is commonly used in hosting companies. It is also used very often for client-server applications. The Nagios plugins package offers a command to check if the PostgreSQL database is working correctly. Its syntax is quite similar to the MySQL command:

```
check_pgsql [-H <host>] [-P <port>] [-w <warn>] [-c <crit>]
            [-t <timeout>] [-d <database>] [-l <logname>]
            [-p <password>]
```

The following table describes the options that this plugin accepts:

Option	Description
-P, --port	The port to use for connections (defaults to 5432)
-d, --database	The database to attempt to connect to
-l, --logname	The username to log in with
-p, --password	The password to log in with

A sample check command that expects user name, password, and database name as arguments is as follows:

```
define command
{
  command_name  check_pgsql
  command_line  $USER1$/check_pgsql -H $HOSTADDRESS$ -l $ARG1$
                -p $ARG2$ -d $ARG3$
}
```

Oracle

Oracle is a popular enterprise-class database server. It is mainly used by medium- and large-sized companies for business critical applications. Therefore, a failure, or even a lack of disk space, for a single database might cause huge problems for a company. Fortunately, a plugin exists to verify various aspects of the Oracle database. And it even offers the ability to monitor tablespace storage and cache usage. The syntax is quite different from most Nagios plugins as the first argument specifies the mode in which the check should be carried out, and the remaining parameters are dependant on the first one. The syntax is as follows:

```
check_oracle --tns <ORACLE_SID>
             --db <ORACLE_SID>
             --oranames <Hostname>
             --login <ORACLE_SID>
             --cache <ORACLE_SID> <USER> <PASS> <CRITICAL> <WARNING>
             --tablespace <ORACLE_SID> <USER> <PASS>
                          <TABLESPACE> <CRITICAL> <WARNING>
```

For all checks, Oracle SID (System Identifier) can be specified in the form of `<ip>` or `<ip>/<database>`. Because the plugin automatically adds the username and password to the identifier, an SID in the form of `<username>[/<password>]@<ip>[/<database>]` should not be specified, and in many cases, will not work.

The `--tns` option checks if a database is listening for a connection based on the `tnsping` command. This can be used as a basic check of both local and remote databases.

Verifying that a local database is running can be done using the `--db` option —in which case, a check is performed by running the Oracle process for a specified database.

Verifying a remote Oracle Names server can be done using the `--oranames` mode.

In order to verify if a database is working properly, a `--login` option can be used— this tries to log in using an invalid username and verifies whether the `ORA-01017` error is received, in which case, the database is behaving correctly.

Verifying cache usage can be done using the `--cache` option, in which case, the cache hit ratio is checked—if it is lower than the specified warning or critical limits, the respective status is returned. This allows the monitoring of bottlenecks within the database caching mechanism.

Similarly, for tablespace checking, a `--tablespace` option is provided—a check is carried out against the available storage for the specified tablespace. If it is lower than the specified limits, a `warning` or `critical` status is returned (as appropriate).

This plugin requires various Oracle commands to be in the binary path (the `PATH` environment variable). Therefore, it is necessary to have either the entire Oracle installation or the Oracle client installation done on the machine that will perform the checks for the Oracle database. Sample definitions to check the login into the Oracle database and the database cache are as follows:

```
define command
{
  command_name  check_oracle_login
  command_line  $USER1$/check_oracle --login $HOSTADDRESS$
}

define command
{
  command_name  check_oracle_tablespace
  command_line  $USER1$/check_oracle --cache $HOSTADDRESS$/$ARG1$
                $ARG2$ $ARG3$ $ARG4$ $ARG5$
}
```

The second example requires the passing of the database name, username, password, and critical/warning limits for the cache hit ratio. The critical value should be lower than the warning value.

Other Databases

Even though Nagios supports verification of some common databases, there are a lot of commonly-used databases for which the standard **nagios-plugins** package does not provide a plugin. For these databases, the first thing worth checking is the Nagios Exchange (visit `http://www.nagiosexchange.org/`) as this has a category for database check plugins, with commands for checking various types of databases (such as DB2, Ingres, Firebird, MS SQL, and Sybase).

In some cases, it might be sufficient to use the `check_tcp` plugin to verify whether a database server is up and running. In other cases, it might be possible to use a dynamic language (such as Python, Perl, or Tcl) to write a small script that connects to your database and performs basic tests. See Chapter 11, *Extending Nagios* for more information on writing Nagios check plugins.

Storage Space

Making sure that a system is not running out of space is very important. A lack of disk space for basic paths such as`/var/spool` or `/tmp` might cause unexpected results throughout the entire system. Quotas that are not properly set up for home directories might also cause disk space to run out in a few minutes under certain circumstances.

Nagios can monitor storage space and warn administrators before such problems happen. It is also possible to monitor remote shares on other disks without mounting them. This would be useful for easily monitoring disk space on Windows boxes, without installing the dedicated Windows Nagios tools described in Chapter 10, *Advanced Monitoring*.

Virtual Memory Monitoring

Making sure that a system is not running out of swap space is essential to the system's correct behavior. Many operating systems have mechanisms that kill the most resource -intensive processes when the system is running out of memory, and this usually leads to many services not functioning properly—many vital processes are not properly respawned in such cases. It is, therefore, a good idea to monitor swap space usage, in order to be able to handle low memory issues on critical systems. Nagios offers a plugin to monitor each swap device independently, as well as the ability to monitor cumulative values. The syntax and description of these options are as follows:

```
check_swap [-a] [-v] -w limit -c limit
```

Option	Description
-a, --all	Compare all swap partitions one by one; if not specified, only total swap sizes are checked.

Values for the `-w` and `-c` options can be supplied in the form of `<value>%`, in which case the `<value>` percent must be free in order not to cause an exception to be generated. They can also be supplied in the form `<value><unit>` (for example, 1000k, 100M, 1G), and in this case, a test fails if less than the specified amount of swap space is available.

A sample definition of a check is as follows:

```
define command
{
  command_name  check_swap
  command_line  $USER1$/check_swap -w $ARG1$ -c $ARG2$
}
```

Monitoring IDE/SCSI SMART

Nagios offers a standard plugin that uses **SMART** (**Self-Monitoring, Analysis, and Reporting Technology System**) technology to monitor and report the failure of disk operations. This plugin operates on top of the SMART mechanism and verifies the status of local hard drives. If supported by the underlying IDE and SCSI hardware, this plugin allows the monitoring of hard disk failures. The syntax is as follows:

```
check_ide_smart [-d <device>] [-i] [-q] [-1] [-O] [-n]
```

The table below provides a description of the accepted options:

Option	Description
-d, --device	The device to verify; if this option is set, no other options are accepted
-i, --immediate	Perform offline tests immediately
-q, --quick-check	Return the number of failed tests
-1, --auto-on	Enable automatic offline tests
-0, --auto-off	Disable automatic offline tests
-n, --nagios	Return output suitable for Nagios

A sample definition of a command to monitor a particular device and report failed tests is as follows:

```
define command
{
  command_name  check_ide_smart
  command_line  $USER1$/check_ide_smart -d $ARG1$ -1 -q -n
}
```

Checking Disk Space

One of the most common checks is checking one or more mounted partitions for available space. Nagios offers a plugin for doing this. This plugin offers very powerful functionality, and can be set up to monitor one, several, or all partitions mounted in a system. The syntax for the plugin is as follows:

```
check_disk -w limit -c limit [-W limit] [-K limit] {-p path | -x
                                                        device}
           [-C] [-E] [-e] [-g group] [-k] [-l] [-M] [-m] [-R path ]
           [-r path] [-t timeout] [-u unit] [-v] [-X type]
           [-d <database>] [-l <logname>] [-p <password>]
```

The most commonly-used options for this plugin are described in the following table:

Option	Description
-w, --warning	Return a warning status if less than the specified percentage of disk space is free
-c, --critical	Return a critical if less than the specified percentage of disk space is free
-W, --iwarning	Return a warning if less than the specified percentage of inodes are free
-K, --icritical	Return a critical if less than specified percentage of inodes are free
-p, --path	The path or partition to verify (option might be specified multiple times)
-M, --mountpoint	Display the mount point instead of the partition in the result
-l, --local	Check only local file systems
-A, --all	Verify all mount points
-r, --ereg-path	Regular expression to find paths/partitions (case sensitive)
-R, --eregi-path	Regular expression to find paths/partitions (case insensitive)

Values for the `-w` and `-c` options can be supplied in the form `<value>%`, in which case `<value>` percent must be free in order not to cause a state to occur. They can also be specified in the form of `<value><unit>` (for example, 800k, 50M, and 4G) in which case, a test fails if the available space is less than the specified amount . Checks for inode availability (options `-W` and `-K`) can only be specified in the form `<value>`.

It is possible to check a single partition or specify multiple `-p`, `-r` or `-R` options, and check if all matching mount points have sufficient disk space. It is sometimes better to define separate checks for each partition so that if the limits are exceeded on several of these, each one is tracked separately. The sample check commands for a single partition and for all partitions are shown in the following examples:

```
define command
{
  command_name  check_partition
  command_line  $USER1$/check_disk -p $ARG1$ -w $ARG2$ -c $ARG3$
}

define command
{
  command_name  check_local_partitions
  command_line  $USER1$/check_disk -A -l -w $ARG1$ -c $ARG2$
}
```

Both of these commands expect warning and critical levels, but the first example also requires a partition path or device as the first argument. It is possible to build more complex checks either by repeating the `-p` parameter or by using `-r` to include several mount points.

Testing Free Space for Remote Shares

Nagios offers plugins that allows the monitoring of remote file systems exported over the SMB/CIFS protocol, the standard protocol for file sharing used by Microsoft Windows®. This allows you to check whether a specified user is able to log on to a particular file server and to monitor the amount of free disk space on the file server. The syntax of this command is as follows:

```
check_disk_smb -H <host> -s <share> -u <user> -p <password>
               -w <warn> -c <crit> [-W <workgroup>] [-P <port>]
```

Options specific to this plugin are described in the following table:

Option	Description
-s, --share	SMB share that should be tested
-u, --user	The username to login to the server as (defaults to guest)

Option	Description
-p, --password	The password to use for logging in
-P, --port	The port to be used for connections; defaults to 139

Values for the `-w` and `-c` options can be specified in the form `<value>%`, in which case `<value>` percent must be free in order to not generate an exception. They can also be specified in form of `<value><unit>` (for example, 800k, 50M, and 4G), in which case, the test fails if the available space is less than the specified amount

This command uses the `smbclient` command to communicate over SMB protocol. It is, therefore, necessary to have the Samba client package installed on the machine where the test will be run.

Sample command definitions to check connectivity to a share without checking for disk space, and also to verify disk space over SMB, are as follows:

```
define command
{
  command_name  check_smb_connect
  command_line  $USER1$/check_disk_smb -H $HOSTADDRESS$ -w 100%
                -c 100% -u $ARG1$ -p $ARG2$ -s $ARG3$
}

define command
{
  command_name  check_smb_space
  command_line  $USER1$/check_disk_smb -H $HOSTADDRESS$
                -u $ARG1$ -p $ARG2$ -s $ARG3$ -w $ARG4$ -c $ARG5$
}
```

Both of the commands require the passing of a username, password and share name as arguments. The latter example also requires the passing of warning and critical value limits to check. The first example will only issue a `critical` state if a partition has no space left. It is also worth noting that Samba 3.x servers report quota as disk space, if this is enabled for the specified user. Therefore, this might not always be an accurate way to measure disk space.

Resource Monitoring

For servers or workstations to be responsive and to be kept from being overloaded, it is also worth monitoring system usage using various additonal measures. Nagios offers several plugins to monitor resource usage and to report if the limits set for these checks are exceeded.

System Load

The first thing that should always be monitored is the system load. This value reflects the number of processes and the amount of CPU capacity that they are utilizing. This means that if one process is using up to 50% of the CPU capacity, the value will be around 0.5; and if four processes try to utilize the maximum CPU capacity, the value will be around 4.0. The system load is measured in three values—the average loads in the last minute, last 5 minutes, and the last 15 minutes. The syntax of the command is as follows:

```
check_swap [-r] -w wload1,wload5,wload15 -c cload1,cload5,cload15
```

Option	Description
-r, --percpu	Divide the load averages by the number of CPUs

Values for the `-w` and `-c` options should be in the form of three values separated by commas. If any of the load averages exceeds the specified limits, a warning, or critical status will be returned, respectively. Here is a sample command definition that uses warning and critical load limits as arguments:

```
define command
{
  command_name  check_load
  command_line  $USER1$/check_load -w $ARG1$ -c $ARG2$
}
```

Checking Processes

Nagios also offers a way to monitor the total number of processes. Nagios can be configured to monitor all processes, only running ones, those consuming CPU, those consuming memory, or a combination of these criteria. The syntax and options are as follows:

```
check_procs -w <range> -c <range> [-m metric] [-s state]
            [-p ppid] [-u user] [-r rss] [-z vsz] [-P %cpu]
            [-a argument-array] [-C command] [-t timeout] [-v]
```

Option	Description
-m, --metric	Select which value to use; one of the following: `PROCS`—Number of processes (the default) `VSZ`—Virtual memory size of matching process `RSS`—Resident set memory size of matching process `CPU`—Percentage CPU time of matching process `ELAPSED`—Time elapsed in seconds of matching process

Option	Description
-s, --state	Only check processes that have the specified status; this is the same as the status in the ps command
-p, --ppid	Check the children of the indicated process IDs
-z, --vsz	Check processes with a virtual memory size exceeding value
-r, --rss	Check processes with the resident set memory exceeding value
-P, --pcpu	Check processes with the CPU usage exceeding value
-u, --user	Check processes owned by a specified user
-a,--argument-array	Check processes whose arguments contain a specified value
-C, --command	Check processes with exact matches of the specified value as a command

Values for the `-w` and `-c` options can either take a single value, or take the form of `<min>:<max>`. In the first case, a `warning` or `critical` state is returned if the value (number of processes by default) exceeds the specified number. In the second case, the appropriate status is returned if the value is lower than `<min>` or higher than `<max>`. Sample commands to monitor the total number of processes and to monitor the number of specific processes are as follows. The second code, for example, can be used to check to see if the specific server is running, and has not created too many processes. In this case, warning or critical values should be specified ranging from 1.

```
define command
{
  command_name   check_procs_num
  command_line   $USER1$/check_procs -m PROCS -w $ARG1$ -c $ARG2$
}

define command
{
  command_name   check_procs_cmd
  command_line   $USER1$/check_procs -C $ARG1$ -w $ARG1$ -c $ARG2$
}
```

Monitoring Logged-in Users

It is also possible to use Nagios to monitor the number of users currently logged in to a particular machine. The syntax is very simple and there are the no options, except for `warning` and `critical` limits.

```
check_users -w limit -c limit
```

A command definition that uses `warning` or `critical` limits specified in the arguments is as follows:

```
define command
{
  command_name  check_users
  command_line  $USER1$/check_users -w $ARG1$ -c $ARG2$
}
```

Miscellaneous Plugins

Nagios also offers plugins for many other operations that are common to daily system monitoring and activities; this section covers only a few of them. It is recommended that you look for remaining commands in both the Nagios-plugins package as well as on the NagiosExchange web site.

APT Updates Checking

Many Linux distributions use **APT** (**Advanced Packaging Tool**) for handling package downloads (visit `http://en.wikipedia.org/wiki/Advanced_Packaging_Tool`). This tool is used by default on Debian and its derivatives. It allows the handling of upgrades and download of packages. It also allows the synchronization of package lists from one or more remote sources. Nagios provides a plugin that allows you to monitor, if any upgrades are available, and/or perform upgrades automatically. The syntax and options are as follows:

```
check_apt [-d|-u|-U [<opts>]] [-n] [-t timeout]
          [-i <regex>] [-e <regex>] [-c <regex>]
```

Option	Description
-u, --update	Perform an apt update operation prior to other operations
-U,--upgrade	Perform an apt upgrade operation
-d,--dist-upgrade	Perform an apt dist-upgrade operation
-n, --no-upgrade	Do not run upgrade or dist-upgrade; useful only with `-u`
-i, --include	Include only packages matching a regular expression
-c, --critical	If any packages match a regular expression, a critical state is returned.
-e, --exclude	Exclude packages matching a regular expression

If the `-u` option is specified, the command first attempts to update apt package information. Otherwise, the package information currently in cache is used. If the `-U` or `-d` option is specified, the specified operation is performed. If `-n` is specified, only an attempt to run the operation is made, without actually upgrading perform monitoring (and not upgrade) activities system. The plugin might also be based on daily apt updates/upgrades and only monitor.

The following is a command definition for a simple dist-upgrade, as well as for monitoring available packages and issuing a critical state if the Linux images are upgradeable (that is, if newer packages exist). However, this command does not perform the actual upgrades.

```
define command
{
  command_name  check_apt_upgrade
  command_line  $USER1$/check_apt -u -d
}

define command
{
  command_name  check_apt_upgrade2
  command_line  $USER1$/check_apt -n -u -d
                -c "^linux-(image|restrict)"
}
```

UPS Status Checking

Another useful feature is that of Nagios being able to monitor UPS status over the network. This requires the machine with UPS to have the Network UPS Tools package (visit `http://www.networkupstools.org/`) installed and running, so that it is possible to query the UPS parameters. It is also possible to monitor local resources using the same plugin. The syntax and options are as follows:

```
check_ups -H host -u ups [-p port] [-v variable] [-T]
          [-w <warn time>] [-c <crit time>] [-t <timeout>]
```

Option	Description
-u, --ups	The name of the UPS to check
-p, --port	The port to use for TCP/IP connection; Defaults to 3493
-T, --temperature	Report the temperature in Celsius degrees
-v, --variable	Variable to output; one of: `LINE`, `TEMP`, `BATTPCT` or `LOADPCT`.

The name of the UPS is usually defined in the `ups.conf` file on the machine that the command is connecting to. The plugin will return an `ok` state if the UPS is calibrating or running on AC power. A `warning` state is returned if the UPS claims to be running on batteries, and a `critical` state is returned in the case of a low battery or if the UPS is off.

The following is a sample definition of a check command that gets passed the UPS name as an argument:

```
define command
{
  command_name  check_ups
  command_line  $USER1$/check_ups -H $HOSTADDRESS$ -u $ARG1$
}
```

LM Sensors

This is a Linux-specific plugin that uses the lm-sensors package (visit `http://www.lm-sensors.org/`) to monitor hardware health.

The command issues an `unknown` state if the underlying hardware does not support health monitoring or if the lm-sensors package is not installed, a `warning` if a non-zero error is returned by the `sensors` command, and a `critical` staus if the string ALARM is found within the output from the command.

The plugin does not take any arguments and simply reports information based on the `sensors` command.

The command definition is as follows:

```
define command
{
  command_name  check_sensors
  command_line  $USER1$/check_sensors
}
```

Dummy Check Plugin

Nagios also offers a dummy checking plugin. It simply takes an exit code (which is described on page X). It is useful for testing dependencies between hosts and /or services, verifying notifications, and can also be used for a service that will be measured using passive checks only. The syntax of this plugin is as follows:

```
check_dummy <exitcode> [<result string>]
```

A sample commands to return an `ok` status as well as `critical` with a status text supplied as an argument is shown below:

```
define command
{
  command_name  check_dummy_ok
  command_line  $USER1$/check_dummy 0
}
```

```
define command
{
  command_name  check_dummy_critical
  command_line  $USER1$/check_dummy 0 $ARG1$
}
```

Manipulating Other Plugins' Output

Nagios offers an excellent plugin that simply invokes other checks and converts their status accordingly. This might be useful when a failed check from a plugin is actually an indication that the service is working correctly. This can, for example, be used to make sure that non-authenticated users can't send emails while valid users can. The syntax and options are as follows:

```
negate [-t timeout] [-o|-w|-c|-u state] <actual command to run>
```

Option	Description
-o, --ok	State to return to when the actual command returns an ok state
-w, --warning	State to return to when the actual command returns a warning state
-c, --critical	State to return to when the actual command returns a critical state
-u, --unknown	State to return to when the actual command returns an unknown state

The states to return can either be specified as exit code number or as a string. If no options are specified, only the `ok` and `critical` states are swapped. If at least one status change option is specified, only the specified states are mapped.

Sample command definitions to check that an SMTP server is not listening, and to verify that a user can't log into a POP3 server are as follows:

```
define command
{
  command_name  check_nosmtp
  command_line  $USER1$/negate $USER1$/check_smtp -H $HOSTADDRESS$
}

define command
{
  command_name  check_pop3loginfailure
  command_line  $USER1$/negate -o critical -w ok -c critical
                $USER1$/check_pop -H $HOSTADDRESS$ -E
                -s "USER $ARG1$\r\nPASS $ARG2$\r\n" -d 5
                -e "ogged in"
}
```

The first example does not use state mapping, and the default `ok` for `critical` state replacement is done. The second example maps the states so that if a server is not listening or if the user is actually able to log in, it is considered a `critical` status for the service.

Summary

The Nagios Plugins Package offers a large variety of checks that can be performed to monitor your infrastructure. Whether you are an administrator of an IT company managing a large network, or just want to monitor a small server room, these plugins will allow you to check the majority of the services that you are currently using.

Nagios offers many plugins for monitoring network-aware applications. These include generic TCP and UDP checks—whether a service is accepting connections or not, as well as more complex checks—whether POP3 service accepts a specific username and password. These also include database monitoring checks for commonly-used database servers. Network-based checks can be used to monitor all of the hosts within your network from a single Nagios server. This makes them much easier to be set up.

Another type of check commands are plugins that return information on local resources—such as CPU usage, disk space, or patches that need to be installed. These plugins need to be run on the same machine that the results are for. However, using the techniques that we will cover in Chapters 7 and 8, they can also be used to monitor resources on all machines across your network.

Choosing which plugin to use for performing a check is usually not a difficult thing to do. However, it requires learning what each plugin can check. This allows you to familiarize yourself with the advanced features of the plugin, such as monitoring replication for MySQL, and how to filter processes when monitoring resources. Having such knowledge will definitely allow to monitor your infrastructure much more efficiently.

5 Advanced Configuration

Any experienced administrator knows that there is a huge difference between a working system and a properly configured system. This chapter describes some guidelines which will help you migrate from small (and increasing over time) Nagios setups to a flexible model using templates and grouping effectively. Using this advice will help you and your team to survive the switch from monitoring only critical services to checking the health of the majority of your IT infrastructure.

Things that worked fine when you monitored ten hosts and fifty services might not work when your configuration grows. It is possible to define hundreds of hosts along with thousands of services by hand. Maintaining and applying changes to such configurations is a nightmare, though—imagine going through all of these host definitions just to change the notification interval or retry count for all of them.

When you manage a large number of objects, it is essential to be able to set parameters for each of them in an easy way. This is where the Nagios templates come in handy. You can either use a hierarchical structure, or a flat structure for all of the actual object definitions. Nagios 3 also offers you the possibility to use more than one template at once, which is a huge improvement for large configurations. Setting up templates in your environment may vary depending upon a number of things including your personal preferences.

Defining how to create groups, and which objects should be members of which groups is also a key factor to a good configuration. These groups can be used to manage downtimes and to create statistics and reports. They can also be used to limit the view of an infrastructure to a particular set of machines. A typical example would be to group hosts per branch of the company they are in—in this way, viewing machines only in Chicago is much easier. Groups also allow setting up escalations in a more convenient way—you might want all of your core routers failing to be escalated to higher management much earlier than a backup server being offline.

If you are going to manage all configuration files manually, then it is very important to plan how to store all your configuration files properly. Larger configurations call for better file placing and naming conventions. Otherwise, it is easy to get lost in all the files and directories that various people create in any way they prefer.

This chapter mainly focuses on how to set up templates, groupings, and the directory structure. However, creating a robust monitoring system involves much more—be sure to read the following chapters that talk about monitoring other servers, setting up multiple hosts that use Nagios to monitor your network and report to a single central machine, as well as how to monitor hosts running the Microsoft Windows operating system.

Maintainable Configurations

The effort involved in setting up and maintaining a system that monitors your company's IT infrastructure is enormous. Usually, it can take months to configure it for several hundred machines. The effort required will also depend upon the scope of hosts and services that should be tracked—the more precise the checks need to be, the more the time needed to set these up.

If your company plans to monitor a wide range of hosts and services, you should consider setting up a machine dedicated to Nagios that will only take care of this single job. Even though a small Nagios installation consumes little resources, as it grows, Nagios will start using up more resources. If you set it up to run on the same machine as business-critical applications, it can lead to problems. Therefore, it is always best to set up a dedicated Nagios box, even if this is on a slower machine, right from the beginning.

Very often, a good approach is to start with monitoring only critical parts of your network, such as routers and main servers. You can also start off with only making sure essential services are working—DHCP, DNS, file sharing, and databases are good examples of what is critical. Of course, if your company does not use file servers, or databases are not critical to the production environment, you can also skip these. The next step would be to set up parenting and start adopting more hosts. At some point, you will also need to start planning how to group hosts and services. In the beginning, the configuration might simply be definitions of people, hosts and services. After several iterations of setting up more hosts and services to be monitored, you should get to a point where all of the things that are critical to the company's business are monitored. This should be an indication that your setting up of Nagios configuration is complete.

As the number of objects grows, you will need to group them. Contacts need to be defined as groups because if your team consists of more than one to two people, they will likely rotate over time. So it's better to maintain a group than change the people responsible for each host individually. Hosts and services should be grouped for many reasons. Firstly, it makes viewing the status and infrastructure topology on the web interface much easier. Secondly, after you start defining escalations for your objects, it is much easier to manage these using groups.

You should take some time to plan how group hosts and services should be set up. How will you use the groupings? For escalations? For viewing single host groups via the web interface? Learn how you can take advantage of this functionality and then plan how you will approach the set-up of your groups.

When defining objects that Nagios should monitor, you often come across a service that is common to all types of machines—such as the SSH server for all Linux servers and telnet for all **AIX** (**Advanced Interactive eXecutive**) ones. In such cases, it is possible to define a service only once and tell Nagios which hosts or host groups the service should be bound to. For example, by telling it that all Linux servers offer SSH, and that all AIX servers offer telnet, it will automatically add such services to all of the machines in these groups. Therefore, if your network has some common services, it is better to define them for particular groups, but only once.

In such cases, you should either set up a new host group or use an existing one to keep track of the hosts offering a particular service. Combined with keeping a list of host groups inside each host definition, this makes things much easier to manage—disabling a particular host also takes care of the corresponding service definitions.

It is also worth mentioning that Nagios performs and schedules service checks in a much better way than it does host checks. In Nagios version 1 and 2, only a single host check could be running at a time, with all other service checks at halt. That is why, it is recommended that you do not schedule host checks at all. You can set up a separate service for your hosts that will send a ping to them and report how many packets have returned, and the approximate time taken for them to return.

Nagios can be set up to schedule host checks only of one of the hosts is failing (is not responding to the pings). A host will be periodically checked until it recovers. In this way, problems with hosts will still be detected, but host checks will only be scheduled on demand. This will cause Nagios to perform much better than it would if regular checks of all hosts on your network are made. To disable regular host checks, simply don't specify check interval for the hosts that you want checked only on demand.

Nagios 3 includes many improvements in this area, but it is still recommended that you schedule service checks regularly and don't tell Nagios to perform regular host checks. This is especially good in environments that have a lot of hosts.

Configuration File Structure

A very important issue is how to store all our configuration files. We can put every object definition in a single file, but this will not make it easy to manage. As mentioned in Chapter 2, *Installation and Configuration*, the recommendation is to store different types of objects in separate folders.

Assuming your Nagios configuration is in `/etc/nagios`, it is recommended that you create folders for all types of objects in the following manner:

```
/etc/nagios/commands
/etc/nagios/timeperiods
/etc/nagios/contacts
/etc/nagios/hosts
/etc/nagios/services
```

Of course, these files will need to be added to the `nagios.cfg` file. After having followed the instructions in Chapter 2, these directories should already be added to our main Nagios configuration file.

It would also be worthwhile to use a version control mechanism such as **CVS** (**Concurrent Versions System**, visit `http://www.cvshome.org/`) or **SVN** (**Subversion, visit** `http://subversion.tigris.org/`) to store your Nagios configuration. While this will add overhead to the process for applying configuration changes, it will also save you from someone overwriting a file accidentally. It will also keep track of who changed which parts of the configuration, so you always know whom to blame if things break down.

You might consider writing a simple script that will perform an export from CVS into a temporary directory, verify that Nagios works fine using the `nagios -v` command and, only if that did not fail, copy the new configuration in place of the older one and restart Nagios.

As for naming the files themselves—for time periods, contacts, and commands, it is recommended that you keep single definitions per file, as in `contacts/nagiosadmin.cfg`. This greatly reduces naming collisions and also makes it much easier to find particular object definitions.

Storing hosts and services might be done in a slightly different way—host definitions should go to the `hosts` subdirectory and the file should be named the same as the host name, for example, `hosts/localhost.cfg`. Services can be split into two different types and stored depending on how they are defined and used.

Services that are associated with more than one host should be stored in the services subdirectory. A good example is the SSH service, which is present on the majority of systems. In this case, it should go to `services/ssh.cfg` and use host groups to associate it with the hosts that actually offer connecting over this protocol.

Services that are specific to a host should be handled differently. It's best to store them in the same file as the host definition. A good example might be checking disk space on partitions that might be specific to a particular machine such as checking the `/oracle` partition on a host that's dedicated to Oracle databases.

Our recommendation for handling groups is to create files called `groups.cfg` and define all groups in it, without any members. Then while defining a contact, host, or group, you can define which groups it belongs to by using the `contactgroups`, `hostgroups` or `servicegroups` directives accordingly. This way, if you disable a particular object by deleting or commenting out its definition, the definition of the group itself will still work.

If you plan on having a large number of both check command and notify command definitions, you may want to split this into two separate directories—`checkcommands` and `notifycommands`. You can also use a single commands `subdirectory`, prefix the file names, and store the files in a single directory, for example, `commands/check_ssh.cfg` and `commands/notify_jabber.cfg`.

Defining Dependencies

It is a very common scenario that computers, or the applications they offer, depend on other objects to function properly. A typical example is a database that an email or web server will depend upon. Another one is a host behind a private network depends that on an OpenVPN service to work. As a system administrator, your job is to know these relations—if you plan to reinstall a database cluster, you need to let people know there will be downtime for almost all applications. Nagios should also be aware of such relations.

In such cases, it is very useful for system monitoring software to consider these dependencies. When analyzing which hosts and services are not working properly, it is good to analyze such dependencies and discard things that are not working because of other failures. This way, it will be easier for you to focus on the real problems. Therefore, it allows you to get to the root cause of any malfunction much faster.

Nagios allows you to define how hosts and services depend on each other. This allows very flexible configurations and checks, and distinguishes it from many other less advanced system monitoring applications. Nagios provides very flexible mechanisms for checking hosts and services—it will take all dependencies into account. This means that if a service relies on another one to function properly, Nagios will perform checks to make sure that all dependant services are working properly.

In case a dependant service is not working properly, Nagios may or may not perform checks, and may or may not send out any notifications, depending on how the dependency is defined. This is logical as the service will most probably not work properly if a dependant object is not working.

Nagios also offers the ability to specify parents for hosts. This is, in a way, similar to dependencies, as both specify that one object depends on another object. The main difference is that parents are used to define the infrastructure hierarchy. Parent definitions are also used by Nagios to skip checks for hosts that will obviously be down. Dependencies, on the other hand, can be used to suppress notifications about the problems that are occurring due to dependant services being down, but they do not necessarily cause Nagios to skip checking a particular host or service. Another difference is that parents can only be specified for hosts, whereas dependencies can be set up between hosts and services.

Dependencies also offer more flexibility in terms of how they are configured. It is possible to specify which states of the dependant host or service will cause Nagios to stop sending out notifications. You can also tell Nagios when it should skip performing checks, based on the status of the dependant object.

Dependencies might also be valid only at certain times—for example a back-up service that needs to be monitoring your system all of the time, but that needs to have access to networked storage only between 11 PM and 4 AM.

To aid in describing how objects depend on each other, Nagios documentation uses two terms—*master* and *dependent* objects. When defining dependency, a master object is the object that needs to be working correctly in order for the other object to function. Similarly, the dependent object is the one that needs another object in order to work. This terminology will be used throughout this section, to avoid confusion.

Let's start with host dependency definitions. These are objects that have several attributes, and each dependency can actually describe one or more dependencies—for example, it is possible to tell Nagios that 20 machines rely on a particular host in a single dependency definition.

Here is an example of a dependency specifying that during maintenance, a Windows backup storage server in another branch depends upon a VPN server.

```
define hostdependency
{
  dependent_host_name            backupstorage-branch2
  host_name                      vpnserver-branch1
  dependency_period              maintenancewindows
}
```

The following table describes all of the available directives for defining a host dependency. Items in bold are required when specifying a dependency:

Option	Description
dependent_host_name	Defines host names that are dependent on the master hosts, separated by commas
dependent_hostgroup_name	Defines host group names whose members are dependent on the master hosts, separated by commas
host_name	Defines master hosts, separated by commas
hostgroup_name	Defines host groups whose members are to be master hosts, separated by commas
inherits_parent	Whether dependency should inherit dependencies of master hosts
execution_failure_criteria	Specifies which master host states should prevent Nagios from checking the dependant hosts, separated by commas; can be one or more of the following: n—none; checks should always be executed p—pending state (no check has yet been done) o—host UP state d—host DOWN state u—host UNREACHABLE state
notification_failure_criteria	Specifies which master host states should be prevented from generating notifications about dependent host status changes, separated by commas; can be one or more of the following: n—none; notification should always take place p—pending state (no check has yet been done) o—host UP state d—host DOWN state u—host UNREACHABLE state
dependency_period	Specifies time periods during which the dependency will be valid; if not specified, the dependency is always valid

The question is where to store such dependency files. As for service definitions, it is recommended that you store dependencies specific to a particular host in the file containing the definition of the dependent host. For the previous example, we would put it in the `hosts/backupstorage-branch2.cfg` file.

When defining a dependency that will describe a relationship between more than one master or dependant host, it's best to put these into a generic file for dependencies—for example, we can put it in `hosts/dependencies.cfg`. Another good option is to put dependency definitions that only affect a single master host in the master host's definition.

If you are defining a dependency that covers more than one master or dependent host, it is best to use host groups to manage the list of hosts that should be included in dependency's definition. This can be one or more host group names, and very often, these groups will also be the same as for the service definitions.

Service dependencies work in a similar way as host dependencies. For hosts, you need to specify one or more master hosts and one or more dependant hosts; for services, you need to define a master service and a dependent service.

Service dependencies can be defined only for a single service, but on multiple hosts. For example, you can tell Nagios that POP3 services on the `emailservers` host group depend on the LDAP service on the `ldapserver` host.

Here is an example of how to define such a service dependency:

```
define servicedependency
{
  host_name                       ldapserver
  service_description             LDAP
  dependent_hostgroup_name        emailservers
  dependent_service_description   POP3
  execution_failure_criteria      c,u
  notification_failure_criteria   c,u,w
}
```

The following table describes all available directives for defining a service dependency. Items in bold are required when specifying a dependency.

Option	Description
dependent_host_name	Defines host names whose services should be taken into account for this dependency, separated by commas
dependent_hostgroup_name	Defines host group names whose members' services should be taken into account for this dependency, separated by commas
dependent_service_description	Defines service that should be the dependent service for all specified dependant hosts

Option	Description
host_name	Defines the master hosts whose services should be taken into account by this dependency, separated by commas
hostgroup_name	Defines the master host groups whose members' services should be taken into account by this dependency separated by commas
service_description	Defines the service that should be the master service for all provided master hosts
inherits_parent	Specifies whether this dependency should inherit the dependencies of master hosts
execution_failure_criteria	Specifies which master service states should prevent Nagios from checking dependent services, separated by commas; can be one or more of the following: n – none; checks should always be executed p – pending state (no check has yet been done) o – service OK state w – service WARNING state c – service CRITICAL state u – service UNKNOWN state
notification_failure_criteria	Specifies which master service states should be prevented from generating notifications for dependent service status changes, separated by commas; can be one or more of the following: n – none; checks should always be executed p – pending state (no check has yet been done) o – service OK state w – service WARNING state c – service CRITICAL state u – service UNKNOWN state
dependency_period	Specifies the time periods during which the dependency will be valid; if not specified, the dependency is always valid

Similar to host dependencies, there is a question on where to store service dependency definitions. A good answer to this is to store dependencies in the same files where the dependent service definitions are kept. If you are following the previous suggestions regarding how to keep services in the file structure, then for a service bound to a single host, both service and the related dependencies should be kept in the same file as the host definition itself. If a service is used by more than one host, it is kept in a separate file. In this case, dependencies related to that service should also be kept in the same file as the service.

Using Templates

Templates in Nagios allow you to create a set of parameters that can then be used in the definitions of multiple hosts, services, and contacts. The main purpose of templates is to keep parameters that are generic to all objects, or a group of objects, in one place. This way, you can avoid putting the same directives in hundreds of objects, and your configuration is more maintainable.

It is also good to start using templates for hosts and services, and decide how they should be used. Sometimes, it is better to have one template inherit another and create a hierarchical structure. In many cases, it is more reasonable to create hosts so that they use multiple templates—this is new functionality in Nagios 3, so it will not work for Nagios 2 configurations. This functionality allows inheriting some options from one template, and some parameters from another template.

The following is an illustration of how the templates can be structured using both techniques:

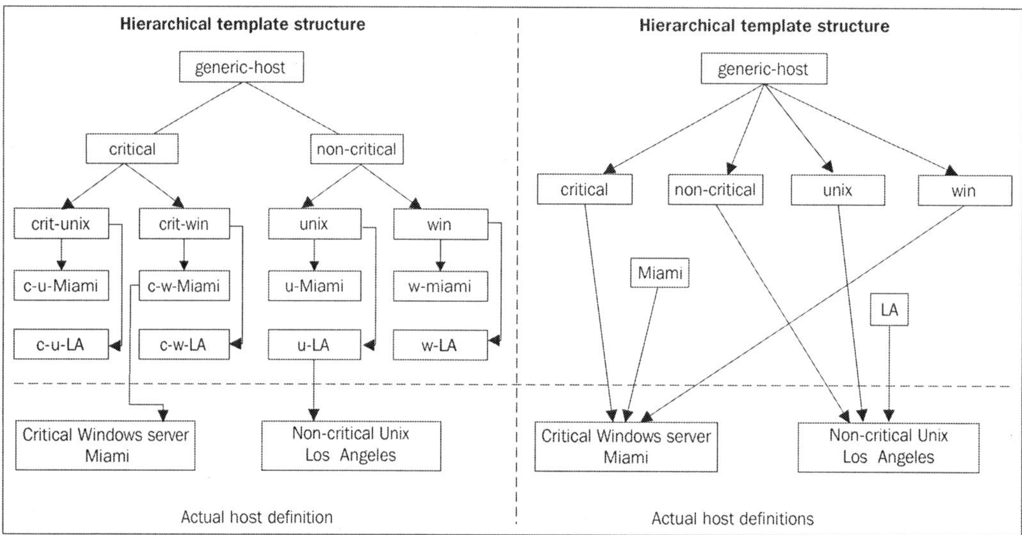

This example illustrates how the templates can be structured using both hierarchy and multiple templates inheritance. This diagram shows how to use templates for host definitions. Similar rules apply for services as well, but the inheritance structure might be quite different.

In both of the methods shown above, there is a distinction between `critical` and `non-critical` servers. Hosts are also split into ones that are UNIX based and ones that are Microsoft Windows based. There is also a distinction between the two branches that are configured—`Miami` and `LA` (Los Angeles). Furthermore, there is also a `generic-host` template that is used by every other template.

Usually, such distinctions make sense as Windows and UNIX boxes might be checked differently. Based on the operating system and the location of the machine, different people should be assigned as contacts in case of problems. There may also be different time periods during which these hosts should be checked.

The example on the left shows the inheritance of one type of parameter at a time. First, a distinction is made between critical and non-critical machines. Usually, both types have different values for the notification and check intervals, as well as the number of checks to perform before generating a notification for a problem. The next step is to differentiate between Microsoft Windows and UNIX based servers—this might involve `check` command to verify that a server is up. The last step is to define templates for each system in both of the branches (`Miami` and `LA`). The actual host definition inherits from one template in the final set of templates.

The example on the right uses a slightly different approach. It first defines different templates for UNIX and Windows systems. Next, a pair of templates for critical and noncritical machines is also defined. Finally, a set of templates defines the branches—`Miami` and `LA`. The actual host definition inherits templates for the operating system, for the level of criticality, and for the branch it belongs to. It inherits parameters partially from each of the templates.

In both cases, attributes that are passed at different levels are the same, even though the approach is different. Usually, the templates that define the operating system also define how a host check should be done. They might also indicate the time period over which a host should be checked.

Templates for critical and noncritical machines usually specify how notifications should be carried out. If a host is crucial to infrastructure, its owners should be notified in a more aggressive way. Similarly, machines that are not affecting business directly do not need that much attention.

Templates for locations usually define the owners of the machines. The locations are not always branches, as in this example; they can be branches, floors, or even network connection types. Locations can also point machines to their parent hosts—usually computers located in the same place that are connected to the same router.

Even though the previous example shows an approach typical of hosts, templates for other types of objects work in a similar way. The main difference is that templates for contacts and services are usually less structured.

Contacts usually use only a couple of templates. They depend on the working hours and the notification preferences. The remaining parameters can be kept in an individual contact's definition. Very often, users may have their own preferences on how they should be notified, so it's better not to try and design templates for that.

Services usually use a similar approach as the one for hosts. It is a good idea to define templates for branches depending on the priority of service. Good configurations tend to have many more hosts than service definitions. This is because it's better to define services common to multiple machines once, and to use groups to manage hosts that should be associated with this service.

Defining templates in Nagios is very similar to defining actual objects. You simply define the template as the required object type. The only difference is that you need to specify the `register` directive and specify a value, of `0` for it. This will tell Nagios that it should not treat this as an actual object, but as a template. You will also need to use the `name` directive for defining template names. You do not need to specify other directives for naming objects such as `host_name`, `contact_name`, or `service_description`.

When defining an object, simply include the `use` directive and specify all of the templates to be used as its value. If you want to inherit from multiple templates, separate all of them by commas.

The following is an example on how to define a template for a Linux server and then use this in an actual host definition:

```
define host
{
  register               0
  name                   generic-servers
  check_period           24x7
  retry_interval         1
  check_interval         15
  max_retry_attempts     5
  notification_period    24x7
  notification_interval  60
  notification_options   d,r
}

define host
{
  register               0
  use                    generic-servers
  name                   linux-servers
  check_command          check-host-alive
  contact_groups         linux-admins
}

define host
{
  use                    linux-servers
  host_name              ubuntu1
  address                192.168.2.1
}
```

As mentioned earlier, templates use name for defining the template, and the actual host uses the host_name directive.

Nagios 3 allows you to inherit from multiple templates, and templates using other (nested) templates. It's good to know how Nagios determines the order in which every directive is looked for in each of the templates. When inheriting attributes from more than one template, Nagios tries to find the directive in each of the templates, starting from the first one. If it is found in the first template, that value is used; if not, Nagios checks for a value in the second one. This cycle continues until the last template in the list. If any of the templates is also inheriting from another template, then a check for the second level of templates is done recursively. This means that checking for a directive will perform a recursive check of all of the templates that are inherited from the currently-checked one.

The following illustration shows an example of this situation. The actual host definition inherits three templates—B, F, and G. Template B inherits A, F inherits D and E and finally, D inherits attributes from template C.

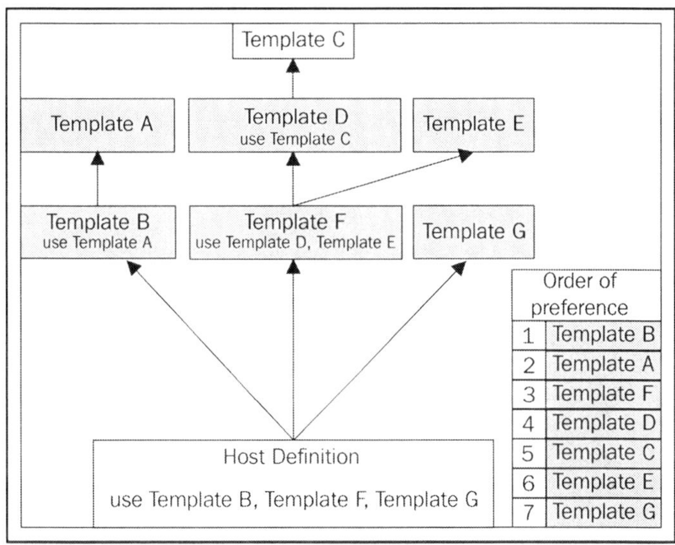

If Nagios tries to find any directive related to this host, the first thing that will be checked is the actual host definition. If the host does not include the directive, Nagios will first look under B, as this is the first template that should be used. If it is not found in B, Nagios will recursively try to find the attribute in A, as it is used by template B. The next step is to look in F along with all of the templates it is using. F inherits D and E. The first one to check is B along with all parent templates—this dictates that D, C, and the next E should now be checked. If the attribute is still not found, then template G is used.

Let's assume the following directives (among others) are defined for the previous illustration:

```
define host
{
  register                0
  name                    A
  check_period            workinghours
  retry_interval          1
  check_interval          15
}

define host
{
  register                0
  use                     A
  name                    B
  check_period            24x7
}

define host
{
  register                0
  name                    D
  use                     C
  max_retry_attempts      4
}

define host
{
  register                0
  name                    E
  max_retry_attempts      3
}

define host
{
  register                0
  use                     D,E
  name                    F
  notification_interval   30
}

define host
{
  use                     B,F,G
  host_name               ubuntu1
  address                 192.168.2.1
  notification_interval   20
}
```

For this particular example, the values for address and notification_interval directives are taken directly from the host ubuntu1 definition. Even though notification_interval is also defined in F, it is overwritten by the actual host definition.

The value for max_retry_attempts is taken from the template D—regardless of whether it is also defined in C or not. Even though the template E also defines a value for it, as D is put before E, the values defined in both of them are taken from D.

The value for check_period is taken from B, which overwrites the value defined for the template A. Values for retry_interval and check_interval are taken from A.

Custom Variables

Custom variables allow you to include your own directives when defining objects. These can then be used in commands. This allows you to define objects in a more concise way and define service checks in a more general fashion. This functionality was introduced in Nagios 3, and is not available in the previous versions.

The idea is that you define directives that are not standard Nagios parameters in host, service, or contact objects, and they can then be accessed from all commands—check commands, notifications, and event handlers. This is very useful for complex Nagios configurations where you might want commands to perform nontrivial tasks for which they will require additional information.

Let's assume we want Nagios to check that hosts have correct MAC addresses. In Nagios 2, we would need to use a separate service check definition for each host and specify the MAC address in each of them. With Nagios 3, we can define a custom variable to store the MAC address for all or some of the hosts. We can then define a service once and use that custom variable for the check command.

When defining an object, a custom variable needs to be prefixed with an underscore and written in upper case. Custom variables are then accessible from check commands as the following macros:

- $_HOST<variable>$—for directives defined within a host object
- $_SERVICE<variable>$—for directives defined within a service object
- $_CONTACT<variable>$—for directives defined within a contact object

For the example above, a macro definition would be $_HOSTMAC$.

The following is an example of a contact and notification command that uses a custom variable for the Jabber address:

```
define contact
{
  contact_name                jdoe
  alias                       John Doe
  host_notification_commands host-notify-by-jabber
  _JABBERID                   jdoe@jabber.yourcompany.com
}

define command
{
  command_name        host-notify-by-jabber
  command_line        $USER1$/notify_via_jabber $_CONTACTJABBERID$
                      "Host $HOSTDISPLAYNAME$ changed state to
                       $HOSTSTATE$"
}
```

Of course, you will also need a plugin to send notifications over Jabber. This can be downloaded from the Nagios project on SourceForge (visit `http://nagios.sf.net/download/contrib/notifications/notify_via_jabber`). The previous example will work with any other protocol you might be using. All that's needed is a plugin that will send commands over such a protocol.

A very useful client called EKG2 (visit `http://www.ekg2.org/`) allows you to send messages over various protocols including, Jabber, and has a pipe that can be used to send messages over these protocols. A sample command to do this can be as follows:

```
define command
{
  command_name        host-notify-by-ekg2
  command_line        /usr/bin/printf "%b" "msg $_CONTACTEKGALIAS$
                      Host $HOSTDISPLAYNAME$ changed state to
                      $HOSTSTATE$\n" >>~/.ekg2/.pipe
}
```

A major benefit of custom variables is that they can also be changed on the fly over an external command pipe. This way, the custom variables functionality can be used in more complex configurations. Event handlers may trigger changes in the attributes of other checks.

An example might be that a ping check with 50ms and 20% packet loss limits is made to ensure that the network connectivity is working correctly. However, if the main router is down and a failover connection is used, the check is set to a more relaxed limits of 400ms and 50% packet loss.

An example configuration might be as follows:

```
define service
{
  host_name             router2
  service_description PING
  check_command         check_ping_limits
  _LIMITS               50.0,20%
}

define command
{
  command_name          check_ping_limits
  command_line          $USER1$/check_ping -H $HOSTADDRESS$
                        -w $_SERVICELIMITS$ -c $_SERVICELIMITS$
}
```

Then, when a service that checks if the main router is up, is in a hard critical state, an event handler will invoke a change in the limits by sending a `CHANGE_CUSTOM_SVC_VAR` command (`http://www.nagios.org/developerinfo/externalcommands/commandinfo.php?command_id=140`) over the external commands pipe to set the `_LIMITS` custom variable.

Chapter 6, *Notification and Events* covers event handlers and external commands pipe in more detail. So it is recommended that you read this chapter in order to better understand this approach.

Flapping

Flapping is a situation where a host or service changes states very rapidly—constantly switching between working correctly and not working at all. This can happen for various reasons—a service might crash after a short period of operating correctly or due to performing some maintenance by system administrators.

Nagios can detect that a host or service is flapping, if Nagios is configured to do so. It does so by analyzing previous results, in terms of how many state changes between have happened and within a specific period of time. Nagios keeps a history of the 21 most recent checks and analyzes changes within that history.

The following is an image illustrating the 21 most recent check results, which means that Nagios can detect up to 20 state changes in the recent history of an object. It also shows how Nagios detects state transitions:

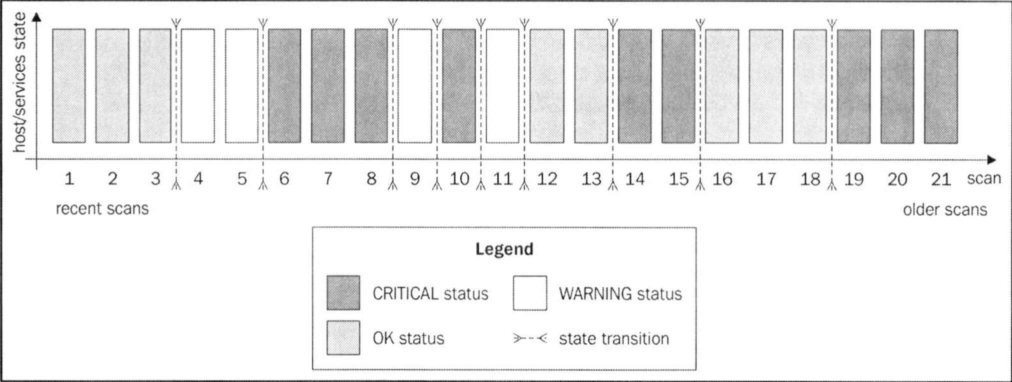

Nagios then finds all of the changes between different states, and uses them to determine if a host or service is flapping—it checks too see if a state is the same as the result from the previous check, and if it has changed, a state transition is counted at this place. In the example above, we have three transitions in all.

Nagios calculates a flapping threshold based on this information—the value reflects how many of the state changes have occurred recently. If there are no changes in the last 21 state checks, the value would be 0%. If all checks have different states, the flapping threshold would be 100%.

Nagios also differentiates older results from newer ones. This means that a state transition that took place during the 18th previous check will cause the flapping threshold to be much lower than a transition that took place during the 3rd previous check.

In our case, if Nagios would only take the number of transitions into account, the flapping threshold would be 45%. The weighted algorithm used in Nagios would calculate the flapping threshold as being more than 45% as there have been many changes in the more recent checks.

Nagios takes threshold values into consideration when estimating whether a host or service has started or stopped flapping. The configuration for each object allows the definition of low and high flapping thresholds.

If an object was not previously flapping, and the current flapping threshold is equal to or greater than the high flap threshold, Nagios assumes that the object has just started flapping. If an object was previously flapping, and the current threshold is lower than the low flap threshold, Nagios assumes the object has just stopped flapping.

The following chart shows how the flapping threshold for an object has changed over time, and when Nagios assumed it started and stopped flapping. In this case, the high flap threshold is set to 40%, and the low flap threshold is set to 25%. Red vertical lines indicate when Nagios assumed the flapping to have started and stopped, and the grey area shows where the service was assumed to be flapping.

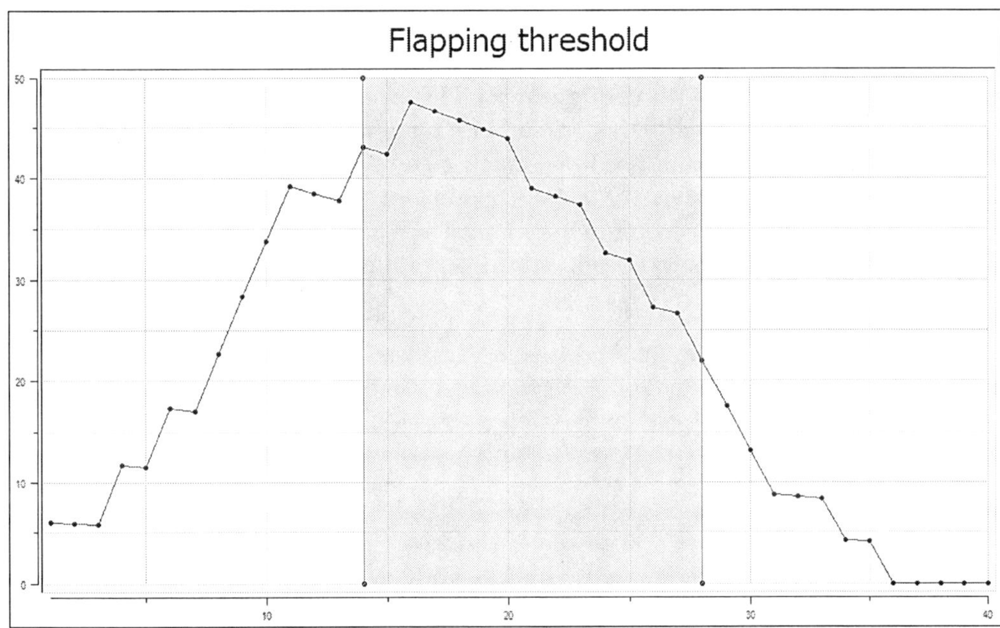

It is worth noting that the low flap threshold should be lower than the high flap threshold. This prevents the situation where after one state transition, flapping would be detected and the next check would tell Nagios that the object has stopped flapping. If both the attributes are set to the same value, an object might be identified as having started and stopped flapping often. This can happen when the flapping threshold changes from below threshold to above threshold, or vice-versa. This might cause Nagios to send out large number of notifications and cause its performance to degrade.

Summary

Nagios configuration can either be your friend or your enemy. We recommend getting be friends with it as it can be a lifesaver.

When deploying Nagios in your company, it would be worthwhile planning the layout of your entire configuration. Some people recommend one file for each single definition, while others recommend storing things in a single file per host. We recommend keeping similar things in the same file and maintaining a directory-based set of files.

Defining parent hosts and dependencies between hosts and services would also be beneficial if you want Nagios to help you track down the root cause of a problem. This will skip check against hosts and services that are in error due to the other problems in your network. Of course, if you don't define those, Nagios will still work, will still perform very useful checks, but you will be on your own in analyzing what happened because of what.

In order for Nagios and you to get along well, it would also be good to use templates for the things you define in the configuration. This allows you to have various directives in one or more templates instead of having them scattered across the entire configuration. Such configurations have much greater flexibility and are easier to maintain over time. The drawback is that if your company won't have any guidelines as to how templates should be created and used—in terms of approach, naming and file locations—you might still run into having a configuration that's a nightmare to update.

A great feature added in Nagios 3 is custom variables. These allow you to put any data you like into your object configurations and use them inside commands. These values can also be modified on the fly from event triggers or external applications, and allow more complex solutions to be built based on Nagios.

Nagios also offers a way to detect flapping—a situation where a host or service constantly switches states—for example, between working correctly and failing. Nagios can be configured to ignore this, act upon it, and how Nagios detects the case can also be fine-tuned to your needs.

6
Notifications and Events

We already know how notifications work in Nagios. The previous chapters described how Nagios sends information to the users when a problem occurs, and how it decides to notify people. Previously, our examples were limited to sending an email 24 hours a day or only during working days.

There is a lot more to what Nagios can do, and how it can make your life easier. Imagine that you set up Nagios to send a text message to your mobile during day time. It can also send you a message on Jabber or MSN. Imagine that you also make Nagios stop notifying you when your workstation is not online.

Even though the above examples above seem complicated, they are actually quite simple to implement. It's a matter of combining event handlers with custom variables, and a little ingenuity. A service that will check if a user's workstation is present can have an event handler to automatically enable and disable host and/or service notifications for a contact or contact group.

It's also possible to set up your monitoring to notify managers if the issue has not been fixed within a certain period of time. Based on the importance of a host or service, these can be different managers that are notified and different time periods after which the notification is sent. Nagios can also be used to notify emergency response teams so that if a problem is not fixed in a short period of time, they will assist in recovering from the potential after effects of this problem.

There are cases when you want Nagios to perform one or more actions if a service starts or stops malfunctioning. For instance, you might have a web server set up to retry five times before a failure becomes a hard state for Nagios. In such a case, you can also configure Nagios to try restarting itself after the third soft failure—if it fails, it will move to a hard state after the next two failures. In case the restart succeeds, a hard state will not even get recorded and only a soft failure will get logged.

Nagios is able to integrate itself with other applications that can send commands to Nagios directly and can report the status of host or service checks. Sending commands can be used by Nagios web interface, but you might as well use it inside your application or event handlers for various objects.

Effective Notifications

This section covers notifications in more depth and describes the details of how Nagios can tell other people about what is happening. We will discuss a simple approach, as well as a more complex approach on how notifications can make your life easier.

Probably, most people already know that a plain email notification about a problem may not always be the right thing to do. As people's inboxes get cluttered with emails, the usual approach is to create rules to move certain messages that they don't even look at to separate folders. There's a pretty good chance that if people start getting a lot of notifications that they won't need to react to, they'll simply ask their favorite mailing program to move these messages into a 'do not look in here unless you have plenty of time' folder. Moreover, in such cases, if there is an issue they should be handling, they will most probably not even see the notification email.

This section talks about the things that can be implemented in your company to make notifications more convenient to the IT staff. Limiting the amount of irrelevant information sent to various people tends to increase their response time, as they will have much less information to filter out.

The first issue that many Nagios administrators overlook is the ability to create more than one notification command. In this way, Nagios can try to notify you on both instant messaging (such as Jabber/Gtalk, MSN, or Yahoo) and email. It can also send you an SMS. A disadvantage is that at some point, you might end up receiving SMSes at 2 AM about an outage of a machine that may well be down for the next 3 days and is not critical.

At this point, it's worth mentioning that there's another easy solution. Again, most people do not use it even though it offers a very flexible set up in an easy way. The approach is to create multiple contacts for a single person. For example, you can set up different contacts when you're at work, when you're offline, and define a profile to not to disturb you too much during the night.

For example you can set up the following contacts to handle various times of the day in a different fashion:

- `jdoe-workhours` would be a contact that will only receive notifications during working hours; notifications will be carried out using both the corporate IM system and an email

- `jdoe-daytime` would be a contact that will only receive notifications between 7 AM and 10 PM, excluding working hours; notifications will be sent as a text or a pager message, and an email
- `jdoe-night` would be a contact that will only receive notifications between 10 PM and 7 AM; notifications will only be sent out as an email

All entries would also contain `contactgroups` pointing to the same groups that the single `jdoe` contact entry used to contain. This way, the other objects such as hosts, services, or contact groups related to this user would not be affected. All entries would also reside in the same file; for example, `contacts/jdoe.cfg`.

The main drawback of this approach is that logging on to the web interface would require using one of the users above or keeping the `jdoe` contact without any notifications, just to be able to log on to the interface.

The example above combined both the creation of multiple contacts and use of multiple notification commands to achieve a convenient way of getting notified about a problem. Using only multiple contacts also works fine. Another approach to the problem is to define different contacts for different ways of being notified—for example, `jdoe-email`, `jdoe-sms`, and `jdoe-jabber`. This way, you can define different contact methods for various time periods—instant messages during working hours, SMSes while on duty, and an email when not at work.

Another important issue is to make sure that as few people as possible are notified of the problem. Imagine there is a host without an explicit administrator assigned to it. A notification about a problem gets sent out to 20 different people. In such a case, either each of them will assume that someone else will resolve the problem, or people will run into a communication problem over discussing who will actually handle it.

Teams that cooperate tightly with each other usually solve these issues naturally—knowledgeable people start discussing a solution and a natural person to solve the issue comes out of the discussion. However, the teams that are distributed across various locations or that have poor communication skills will run into problems in such cases.

This is why, it is a good idea to either nominate a coordinator who will assign tasks as they arise, or try to maintain a short list of people responsible for each machine. If you need to make sure that other people will investigate the problem if the original owner of the machine cannot do it immediately, then it is a good idea to use escalations for this purpose. These are described later in this chapter.

Previously, we mentioned that notifications only via email may not always be the best thing to do. For example, they don't work well for situations that require fast response times. There are various reasons behind this. Firstly, emails are slow—even though the email lands on your mail server in a few seconds, people usually only poll their emails every few minutes. Secondly, people tend to filter emails and skip those that they are not interested in.

Another good reason why emails should not always be used is that they stay on your email account until you actually fetch and read them. If you have been on a 2-week vacation and a problem has occurred, should you still be worried when you read it after you get back? Has the issue been resolved already?

If your team needs to react to problems promptly, using email as the basic notification method is definitely not the best choice. Let's consider what other possibilities exist to notify users of a problem effectively.

As already mentioned, a very good choice is to use instant messaging or **SMS** (**Simple Messaging Service**) messages as the basic means of notification, and only use email as a last resort. Some companies might also use the client-server approach to notify the users of the problems, perhaps integrated with showing Nagios' status only for particular hosts and services. **NagiosExchange** has plenty of available solutions you can use for handling notifications effectively. Visit `http://www.nagiosexchange.org/` for more details.

The first and the most powerful option is to use **Jabber** (visit `http://www.jabber.org/`) for notifications. There is an existing script for this that is available in the contributions repository on the Nagios project website (visit `http://nagios.sf.net/download/contrib/notifications/notify_via_jabber`). This is a small Perl script that sends messages over Jabber. You may need to install additional system packages to handle Jabber connectivity from Perl. On Ubuntu, this requires running the following command:

```
root@ubuntu1:~# apt-get install libnet-jabber-perl
```

If you are using **CPAN** (visit `http://www.cpan.org/`) to install Perl packages, then simply run the following command:

```
root@ubuntu1:~# cpan install Net::Jabber
```

In order to use the notification plugin, you will need to customize the script—change the `SERVER`, `PORT`, `USER`, and `PASSWORD` parameters to an existing account. Our recommendation is to create a separate account to use only for Nagios notifications—you will need to set up authorization for each user that you want to send notifications to.

As you plan to monitor servers and potentially even outgoing Internet connectivity, it would not be wise to use public Jabber servers for reporting errors. Therefore, it would be a good idea to set up a private Jabber server, probably on the same host on which the Nagios monitoring system is running.

If you plan to have a more comfortable setup, you can also use **Tkabber** (visit `http://tkabber.jabber.ru/`) as a Jabber client, and write a plugin that reads object's cache and the current status from the Nagios host and shows an up-to-date report for hosts that you are the owner of. Information on reading Nagios output can be found on my **Tclmentor** blog at `http://tclmentor.kocjan.org/search/label/nagios`.

Another possibility is to send messages over **SMB/CIFS** protocol (visit `http://en.wikipedia.org/wiki/Server_Message_Block`). This way, you can send messages directly to the computers, assuming people are running the Microsoft Windows operating system. There is also the possibility of receiving messages using Samba package on UNIX machines. This requires having the `smbclient` command installed. On Ubuntu, this requires running the following command:

```
root@ubuntu1:~# apt-get install smbclient
```

A simple command definition example that uses `smbclient` directly to send messages to the specified host name is as follows:

```
define command
{
  command_name  notify_host_via_smbclient
  command_line  printf "Host notification: $NOTIFICATIONTYPE$\n\n
                       Host:     $HOSTNAME$\n
                       State:    $HOSTSTATE$
                       Address:  $HOSTADDRESS$\n
                       Info:     $HOSTOUTPUT$" |
                       smbclient -M $_CONTACTSMBHOSTNAME$
}
```

The preceding example uses the `$_CONTACTSMBHOSTNAME$` macro definition. It maps to the `_SMBHOSTNAME` custom variable defined for a specified contact.

In order for Windows XP and 2003 to show the messages from other users correctly, you will need to enable the `Messenger` service. This can be done by running the following command as the system administrator, or as a user with administrator privileges:

```
C> net start Messenger
```

Another way to communicate problems to the users is to use text messages, also known as SMS. This is a very sensitive issue because if your system is not properly configured, it can send a message in the middle of a night about a noncritical thing that can be fixed within the next 5 working days.

There is a very useful package for handling of SMS sending called **SMSServerTools** (visit `http://smstools.meinemullemaus.de/`). It allows the configuration of email and web gateways, as well as sending text messages over dedicated **GSM (Global System for Mobile Communication**; visit `http://en.wikipedia.org/wiki/GSM`) terminals. The tool offers the ability to queue text messages so that it handles a higher number of messages to be sent by the appropriate means.

GSM terminals work in a manner similar to a typical mobile phone. They use a standard SIM card and have a normal GSM phone module that is used to send SMS messages. Terminals are usually connected via a serial port or USB connection. Your server can then send messages by sending commands to the terminal. GSM terminals use the same command convention as phone modems, although each model uses a different set of commands. For information on how you can send SMS messages over it, please refer the terminal's user manual.

Current mobile phones also offer cheap Internet connectivity, and smart devices offer the possibility to write custom applications in Java, .NET, and many other languages including Python and Tcl. Therefore, you can also make a client-server application that queries the server for the status of selected hosts and services. It can even be unified with a notification command that pushes the changes down to the application immediately.

These are only a few of the possibilities that you can use to communicate problems more effectively.

Other possibilities include a ready-to-use client-server application (visit `http://www.nagiosexchange.org/Notifications.35.0.html?&tx_netnagext_pi1[p_view]=182`) that allows the sending of notifications to people directly to their desktop machines. One interesting notification command allows you to choose other commands to use based on user availability on Jabber—this sends messages over Jabber if the user is are available and uses SMSes or emails otherwise. (visit `http://www.nagiosexchange.org/Notifications.35.0.html?&tx_netnagext_pi1[p_view]=1036`)

There are also tools to send messages to ICQ users and ones that use VoIP technology to provide you with predefined wave messages or output from a speech synthesis system.

Escalations

A common problem with resolving problems is that a host or a service may have blurred ownership. Often, there is no single person responsible for a host or service, which makes things harder. It is also typical to have a service with subtle dependencies on other things, which by themselves are small enough not to be monitored by Nagios. In such a case, it is good to include lower management in the escalations so that they are able to focus on problems that haven't been resolved in a timely manner.

Here is a good example: a database server might fail because a small Perl script that is run prior to actual start and clean things up has entered an infinite loop. The owner of this machine gets notified. But the question is, who should be fixing it? The script owner? Or perhaps the database administrator? In IT reality, this often ends up in a series of throwing ball into each other's yards without solving anything.

In such cases, escalations are a great way to solve such complex problems. In the previous example, if the problem is not been resolved after two hours, the IT team coordinator or manager would be notified. Another hour later, he would get another email. At that point, he would schedule an urgent meeting with the developer who owns the script, and the database admin, to discuss how this could be solved.

Of course, in real-world scenarios, escalating to management alone would not solve all problems. However, often, situations need a coordinator that will take care of communicating issues between teams and trying to find a company-wide solution. Business-critical services also require much higher attention. In such cases, it is a real benefit for the company if it has an escalation ladder that can be followed for all major problems.

Nagios offers many ways to set up escalations, depending on your needs. Escalations do not need to be sent out just after a problem occurs—that would create confusion and prevent smaller problems from being solved. Usually, escalations are set up so that additional people are informed only if a problem has not been resolved after a certain amount of time.

From a configuration point of view, all escalations are defined as separate objects. There are two types of objects—`hostescalation` and `serviceescalation`. Escalations are configured so that they start and stop being active along with the normal host or service notifications. This way, if you change the `notification_interval` directive in host or service definition, the times at which escalations start and stop will also change.

A sample escalation for company's main router is as follows:

```
define hostescalation
{
  host_name              mainrouter
  contactgroups          it-management
  first_notification     2
  last_notification      0
  notification_interval  60
  escalation_options     d,u,r
}
```

The following table describes all available directives for defining a host escalation. Items in bold are required when specifying an escalation.

Option	Description
host_name	Defines the host names that escalation should be defined for; separated by commas
hostgroup_name	Defines the host group names of the groups for whose members the escalation should be defined; separated by commas
contacts	List of all contacts that should receive notifications related to this escalation; separated by commas; at least one contact or contact group needs to be specified for each escalation
contactgroups	List of all contacts groups that should receive notifications related to this escalation, separated by commas; at least one contact or contact group needs to be specified for each escalation
first_notification	The number of notifications after which this escalation becomes active; setting this to 0 causes notifications to be sent until host recovers from the problem; see the following description
last_notification	The number of notifications after which this escalation stops being active; see the following description below
notification_interval	Specifies the number of minutes between sending notifications related to this escalation
escalation_period	Specifies the time period during which this escalation should be valid; if not specified, this defaults to 24 hours a day 7 days a week
escalation_options	Specifies the host states for which notification types should be sent, separated by commas; this can be one or more of the following: d - host DOWN state u - host UNREACHABLE state r - host recovery (UP state)

Service escalations are defined in a very similar way to host escalations. You can specify one or more hosts or host groups, as well as a single service description. Service escalation will be associated with this service on all hosts mentioned in the `host_name` and `hostgroup_name` attributes.

The following is an example of a service escalation for an OpenVPN check on the company's main router:

```
define serviceescalation
{
  host_name              mainrouter
  service_description    OpenVPN
  contactgroups          it-management
  first_notification     2
  last_notification      0
  notification_interval 60
  escalation_options     w,c,r
}
```

The following table describes all available directives for defining a service escalation. Items in bold are required when specifying an escalation.

Option	Description
host_name	Defines the host names that the escalation should be defined for, separated by commas
hostgroup_name	Defines the host group names of the groups for whose members the escalation should be defined, separated by commas
service_description	The service for which the escalation is being defined
contacts	List of all contacts that should receive notifications related to this escalation, separated by commas; at least one contact or contact group needs to be specified for each escalation
contactgroups	List of all contact groups that should receive notifications related to this escalation, separated by commas; at least one contact or contact group needs to be specified for each escalation
first_notification	The number of notifications after which this escalation becomes active; see the following description
last_notification	The number of notifications after which this escalation stops being active; setting this to 0 causes notifications to be sent until the service recovers from the problem; see the following description
notification_interval	Specifies the number of minutes between sending notifications related to this escalation

Option	Description
escalation_period	Specifies the time period during which escalation should be valid; if not specified, this defaults to 24 hours a day 7 days a week
escalation_options	Specifies which notification types for service states should be sent, separated by commas; this can be one or more of the following: r—service recovers (OK state) w—service WARNING state c—service CRITICAL state u—service UNKNOWN state

Let's consider the following configuration—a service along with two escalations:

```
define service
{
  use                    generic-service
  host_name              mainrouter
  service_description    OpenVPN
  check_command          check_openvpn_remote
  check_interval         15
  max_check_attempts     3
  notification_interval 30
  notification_period    24x7
}

# Escalation 1
define serviceescalation
{
  host_name              mainrouter
  service_description    OpenVPN
  first_notification     4
  last_notification      8
  contactgroups          it-escalation1
  notification_period    24x7
  notification_interval 15
}

# Escalation 2
define serviceescalation
{
  host_name              mainrouter
  service_description    OpenVPN
  first_notification     8
  last_notification      0
  contactgroups          it-escalation2
  notification_period    24x7
  notification_interval 120
}
```

In order to show how the escalations work, let's take an example—a failing service. A service fails for a total of 16 hours and then recovers—for the clarity of the example, we'll skip the soft and hard states and the timing required for hard state transitions.

Service notifications are set up so that the first notification is sent out 30 minutes after failure. Later on, they are repeated every 60 minutes, then the next notification is sent 1.5 hours after the actual failure and so on. The service also has two escalations defined for it.

`Escalation 1` is first triggered along with the fourth service notification that is sent out. Escalation stops being active after the eighth service notification on the failure. It only sends out reports about problems, not recovery. The interval for this escalation is configured to be 15 minutes.

`Escalation 2` is first triggered along with the eighth service notification and never stops— the `last_notification` directive is set to `0`. It sends out reports about problems and recovery. The interval for this escalation is configured to 2 hours.

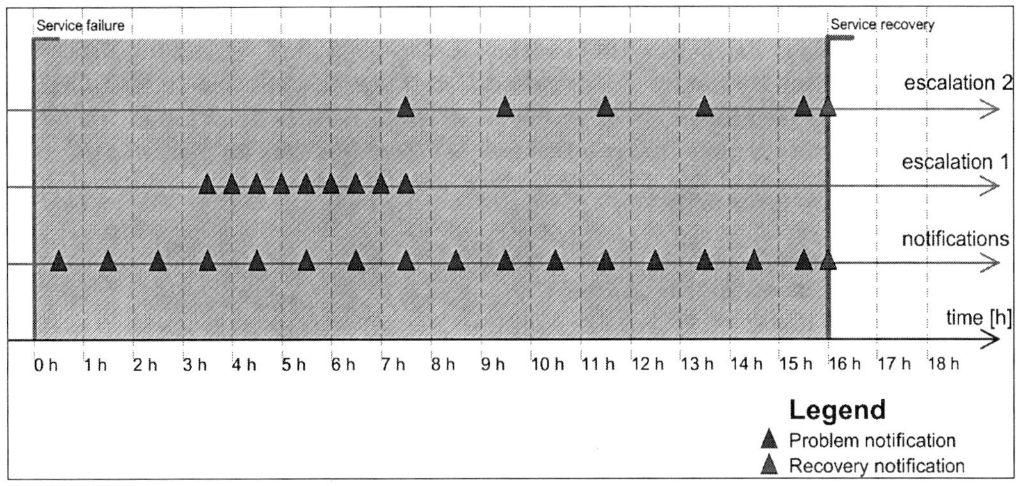

The diagram above shows when both escalations are sent out. Notifications for the service itself are sent out 0.5, 1.5, 2.5, 3.5 ... hours after the occurrence of the initial service failure.

`Escalation 1` becomes active after 3.5 hours—which is when the fourth service notification is sent out. The last notification related to `escalation 1` is sent out 7.5 hours after the initial failure—this is the time when the eighth service notification is sent out. It is sent every 30 minutes; so a total of nine notifications related to `escalation 1` are sent out.

`Escalation 2` becomes active after 7.5 hours - which is when the eighth service notification is sent out. The last notification related to `escalation 2` is sent out when the problem is resolved, and concerns the actual problem resolution. It is sent every two hours, so a total of four notifications related to `escalation 2` are sent out.

Escalations can be defined to be independent of each other—there is no reason why `Escalation 2` cannot start after the sixth service notification is sent out. There are also no limits on the number of escalations that can be set up for a single host or service.

The main point is that escalations should be defined reasonably, so that they don't bloat management or other teams with problems that would be solved without their interference anyway.

Escalations can also be used to contact different people for a certain set of objects, based on time periods. If an escalation has the `first_notification` set to `1` and the `last_notification` set to `0`, then all notifications related to this escalation will be sent out exactly in the same way as notifications for the service itself.

For example, normal IT staff may be handling problems normally, but during holidays, if notifications about problems should also go to the CritSit team, then you can simply define an escalation saying that during the `holidays` time period, CritSit group should also be notified about problems when the first notification is sent out. The following is an example that is based on the OpenVPN service defined earlier:

```
define serviceescalation
{
  host_name             mainrouter
  service_description   OpenVPN
  first_notification    1
  last_notification     0
  contactgroups         CritSit
  notification_period   holidays
  notification_interval 30
  escalation_options    w,c,r
}
```

The definitions above specify both the service and its escalation. Please note that the `notification_interval` is set to the same value in both the object and the escalation.

External Commands

Nagios offers a very powerful mechanism for receiving events and commands from external applications—the external commands pipe. This is a pipe file created on a file system that Nagios uses to receive incoming messages. The name of the file is `rw/nagios.cmd` and it is located in the directory passed as the `localstatedir` option during compilation. If you have followed the compilation and installation instructions given in Chapter 2 of this book, the file name will be `/var/nagios/rw/nagios.cmd`.

The communication does not use any authentication or authorization—the only requirement is to have write access to the pipe file. An external command file is usually writable by the owner and the group; the usual group used is `nagioscmd`. If you want a user to be able to send commands to the Nagios daemon, simply add that user to this group.

A small limitation of the command pipe is that there is no way to get any results back and so it is not possible to send any query commands to Nagios. Therefore, by just using the command pipe, you have no verification that the command you have just passed to Nagios has actually been processed, or will be processed soon. It is, however, possible to read the Nagios log file and check if it indicates that the command has been parsed correctly, if necessary.

An external command pipe is used by the web interface to control how Nagios works. The web interface does not use any other means to send commands or apply changes to Nagios. This gives a good understanding of what can be done with the external command pipe interface.

From the Nagios daemon perspective, there is no clear distinction as to who can perform what operations. Therefore, if you plan to use the external command pipe to allow users to submit commands remotely, you need to make sure that the authorization is in place as well so that it is not possible for unauthorized users to send potentially dangerous commands to Nagios.

The syntax for formatting commands is easy. Each command must be placed on a single line and end with a newline character. The syntax is as follows:

```
[TIMESTAMP] COMMAND_NAME;argument1;argument2;...;argumentN
```

`TIMESTAMP` is written as UNIX time—that is the number of seconds since 1970-01-01 00:00:00. This can be created by using the `date +%s` system command. Most programming languages also offer the means to get the current UNIX time. Commands are written in upper case. This can be one of the commands that Nagios should execute, and the arguments depend on the actual command.

For example, to add a comment to a host stating that it has passed a security audit, one can use the following shell command:

```
echo "['date +%s'] ADD_HOST_COMMENT;somehost;1;Security Audit;
      This host has passed security audit on 'date +%Y-%m-%d'"
      >/var/nagios/rw/nagios.cmd
```

This will send an `ADD_HOST_COMMENT` command (visit `http://www.nagios.org/developerinfo/externalcommands/commandinfo.php? command_id=1`) to Nagios over the external command pipe. Nagios will then add a comment to the host, `somehost`, stating that the comment originated from `Security Audit`. The first argument specifies the host name to add the comment to; the second tells Nagios if this comment should be persistent. The next argument describes the author of the comment, and the last argument specifies the actual comment text.

Similarly, adding a comment to a service requires the use of the `ADD_SVC_COMMENT` command (visit `http://www.nagios.org/developerinfo/externalcommands/commandinfo.php? command_id=1`). The command's syntax is very similar to the `ADD_HOST_COMMENT` command except that the command requires the specification of the host name and service name.

For example, to add a comment to a service stating that it has been restarted, you should use the following:

```
echo "['date +%s'] ADD_SVC_COMMENT;router;OpenVPN;1;nagiosadmin;
Restarting the OpenVPN service" >/var/nagios/rw/nagios.cmd
```

The first argument specifies the host name to add the comment to; the second is the description of the service to which Nagios should add the comment. The next argument tells Nagios if this comment should be persistent. The fourth argument describes the author of the comment, and the last argument specifies actual comment text.

You can also delete a single comment or all comments using the `DEL_HOST_COMMENT` (visit `http://www.nagios.org/developerinfo/externalcommands/commandinfo.php? command_id=3`), `DEL_ALL_HOST_COMMENTS` (visit `http://www.nagios.org/developerinfo/externalcommands/commandinfo.php? command_id=13`), and `DEL_SVC_COMMENT` (visit `http://www.nagios.org/developerinfo/externalcommands/commandinfo.php? command_id=4`) or `DEL_ALL_SVC_COMMENTS` commands (visit `http://www.nagios.org/developerinfo/externalcommands/commandinfo.php? command_id=14`).

Other commands worth mentioning are related to scheduling checks on demand. Very often, it is necessary to request that a check be carried out as soon as possible; for example, when testing a solution.

This time, let's create a script that schedules a check of a host, all services on that host, and a service on a different host, as follows:

```
#!/bin/sh

NOW='date +%s'

echo "[$NOW] SCHEDULE_HOST_CHECK;somehost;$NOW" \
     >/var/nagios/rw/nagios.cmd
echo "[$NOW] SCHEDULE_HOST_SVC_CHECKS;somehost;$NOW" \
     >/var/nagios/rw/nagios.cmd
echo "[$NOW] SCHEDULE_SVC_CHECK;otherhost;Service Name;$NOW" \
     >/var/nagios/rw/nagios.cmd

exit 0
```

The commands `SCHEDULE_HOST_CHECK` (visit `http://www.nagios.org/developerinfo/externalcommands/commandinfo.php? command_id=127`) and `SCHEDULE_HOST_SVC_CHECKS` (`http://www.nagios.org/developerinfo/externalcommands/commandinfo.php? command_id=30`) accept a host name and the time at which the check should be scheduled. The `SCHEDULE_SVC_CHECK` command (visit `http://www.nagios.org/developerinfo/externalcommands/commandinfo.php? command_id=29`) requires the specification of a service description as well as the name of the host to schedule the check on.

Normal scheduled checks, such as the ones scheduled above, might not actually take place at the time that you scheduled them. Nagios also needs to take allowed time periods into account as well as checking whether checks were disabled for a particular object or globally for the entire Nagios.

There are cases when you'll need to force Nagios to do a check—in such cases, you should use `SCHEDULE_FORCED_HOST_CHECK` (visit `http://www.nagios.org/developerinfo/externalcommands/commandinfo.php? command_id=128`), `SCHEDULE_FORCED_HOST_SVC_CHECKS` (visit `http://www.nagios.org/developerinfo/externalcommands/commandinfo.php? command_id=130`) and `SCHEDULE_FORCED_SVC_CHECK` (visit `http://www.nagios.org/developerinfo/externalcommands/commandinfo.php? command_id=129`) commands. They work in exactly the same way as described above, but make Nagios skip the checking of time periods, and ensure that the checks are disabled for this particular object. This way, a check will always be performed, regardless of other Nagios parameters.

Other commands worth using are related to custom variables, introduced in Nagios 3. This feature is described in more detail in Chapter 5, *Advanced Configuration*. When you define a custom variable for a host, service, or contact, you can change its value on the fly with the external command pipe.

As these variables can then be directly used by check or notification commands and event handlers, it is possible to make other applications or event handlers change these attributes directly without modifications to the configuration files.

A good example would be that the IT staff registers its presence via an application without any GUI. This application periodically sends information about the latest known IP address, and that information is then passed to Nagios assuming that the person is in the office. This would later be sent to a notification command to use that specific IP address while sending a message to the user.

Assuming that the user name is `jdoe` and the custom variable name is `DESKTOPIP`, the message that would be sent to the Nagios external command pipe would be as follows:

```
[1206096000] CHANGE_CUSTOM_CONTACT_VAR;jdoe;DESKTOPIP;12.34.56.78
```

This would cause a later use of `$_CONTACTDESKTOPIP$` to return a value of `12.34.56.78`.

Nagios offers the `CHANGE_CUSTOM_CONTACT_VAR` (visit `http://www.nagios.org/developerinfo/externalcommands/commandinfo.php? command_id=141`), `CHANGE_CUSTOM_HOST_VAR` (visit `http://www.nagios.org/developerinfo/externalcommands/commandinfo.php? command_id=139`), and `CHANGE_CUSTOM_SVC_VAR` (visit `http://www.nagios.org/developerinfo/externalcommands/commandinfo.php? command_id=140`) commands for modifying custom variables in contacts, hosts and, services accordingly.

The commands explained above are just a very small subset of the full capabilities of the Nagios external command pipe. For a complete list of commands, visit `http://www.nagios.org/developerinfo/externalcommands/commandlist.php`, where the External Command List can be seen.

External commands are usually sent from event handlers or from the Nagios web interface. You will find external commands most useful when writing event handlers for your system, or when writing an external application that interacts with Nagios.

Event Handlers

Event handlers are commands that are triggered whenever the state of a host or service changes. They offer functionality similar to notifications. The main difference is that the event handlers are called for each type of change and even for each soft state change. This provides the ability to react to a problem before Nagios notifies it as a hard state and sends out notifications about it. Another difference is what the event handlers should do. Instead of notifying users that there is a problem, event handlers are meant to carry out actions automatically.

For example, if a service defined with `max_check_attempts` set to 4, the `retry_interval` set to 1, and the `check_interval` is set to 5, then the following example illustrates when event handlers would be triggered, and with what values, for `$SERVICESTATE$`, `$SERVICESTATETYPE$`, and `$SERVICEATTEMP$` macro definitions:

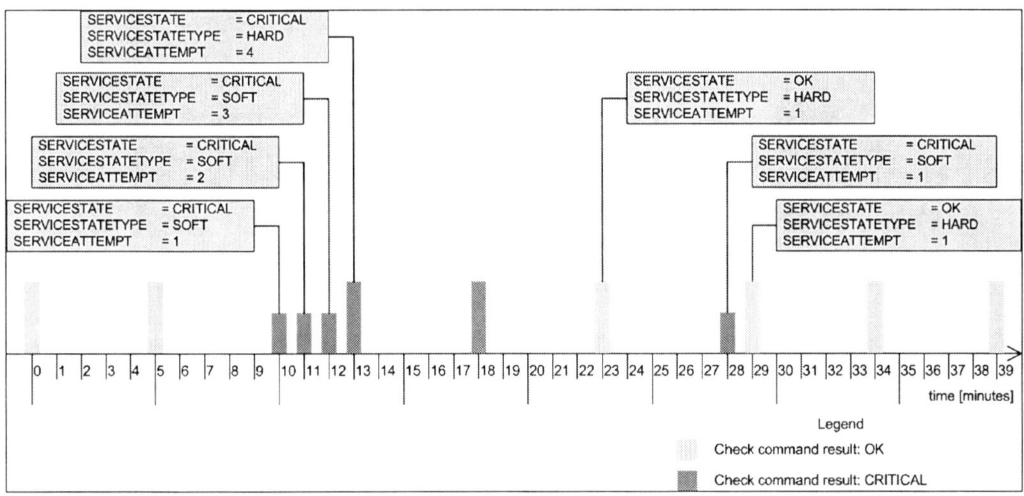

Event handlers are triggered for each state change—for example, in minutes, 10, 23, 28, and 29. When writing an event handler, it is necessary to check whether an event handler should perform an action at that particular time or not. See the following example for more details.

Event handlers are also triggered for each soft check attempt and for soft to hard transitions. In this example, these occur at minutes 11, 12, and 13. It's important to know that the events will not be run if no state changes have occurred, and the object is in a hard state—for example, no events are triggered in minutes 5, 18, 34, and 39.

A typical example might be that your web server process tends to crash once a month. Because this is rare enough, it is very difficult to debug and resolve it. Therefore, the best way to proceed is to restart the server automatically until a solution to the problem is found.

If your configuration has `max_check_attempts` set to 4, as in the example above, then a good place to try to restart the web server is after the third soft failure check—in the previous example, this would be minute 12.

Assuming that the restart has been successful, the diagram shown above would look like this:

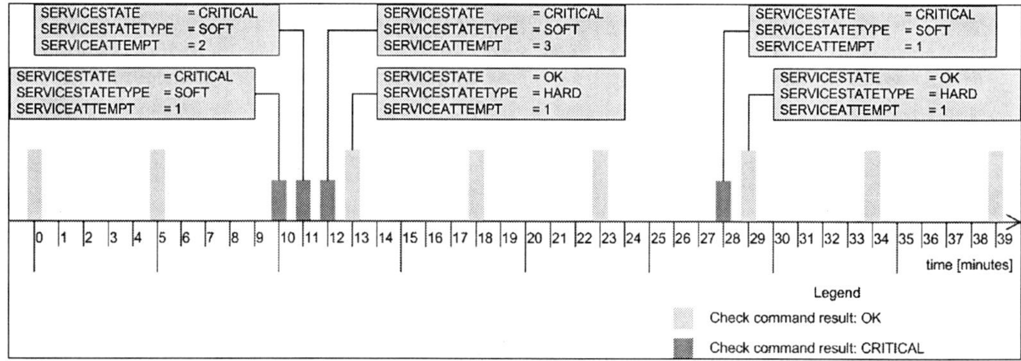

Please note that no hard critical state has occurred since the event handler resolved the problem. If a restart cannot resolve the issue, Nagios will only try it once, as the attempt is done only in the third soft check.

Event handlers are defined as commands, similar to check commands. The main difference is that the event handlers only use macro definitions to pass information to the actual event handling script. This implies that the `$ARGn$` macro definitions cannot be used and arguments cannot be passed in the host or service definition by using the `!` separator.

In the previous example, we would define the following command:

```
define command
{
  command_name restart-apache2
  command_line $USER1$/events/restart_apache2
               $SERVICESTATE$ $SERVICESTATETYPE$ $SERVICEATTEMPT$
}
```

The command would need to be added to the service. For both hosts and services, this requires adding an `event_handler` directive that specifies the command to be run for each event that is fired. In addition, it is good to set `event_handler_enabled` set to 1 to make sure that event handlers are enabled for this object.

The following is an example of a service definition:

```
define service
{
  host_name                 localhost
  service_description       Webserver
  use                       apache
  event_handler             restart-apache2
  event_handler_enabled     1
}
```

Finally, a short version of the script is as follows:

```
#!/bin/sh

# use variables for arguments
SERVICESTATE=$1
SERVICESTATETYPE=$2
SERVICEATTEMPT=$3

# we don't want to restart if current status is OK
if [ "$SERVICESTATE" != "OK" ] ; then

  # proceed only if we're in soft transition state
  if [ "$SERVICESTATETYPE" == "SOFT" ] ; then

    # proceed only if this is 3rd attempt, restart
    if [ "$SERVICESTATEATTEMPT" == "3" ] ; then

      # restarts Apache as system administrator
      sudo /etc/init.d/apache2 restart
    fi

  fi

fi

exit 0
```

As we're using `sudo` here, obviously the script needs an entry in the `sudoers` file to allow the `nagios` user to run the command without a password prompt. An example entry for the `sudoers` file would be as follows:

```
nagios ALL=NOPASSWD: /etc/init.d/apache2
```

This will tell `sudo` that the command `/etc/init.d/apache2` can be run by the user `nagios` and that asking for passwords before running the command will not be done.

According to our script, the restart is only done after the third check fails. Assuming that the restart went correctly, the next Nagios check will notify that Apache is running again. As this is considered a soft state, Nagios has not yet sent out any notifications about the problem.

If the service would not restart correctly, the next check will cause Nagios to set this failure as a hard state. At this point, notifications will be sent out to the object owners.

You can also try performing a restart in the second check. If that did not help, then during the third attempt, the script can forcefully terminate all Apache2 processes using the `killall` or `pkill` command. After this has been done, it can try to start the service again. For example:

```
# proceed only ifthis is 3rd attempt, restart
if [ "$SERVICESTATEATTEMPT" == "2" ] ; then

  # restart Apache as system administrator
  sudo /etc/init.d/apache2 restart
fi

# proceed only ifthis is 3rd attempt, restart
if [ "$SERVICESTATEATTEMPT" == "3" ] ; then
  # try to terminate apache2 process as system administrator
  sudo pkill apache2

  # starts Apache as system administrator
  sudo /etc/init.d/apache2 start
fi
```

Another common scenario is to restart one service if another one has just recovered—for example, you might want to restart email servers that use a database for authentication if the database has just recovered from a failure state. The reason for doing this is that some applications may not handle disconnected database handles correctly—this can lead to the service working correctly from the Nagios perspective, but not allowing some of the users in due to internal problems.

If you have set this up for hosts or services, it is recommended that you keep flapping enabled for these services. It often happens that due to incorrectly planned scripts and the relations between them, some services might end up being stopped and started again.

In such cases, Nagios will detect these problems and stop running event handlers for these services, which will cause fewer malfunctions to occur. It is also recommended that you keep notifications set up so that people also get information on when flapping starts and stops.

Modifying Notifications

An interesting new feature in Nagios 3 is the ability to change various parameters related to notifications. These parameters are modified via an external command pipe, similar to a few of the commands shown in the previous section.

A good example would be when Nagios contact persons have their workstations connected to the local network only when they are actually at work (which is usually the case if they are using notebooks), and turn their computers off when they leave work. In such a case, a ping check for a person's computer could trigger an event handler to toggle that person's attributes.

Let's assume that our user `jdoe` has two actual contacts—`jdoe-email` and `jdoe-jabber`, each for different types of notifications. We can set up a host corresponding to the `jdoe` workstation. We will also set it up to be monitored every five minutes and create an event handler. The handler will change the `jdoe-jabber`'s host and service notification time period to `none` on a hard host down state. On a host up state change, the time period for `jdoe-jabber` will be set to `24x7`. This way, the user will only get Jabber notifications if he or she is at work.

Nagios offers commands to change the time periods during which a user wants to receive notifications. The commands for this purpose are: `CHANGE_CONTACT_HOST_NOTIFICATION_TIMEPERIOD` (visit `http://www.nagios.org/developerinfo/externalcommands/commandinfo.php? command_id=153`) and `CHANGE_CONTACT_SVC_NOTIFICATION_TIMEPERIOD` (visit `http://www.nagios.org/developerinfo/externalcommands/commandinfo.php? command_id=152`). Both commands take the contact and the time period name as their arguments.

An event handler script that modifies the user's contact time period based on state is as follows:

```
#!/bin/sh

NOW='date +%s'
CONTACTNAME=$1-jabber
if [ "$2,$3" = "DOWN,HARD" ] ; then
    TP=none
else
    TP=24x7
fi
echo "[$NOW] CHANGE_CONTACT_HOST_NOTIFICATION_TIMEPERIOD;
       $CONTACT;$TP" \
     >/var/nagios/rw/nagios.cmd
echo "[$NOW] CHANGE_CONTACT_SVC_NOTIFICATION_TIMEPERIOD;
       $CONTACT;$TP" \
     >/var/nagios/rw/nagios.cmd
exit 0
```

The command should pass `$CONTACTNAME$`, `$SERVICESTATE$`, and `$SERVICESTATETYPE$` as parameters to the script.

In case you need a notification about a problem sent again, you should use the `SEND_CUSTOM_HOST_NOTIFICATION` (visit `http://www.nagios.org/developerinfo/externalcommands/commandinfo.php? command_id=134`) or `SEND_CUSTOM_SVC_NOTIFICATION` (visit `http://www.nagios.org/developerinfo/externalcommands/commandinfo.php? command_id=135`) command. These commands take host or host and service names, additional options, author name, and comments that should be put in the notification. Options allow specifying if the notification should also include all escalation levels (a value of 1), if Nagios should skip time periods for specific users (a value of 2) as well as if Nagios should increment notifications counters (a value of 4). Options are stored bitwise so a value of 7 (1+2+4) would enable all of these options. The notification would be sent to all people including escalations; it will be forced, and the escalation counters will be increased. Option value 3 means it should be broadcast to all escalations as well, and the time periods should be skipped.

To send a custom notification about the main router to all users including escalations, you should send the following command to Nagios:

```
[1206096000] SEND_CUSTOM_HOST_NOTIFICATION;router1;3;jdoe;RESPOND ASAP
```

Adaptive Monitoring

Nagios 3 introduces a very powerful feature called adaptive monitoring that allows the modification of various check-related parameters on the fly. This is done by sending a command to the Nagios external command pipe.

The first thing that can be changed on the fly is the command to be executed by Nagios, along with the attributes that will be passed to it—an equivalent of the `check_command` directive in the object definition. In order to do that, you can use the `CHANGE_HOST_CHECK_COMMAND` (visit `http://www.nagios.org/developerinfo/externalcommands/commandinfo.php? command_id=107`) or `CHANGE_SVC_CHECK_COMMAND` (visit `http://www.nagios.org/developerinfo/externalcommands/commandinfo.php? command_id=108`) command. These require the host name, or the host name and service description, and the check command as arguments.

This can be used to actually change how hosts or services are checked, or to only modify parameters that are passed to the check commands—for example, a check for ping latency can be modified based on whether a primary or a backup connection is used. An example to change a check command of a service, which changes the command and its specified parameters, is as follows:

```
[1206096000] CHANGE_SVC_CHECK_COMMAND;linux1;PING;check_ping!500.0,50%
```

A similar possibility is to change the custom variables that are used later in a check command. An example where the following command and service are used is:

```
define command
{
  command_name           check-ping
  command_line           $USER1$/check_ping -H $HOSTADDRESS$
                         -p $_SERVICEPACKETS$ -w $_SERVICEWARNING$
                         -c $_SERVICECRITICAL$

}

define service
{
  host_name                linux2
  service_description      PING
  use                      ping
  _PACKETS                 5
  _WARNING                 100.0,40%
  _CRITICAL                300.0,60%
}
```

This example is very similar to the one we saw earlier. The main benefit is that parameters can be set independently—for example, one event handler might modify the number of packets to send while another one can modify the warning and/or critical state limits.

The following is an example to modify the warning level for the ping service on a linux1 host:

```
[1206096000] CHANGE_CUSTOM_SVC_VAR;linux1;PING;_WARNING;500.0,50%
```

As us the case for check commands, it is also possible to modify event handlers on the fly. This can be used to enable or disable scripts that try to resolve a problem. To do this, you need to use the `CHANGE_HOST_EVENT_HANDLER` (visit `http://www.nagios.org/developerinfo/externalcommands/commandinfo.php?command_id=105`) and `CHANGE_SVC_EVENT_HANDLER` (visit `http://www.nagios.org/developerinfo/externalcommands/commandinfo.php? command_id=106`) commands.

In order to set an event handler command for the Apache2 service mentioned previously, you need to send the following command:

```
[1206096000] CHANGE_SVC_EVENT_HANDLER;localhost;webserver;
restart-apache2
```

Please note that setting an empty event handler disables any previous event handlers for this host or service. The same comment also applies for modifying the check command definition. In case you are modifying commands or event handlers, please make sure that the corresponding command definitions actually exist; otherwise, Nagios might reject your modifications.

Another feature that you can use to fine-tune the execution of checks is the ability to modify the time period during which a check should be performed. This is done with the `CHANGE_HOST_CHECK_TIMEPERIOD` (visit `http://www.nagios.org/developerinfo/externalcommands/commandinfo.php? command_id=138`) and `CHANGE_SVC_CHECK_TIMEPERIOD` (visit `http://www.nagios.org/developerinfo/externalcommands/commandinfo.php? command_id=137`) commands. Similar to the previous commands, these accept the host, or host and service names, and the new time period to be set. See the following example:

```
[1206096000] CHANGE_SVC_CHECK_TIMEPERIOD;localhost;webserver;
workinghours
```

As is the case with command names, you need to make sure that the time period you are requesting to be set exists in the Nagios configuration. Otherwise, Nagios will ignore this command and leave the current check time period.

Nagios also allows modifying intervals between checks—both for the normal checks, and retrying during soft states. This is done through the `CHANGE_NORMAL_HOST_CHECK_INTERVAL` (visit `http://www.nagios.org/developerinfo/externalcommands/commandinfo.php? command_id=109`), `CHANGE_RETRY_HOST_CHECK_INTERVAL` (visit `http://www.nagios.org/developerinfo/externalcommands/commandinfo.php? command_id=136`), `CHANGE_NORMAL_SVC_CHECK_INTERVAL` (visit `http://www.nagios.org/developerinfo/externalcommands/commandinfo.php? command_id=110`), and `CHANGE_RETRY_SVC_CHECK_INTERVAL` (visit `http://www.nagios.org/developerinfo/externalcommands/commandinfo.php? command_id=111`) commands. All of these commands require passing the host, or the host and service names, as well as the intervals that should be set.

A typical example of when intervals would be modified on the fly is when the priority of a host or service relies on other parameters in your network. An example might be a backup server.

Making sure that the host and all of services on it are working properly is very important before actually performing scheduled backups. During idle time, its priority might be much lower. Another issue might be that monitoring the backup server should be performed more often in case the primary server fails.

An example to modify the normal interval for a host to every 15 minutes is as follows:

```
[1206096000] CHANGE_NORMAL_HOST_CHECK_INTERVAL;backupserver;15
```

There is also the possibility to modify how many checks need to be performed before a state is considered to be hard. The commands for this are `CHANGE_MAX_HOST_CHECK_ATTEMPTS` (visit `http://www.nagios.org/developerinfo/externalcommands/commandinfo.php? command_id=112`) and `CHANGE_MAX_SVC_CHECK_ATTEMPTS` (visit `http://www.nagios.org/developerinfo/externalcommands/commandinfo.php? command_id=113`).

The following is an example command to modify max retries for a host to `5`:

```
[1206096000] CHANGE_MAX_HOST_CHECK_ATTEMPTS;linux1;5
```

There are many more commands that allow the fine tuning of monitoring and checks on the fly. It is recommended that you get acquainted with all of the external commands that your version of Nagios supports, as mentioned in the section introducing the external commands pipe.

Summary

Nagios offers several ways to let people know that something is wrong. Notifications can range from simple emails to a complex system that deals with multiple ways to communicate problems, as well as the ability to choose the appropriate way dynamically. This will help eliminate people from having to deal with their emails, and will help in resolving issues much more effectively.

Nagios can deliver information about problems in almost any way you can possibly imagine. Notifications can be sent as emails, instant messages, and Windows messaging texts. You can also have a text message over GSM networks; whatever works best for you and your colleagues. You can even set up VoIP combined with speech synthesis to let people know what the problems are.

Nagios also has a very powerful mechanism for escalating problems. When set up correctly, this is a very useful tool which will aid in complex problem resolution. In the case of larger problems, it can also be used to communicate problems properly so that a continuity plan can be put in place to prevent long outages to critical services.

Escalations also have all of the benefits of normal notifications—they can also be sent out in any way you might think of, and people will have the same power to set it up conveniently for themselves.

Another feature of Nagios that allows great flexibility is the external commands pipe. This offers a simple way to send commands directly to Nagios. It can be used from any programming language. Commands can be sent in various situations. Commands can range from adding a comment to an object, to a complete restart of Nagios. External commands also allow enabling and disabling checks, flapping detection, and many other Nagios functionality.

Sending commands to Nagios also provides Nagios' event handlers with the possibility to send commands that affect how Nagios performs and how it notifies users about problems or problem recoveries. It also allows fine tuning of the monitoring of your network infrastructure.

Nagios 3 provides huge advancements in this area, which makes it much easier to create a complex IT monitoring system. This is of great benefit to medium and large networks, where the ability to dynamically adapt to a situation is a must.

7

Passive Checks and NSCA

Nagios is a very powerful platform because it is easy to extend. The previous chapters talked about check command plugins and how they can be used to check any host or service that your company might be using. Another great feature that Nagios offers is the ability for third-party software or other Nagios instances to report information on the status of services or hosts. This way, Nagios does not need to schedule and run checks by itself, but other applications can report information as it is available to them.

This means that your applications can send problem reports directly to Nagios, instead of just logging them. In this way, your applications can benefit from powerful notification systems as well as dependency tracking. This mechanism can also be used to receive failure notifications from other services or machines—for example, **SNMP** (**Simple Network Management Protocol**) traps. This is described in more detail in Chapter 9.

Nagios also offers a tool for sending passive check results for hosts and services over a network. It is called **NSCA** (**Nagios Service Check Acceptor**). It can be used to send results from one Nagios instance to another. It can also be used by third-party applications running on different machines to send passive check results to a central Nagios server.

This mechanism includes password protection, along with encryption, to prevent injection of false results in to Nagios. In this way, NSCA communication sent over Internet is more secure.

What are Passive Checks?

Previous parts of this book often mentioned Nagios performing checks on various software and machines. In such cases, Nagios decides when a check is to be performed, runs the check and stores the result. These types of checks are called **Active Checks**.

Nagios also offers another way to work with the statuses of hosts and services. It is possible to configure Nagios so that it will receive status information sent over a command pipe. In such a case, checks are done by other programs, and their results are sent to Nagios. Nagios will still handle all notifications, event handlers, and dependencies between hosts and services.

Active checks are most common in the Nagios world. They have a lot of advantages and some disadvantages. One of the problems is that such checks can take only a couple of seconds to complete—a typical timeout for an active check to complete is 10 or 30 seconds. In many cases, the time taken is not enough, as some checks need to be performed over a longer period of time to have satisfactory results. A good example might be running a check that takes several hours to complete—in this case, it does not make sense to raise the global `service_check_timeout` option, but rather to schedule these checks outside of Nagios and only report the results back to it.

There are also different types of checks including external applications or devices that want to report information directly to Nagios. This can be done to gather all critical errors to a single, central place. These types of checks are called **Passive Checks**.

For example, when a web application cannot connect to the database, it will let Nagios know about it immediately. It can also send reports after a database recovery, or periodically, even if connectivity to the database has been consistently available, so that Nagios has an up-to-date status. This can be done in addition to active checks, to identify critical problems earlier.

Another example is where an application already processes information such as network bandwidth utilization. In such a case, adding a module that reports current utilization along with the `OK/WARNING/CRITICAL` state to Nagios seems much easier than using active checks for the same job.

Often, there are situations where active checks obviously fit better. In other cases, passive checks are the way to go. In general, if a check can be done quickly and does not require long running processes, it should definitely be done as an active service. If the situation involves reporting problems from other applications or machines, it is definitely a use case for a passive check. In cases where the checks require the deployment of long-running processes or monitoring information constantly, this should be done as a passive service.

Another difference is that active checks require much less effort to be set up when compared to passive checks. In the first case, Nagios takes care of the scheduling, and the command only needs to perform the actual checks and mark the results as `OK/WARNING/CRITICAL` based on how a check command is configured. Passive checks require all the logic related to what should be reported and when it should be checked to be put in an external application. This usually calls for some effort.

The following diagram shows how both active and passive checks are performed by Nagios. It shows what is performed by Nagios in both cases and what needs to be done by the check command or an external application for passive checks.

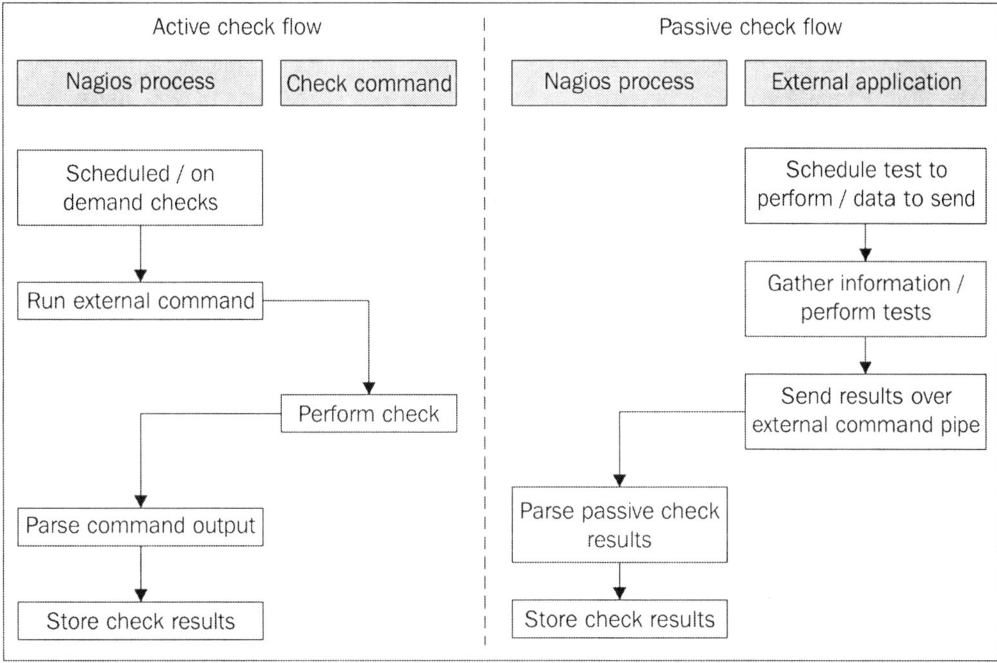

Nagios also offers a way of combining the benefits of both active and passive checks. Often, you have situations where other applications can report if a certain service is working properly or not. But if the monitoring application is not running or some other issue prevents it from reporting, Nagios can use active checks to keep the service status up-to-date.

A good example would be a server that is a part of an application, processing job queues using a database. It can report each problem when accessing the database. We want Nagios to monitor this database, and as the application is already using it, we can add a module that reports this to Nagios.

The application can also periodically let Nagios know if it succeeded in using the database without problems. However, if there are no jobs to process and the application is not using it, Nagios will not have up-to-date information about the database.

Configuring Passive Checks

The first thing that needs to be done in order to use passive checks for your Nagios setup is to make sure that you have the following options in your main Nagios configuration file:

```
accept_passive_service_checks=1
accept_passive_host_checks=1
```

It would also be good to enable the logging of incoming passive checks—this makes determining the problem of not processing a passive check much easier. The following directive allows it:

```
log_passive_checks=1
```

Setting up hosts or services for passive checking requires an object to be defined and set up so as not to perform active checks. The object needs to have the `passive_checks_enabled` option set to `1` for Nagios to accept passive check results over the command pipe.

The following is an example of the required configuration for a host that accepts passive checks and has active checks disabled:

```
define host
{
  use                             generic-host
  host_name                       linuxbox01
  address                         10.0.2.1
  active_checks_enabled           0
  passive_checks_enabled          1
}
```

Configuring services is exactly the same as with hosts. For example, to set up a very similar service, all we need to do is to use the same parameters as those for the hosts:

```
define service
{
  use                             ping-template
  host_name                       linuxbox01
  service_description             PING
  active_checks_enabled           0
  passive_checks_enabled          1
}
```

In this case, Nagios will never perform any active checks on its own and will only rely on the results that are passed to it.

We can also configure Nagios so that if no new information has been provided within a certain period of time, it will use active checks to get the current status of the host or service. If up-to-date information has been provided by a passive check during this period, then it will not perform active checks.

In order to do this, we need to enable active checks by setting the `active_checks_enabled` option to `1` without specifying the `normal_check_interval` directive. For Nagios to perform active checks when there is no up-to-date result from passive checks, you need to set the `check_freshness` directive to `1` and set `freshness_threshold` to the time period after which a check should be performed. The time performed is specified in seconds.

The first parameter tells Nagios that it should check whether the results from the checks are up-to-date. The next parameter specifies the number of seconds after which Nagios should consider the results to be out of date. Attributes can be used for both hosts and services.

A sample definition for a host that runs an active check if there has been no result provided within the last two hours:

```
define host
{
  use                           generic-host
  host_name                     linuxbox02
  address                       10.0.2.2
  check_command                 check-host-alive
  check_freshness               1
  freshness_threshold           7200
  active_checks_enabled         1
  passive_checks_enabled        1
}
```

The following is an illustration showing when Nagios would invoke active checks:

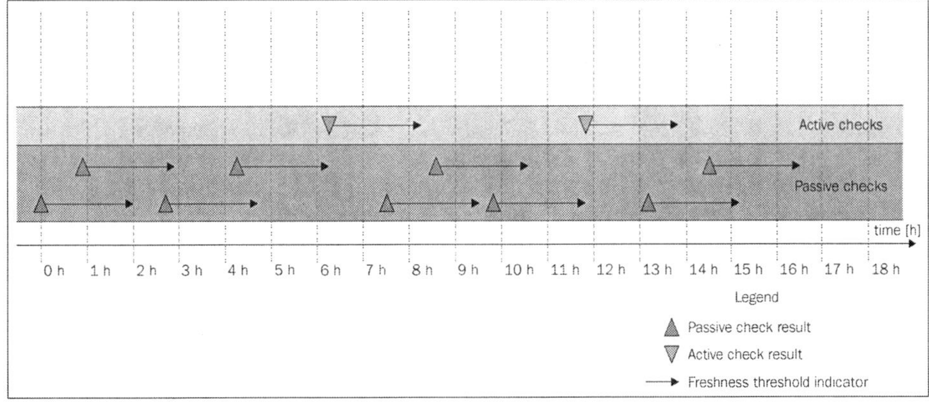

Each time there is at least one passive check result that is still valid (i.e., was received within the past two hours), Nagios will not perform any active checks. However, two hours after the last passive or active check result was received, Nagios would perform an active check to keep the results up-to-date.

Passive Checks—Hosts

Nagios allows applications and event handlers to send out passive check results for host objects. In order to use them, the host needs to be configured to accept passive checks results.

In order to be able to submit passive check results, we need to configure Nagios to allow the sending of passive check results, and set the host objects to accept them.

Submitting passive host check results to Nagios requires sending a command to the Nagios external command pipe. This way, the other applications on your Nagios server can report the status of the hosts.

The command to submit passive checks is `PROCESS_HOST_CHECK_RESULT` (visit `http://www.nagios.org/developerinfo/externalcommands/commandinfo.php?command_id=115`). This command accepts the host name, status code, and the textual output from a check. The host status code should be 0 for an `UP` state, 1 for `DOWN` and 2 for an `UNREACHABLE` state.

The following is a sample script that will accept the host name, status code, and output from a check and will submit these to Nagios:

```
#!/bin/sh

NOW='date +%s'
HOST=$1
STATUS=$2
OUTPUT=$3

echo "[$NOW] PROCESS_HOST_CHECK_RESULT;$HOST;$STATUS;$OUTPUT" \
     >/var/nagios/rw/nagios.cmd

exit 0
```

As an example of the use of this script, the command that is sent to Nagios for `host01`, status code 2 (`UNREACHABLE`) and output `router 192.168.1.2 down` would be as follows:

```
[1206096000] PROCESS_HOST_CHECK_RESULT;host01;2;router
192.168.1.2 down
```

When submitting results, it is worth noting that Nagios might take some time to process them, depending on the intervals between Nagios's checks of the external command pipe.

Unlike active checks, Nagios will not take network topology into consideration by default. This is very important in situations where a host behind a router is reported to be down because the router is actually down.

By default, Nagios handles results from active and passive checks differently. When Nagios plans and receives results from active checks, it takes the actual network topology into consideration and performs a translation of the states based on this. This means that if Nagios receives a result indicating that a host is `DOWN`, it assumes that all child hosts are in an `UNREACHABLE` state.

When a passive result check comes in to Nagios, Nagios expects that the result already has a network topology included. When a host is reported to be `DOWN` as a passive check result, Nagios does not perform a translation from `DOWN` to `UNREACHABLE`. Even if its parent host is currently `DOWN`, the child host state is also stored as `DOWN`.

The following illustration shows how results from active and passive checks are treated differently by Nagios:

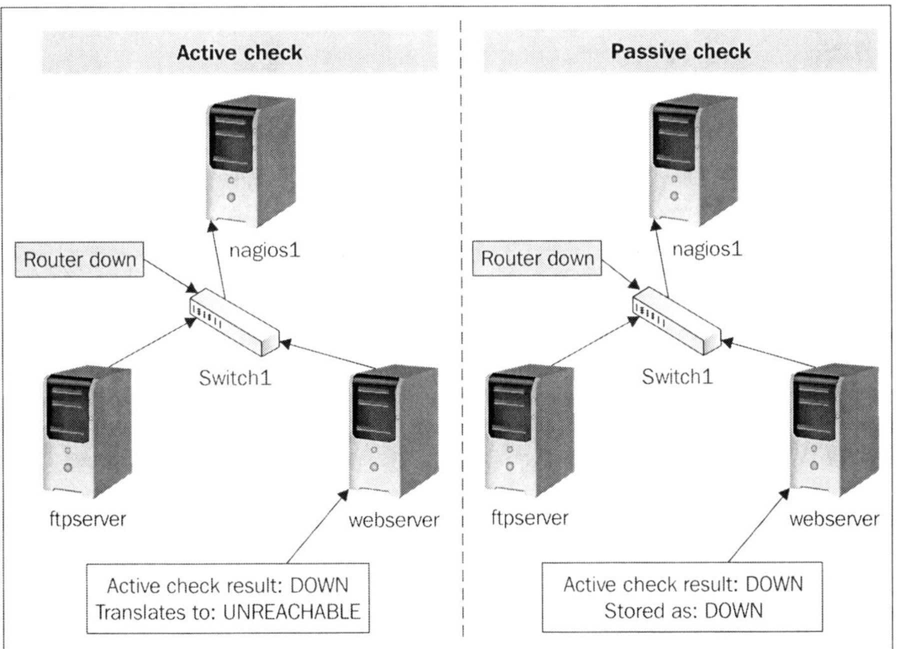

In both the cases, a check result stating that the host is down is received by Nagios. When it comes in as a passive check, no state translation is done and Nagios stores the host and all child nodes being down. When it is an active check result, Nagios takes the fact that `switch1` is down into account and maps the child node's result into an `UNREACHABLE` state.

How Nagios process handles passive check results can be defined in the main Nagios configuration file. In order to make Nagios treat passive host check results in the same way as active check results, we need to enable the following option:

```
translate_passive_host_checks=1
```

By default, Nagios treats host results from passive checks as hard results. This is because, very often, passive checks are used to report host and service statuses from other Nagios instances. In such cases, only reports regarding hard state changes are propagated across Nagios servers.

If you want Nagios to treat all passive check results for hosts as if they were soft results, you need to enable the following option in the main Nagios configuration file:

```
passive_host_checks_are_soft=1
```

Passive Checks—Services

Passive service checks are very similar to passive host checks. In both the cases, the idea is that Nagios receives information about host statuses over the external commands pipe.

As with passive checks of hosts, all that is needed is to enable the global Nagios option to accept passive check results, and also enable this option for each service that should allow the passing of passive check results.

The results are passed to Nagios in the same way as they are passed for hosts. A command to submit passive checks is `PROCESS_SERVICE_CHECK_RESULT` (visit `http://www.nagios.org/developerinfo/externalcommands/commandinfo.php?command_id=114`). This command accepts the host name, service description, status code, and the textual output from a check. Service status codes are the same as those for active checks—0 for `OK`, 1 for `WARNING`, 2 for `CRITICAL`, and 3 for an `UNKNOWN` state.

The following is a sample script that will accept the host name, status code, and output from a check and will submit these to Nagios:

```
#!/bin/sh

CLOCK='date +%s'
HOST=$1
SVC=$2
STATUS=$3
OUTPUT=$4

echo "[$CLOCK] PROCESS_SERVICE_CHECK_RESULT;$HOST;$SVC;$STATUS;
       $OUTPUT"\
     >/var/nagios/rw/nagios.cmd

exit 0
```

As an example of the use of this script, the command that is sent to Nagios for `host01`, service `PING`, status code 0 (`OK`) and output `RTT=57 ms` is as follows:

```
[1206096000] PROCESS_SERVICE_CHECK_RESULT;host01;PING;0;RTT=57 ms
```

A very common scenario for using passive checks is a check that takes a very long time to complete.

As with to submitting host check results, it is worth mentioning that Nagios will take some time to process passive check results as they are polled periodically from the external commands pipe.

A major difference between hosts and services is that service checks differentiate between soft and hard states. When new information regarding a service gets passed to Nagios via the external commands pipe, Nagios treats it the same way as if it had been received by an active check.

If a service is set up with a `max_check_attempts` directive of 5, then the same number of passive check results would need to be passed in order for Nagios to treat the new status as a hard state change.

Passive service checks are often used to report the results of long lasting tests asynchronously. A good example of such a test is checking whether there are bad blocks on a disk. This requires trying to read the entire disk directly from the block device (such as `/dev/sda1`) and checking if the attempt has failed. This can't be done as an active check as reading the device takes a lot of time to complete—larger disks might require several hours to complete.

For this reason, the only way to perform such a check is to schedule them from the system—for example, using the `cron` daemon (visit `http://man.linuxquestions.org/index.php?query=cron`). The script should then post results to the Nagios daemon.

The following is a script that runs the `dd` system command (visit `http://man.linuxquestions.org/index.php?query=dd`) to read an entire block device. Based on whether the read was successful or not, the appropriate status code, along with plugin output, is sent out.

```
#!/bin/sh

 SVC=$1
 DEVICE=$2
 TMPFILE=/tmp/ddlog.$$
 NOW='date +%s'
 PREFIX="['date +%s'] [$NOW] PROCESS_SERVICE_CHECK_
RESULT;localhost;$SVC"

 # try to read the device
 dd if=$DEVICE of=/dev/null >$TMPFILE 2>&1
 CODE=$?
 RESULT='grep copied <$TMPFILE'
 rm $TMPFILE

 if [ $CODE == 0 ] ; then
    echo "$PREFIX;0;$RESULT"
 else
    echo "$PREFIX;2;Error while checking device $DEVICE"
 fi

 exit 0
```

If the check fails, then a `critical` status, along with text stating that there was a problem checking the specific device, is sent out to Nagios. If the check was successful, an output mentioning number of bytes and the speed of transfer is sent out to Nagios. A typical output would be something like this:

```
254951424 bytes (255 MB) copied, 9.72677 seconds, 26.2 MB/s
```

The host name is hardcoded to `localhost`. Using this script requires configuring a service to have active checks disabled and passive checks enabled. As the checks will be done quite rarely, it's recommended to set `max_check_attempts` to 1.

Troubleshooting Passive Checks

It's not always possible to set up passive checks correctly the first time. In such cases, it is a good thing to try to debug the issue one step at a time in order to find any potential problems. Sometimes the problem could be a configuration issue, while in other cases, it could be an issue such as the mistyping of the host or service name.

One thing worth checking is whether the Web UI shows changes after you have sent the passive result check. If it doesn't, then at some point, things are not working correctly.

The first thing you should start with is enabling the logging of external commands and passive checks. To do this, make sure that the following values are enabled in the main Nagios configuration file:

```
log_external_commands=1
log_passive_checks=1
```

In order for the changes to take effect, a restart of the Nagios process is needed. After this has been done, Nagios will log all commands passed via the command pipe and log all of the passive check results it receives.

The first issue, a common problem, is that an application or script cannot write data to the Nagios command pipe. In order to test this, simply change to the user your scripts are running as, and try the following command:

```
user@ubuntuserver:~$ echo "TEST" >/var/nagios/rw/nagios.cmd
```

If the command above runs fine, and no errors are reported, then your permissions are set up correctly. If an error shows up, you should add the user to the `nagioscmd` group as described in Chapter 2, *Installation and Configuration.*

The next thing to do is to manually send a passive check result to the Nagios command pipe and check whether the Nagios log file was received and parsed correctly. To test this, run the following command:

```
echo "['date +%s'] PROCESS_HOST_CHECK_RESULT;host1;2;test" \
  >/var/nagios/rw/nagios.cmd
```

The name, `host1`, needs to be replaced with an actual host name from your configuration. A few seconds after running this command, the Nagios log file should reflect the command that we have just sent. You should see the following lines in your log:

```
EXTERNAL COMMAND: PROCESS_HOST_CHECK_RESULT;host1;2;test
[1220257561] PASSIVE HOST CHECK: host1;2;test
```

If both of these lines are in your log file, then we can conclude that Nagios has received and parsed the command correctly.

If only the first line is present, then it means that either the global option to receive passive host check results is disabled, or it is disabled for this particular object. The first thing you should do is to make sure that your main Nagios configuration file contains the following line:

```
accept_passive_host_checks=1
```

Next, you should check your configuration to see whether the host definition has passive checks enabled as well. If not, simply add the following directive to the object definition:

```
passive_checks_enabled  1
```

If you have misspelled the name of the host object, then the following will be logged:

```
Warning:  Passive check result was received for host 'host01',
but the host could not be found!
```

In this case, make sure that your host name is correct.

Similar checks can also be done for services. You can run the following command to check if a passive service check is being handled correctly by Nagios:

```
echo "['date +%s'] PROCESS_SERVICE_CHECK_RESULT;host1;APT;0;test" \
  >/var/nagios/rw/nagios.cmd
```

Again, `host1` should be replaced by the actual host name, and `APT` needs to be an existing service for that host. After a few seconds, the following entries in Nagios log file would indicate the result has been successfully parsed:

```
EXTERNAL COMMAND: PROCESS_SERVICE_CHECK_RESULT;host1;APT;0;test
PASSIVE SERVICE CHECK: host1;APT;0;test
```

If the second line is not in the log file, either the option to accept service passive checks is disabled on a global basis, or this particular service has the option to accept passive check results disabled. You should start by making sure that your main Nagios configuration file contains the following line:

```
accept_passive_service_checks=1
```

You should also make sure that the service definition has passive checks enabled as well, and if not, add the following directive to the object definition:

```
passive_checks_enabled  1
```

If you have misspelled the name of the host or service, then the following will be logged:

```
Warning:  Passive check result was received for service 'APT' on host
'host1', but the service could not be found!
```

What is NSCA?

Passive checks are sent to Nagios via the external command pipe. As it is a named pipe on a specific machine, the main problem is that all passive check results need to be sent from this machine.

For many Nagios installations, this causes a problem. Very often, a check needs to be done on one or more remote hosts. This requires some mechanism to pass results from the machines that perform the tests to the computers running the Nagios daemon, which will process the results.

This is why **Nagios Service Check Acceptor** (**NSCA**) was developed. It is a client-server application that allows the passing of service and host check results over the network. This protocol allows the use of encryption, so the results are sent securely.

NSCA is an application that allows the sending of results directly to the Nagios external command pipe. NSCA consists of two parts—the server and the client. The part responsible for receiving check results and passing them to Nagios is the server. This listens on a specific TCP port for NSCA clients passing information. It accepts and authenticates incoming connections and passes these results to the Nagios external command pipe. All information is encrypted using the MCrypt library (visit `http://mcrypt.sourceforge.net/`).

The client part accepts one or more host or service check results on a standard input and sends them to the NSCA server using the specified IP address and port. Each line received on the standard input is a single check result that should be sent to the NSCA server. An NSCA client can be used to transmit more than one result over a period of time. Therefore, it is not necessary to launch a new NSCA client instance for each new result.

Authentication is done using the MCrypt libraries for encryption, and NSCA uses a password to verify if the status message is valid. You should either generate a random password or choose a password that is not dictionary-based, and use both upper case and lower case letters, as well as one or more digits. It is necessary to specify the same encryption method along with exactly the same password for both the client and the server in order for it to work properly.

The following illustration shows how passive checks are done on the same host, as well as when sent over the network using NSCA:

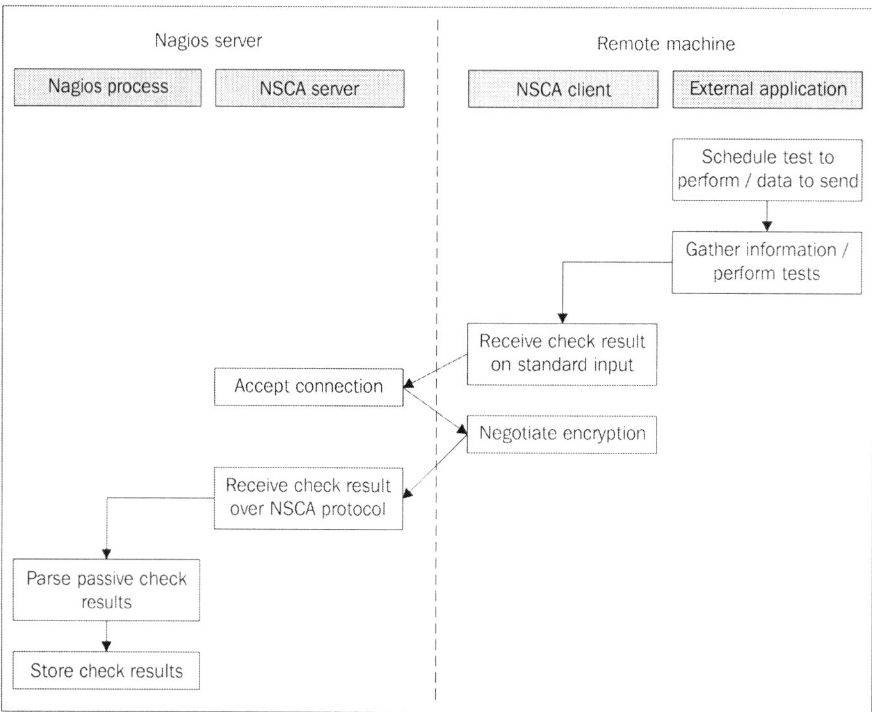

This example shows how the results are passed down directly from an external application to the Nagios daemon. Most complex operations are performed directly by NSCA. The application only needs to gather results from the check or checks, spawn `send_nsca`, and make sure that the results are sent out properly.

NSCA is also commonly used in conjunction with distributed Nagios monitoring. This means that more than one computer runs a Nagios server and the results are distributed between Nagios servers running on different machines. In such cases, NSCA is often used to pass information from one machine to another (this is known as distributed monitoring, and is described in more detail in Chapter 10, *Advanced Monitoring*).

Obtaining NSCA

NSCA project is part of the main Nagios project and can be downloaded from the same Nagios download page as the rest of Nagios.

In order to build NSCA from sources, we will need to download the source code. This can be downloaded from the Nagios project page and can be found in the add-ons section (visit `http://www.nagios.org/download/addons/` for more details). The file is named in the form of `nsca-2.7.2.tar.gz`, where `2.7.2` is the version of NSCA. It is always recommended that you download the latest stable version.

Many Linux distributions already contain prebuilt NSCA binaries. If you are not an experienced user and just want to test NSCA out, you might want to try the prebuilt binaries.

For Ubuntu Linux, the package name is `nsca`. So all that needs to be done is to run the command is:

```
apt-get install nsca
```

For systems that offer `yum` for downloading packages, the command is as follows:

```
yum install nsca
```

NSCA binaries for various operating systems can also be found on NagiosExchange, at `http://www.nagiosexchange.org/`. There is also a binary for Microsoft Windows operating system. This allows the creation of applications that monitor desktop computers and report the results directly to Nagios.

Compiling NSCA

Please note that if you do not plan to compile NSCA from the source and intend to use a pre-built set of binaries, you should continue to the next section.

NSCA requires a small set of prerequisites to be installed on the system. NSCA requires a standard set of tools, required for compilation, to be present on the system. For encryption, the `libmcrypt` package, along with the development files, needs to be installed as well.

On an Ubuntu Linux system, this requires the installation of the packages by performing the following command:

```
apt-get install gcc make binutils cpp pkg-config libmcrypt-dev libc6-dev
```

For other systems, the commands and package names might differ a bit, but their names should be very similar.

Please make sure that you install the standard compilation utilities as, very often, you might be building NSCA for machines that you did not compile Nagios on. This means that they might not have the basic development libraries and compiler installed.

The next step is to run the configuration script to set up parameters for the compilation process. Assuming that we want NSCA to be installed in the same way as the Nagios setup (detailed in Chapter 2), the following configure script should be run:

```
sh configure \
    --sysconfdir=/etc/nagios \
    --prefix=/opt/nagios \
    --localstatedir=/var/nagios \
    --libexecdir=/opt/nagios/plugins \
    --with-nsca-user=nagios \
    --with-nsca-grp=nagioscmd
```

In case any of the tools or files are missing, the configuration script will abort indicating what the missing part is. If this happens, you should install the missing binaries or libraries—how you should do this depends on the exact operating system and distribution used. For Ubuntu systems, it should be by using the same command as the one used for building Nagios:

```
apt-get install gcc make binutils cpp libpq-dev libmysqlclient15-dev\
                libssl0.9.8 libssl-dev pkg-config apache2 \
                libgd2-xpm libgd2-xpm-dev libgd-tools \
                libpng12-dev libjpeg62-dev \
                perl libperl-dev libperl5.8 libnet-snmp-perl
```

After a successful run of the configuration script, you should see a message stating that you can now build NSCA binaries.

The next step is to run the following `make` command to build the NSCA client and server:

```
make all
```

If you plan to build only the client or server part, use the `make send_nsca` or `make nsca` commands, respectively.

Binaries are built as `src/send_nsca` and `src/nsca`. The first one is the NSCA client, and the other one is the server.

You can install the binaries by running the following command:

```
make install
```

You can also copy the binaries manually—copy the `send_nsca` client to the machines that will send the results to Nagios, and send `nsca` to the machine where Nagios is running.

Configuring the NSCA Server

You now have working binaries for the NSCA server—either compiled from sources or installed from packages. We can now proceed with configuring the NSCA server to listen for incoming connections.

There are a couple of ways in which it can be set up—either as a standalone process that handles incoming connections, as part of `inetd` (visit `http://en.wikipedia.org/wiki/inetd`), or as the `xinetd` setup (visit `http://www.xinetd.org/`). In either cases, we will need a configuration file that will tell it which encryption algorithm to use, and the password that will be used to authenticate NSCA client connections. NSCA also needs to know the path of the Nagios command line.

The main difference between these two installation types is that the standalone version requires fewer resources to handle a larger number of incoming connections. On the other hand, `inetd` or `xinetd` based NSCA is much easier to set up. An `inetd` based setup is easier to maintain. Several `inetd` implementations also allow the configuration of connections only from specific IP addresses, or the acceptance of connections only from specific users for UNIX systems. There is no best way in which NSCA should be set up.

The configuration file is similar to the main Nagios configuration file—each parameter is written in the form of `<name>=<value>`. If you compiled NSCA from the source, a default configuration can be found in the `sample-config/nsca.cfg` file.

The first parameter that should be set is `password`. This should be set to the same value for the NSCA server and all NSCA clients. It's best to set it to a random string. Using a dictionary-based password might leave your Nagios setup susceptible to attacks—malicious users might send fake results that cause event triggers to perform specific actions.

Another option that needs to be set is `decryption_method`, which specifies the algorithm to be used for encryption. This is an integer value—a list of possible values and what they mean can be found in the sample configuration file. Both `decryption_method` and `password` need to be specified as the same on the server side and the client side.

A sample configuration is as follows:

```
server_address=192.168.1.1
server_port=5667
nsca_user=nagios
nsca_group=nagioscmd
command_file=/var/nagios/rw/nagios.cmd
password=ok1ij2uh3yg
decryption_method=1
```

The option `server_address` is optional, and specifies the IP address that NSCA should listen on. If omitted, NSCA will listen on all available IP addresses for incoming connections. When it is specified, NSCA will only accept connections on the specified IP address.

The remainder of this section will assume that the NSCA server configuration file is located as `/etc/nagios/nsca.cfg`. At this point, it is good to create an NSCA configuration based on the example above or the sample NSCA configuration file.

The fastest way to start NSCA is to start it manually in standalone mode. In this mode, NSCA handles listening on the specified TCP port and changing the user/group by itself.

To do this, simply run the NSCA binary with the following parameters:

```
/opt/nagios/bin/nsca -c /etc/nagios/nsca.cfg --daemon
```

If you plan to have NSCA start up along with Nagios, it is a good idea to add a line to your `/etc/init.d/nagios` script that runs Nagios at system boot. Running NSCA should go in the `start` section, and stopping NSCA (via `killall` (see `http://en.wikipedia.org/wiki/killall`) command or using Pid File) should be put in the `stop` section of the `init` script. The NSCA source distribution also comes with a script that can be placed as `/etc/init.d/nagios` to start and stop the NSCA server.

Another possibility is to configure NSCA to run from the `inetd` or `xinetd` super-server daemons. This requires adding the definition of the NSCA server to the proper configuration files, and those daemons will handle accepting connections and spawning actual NSCA processes when needed.

In order to add the NSCA definition to `inetd` or `xinetd`, we first need to add a service definition of the TCP port used. In order to do that, we need to add the following line to the `/etc/services` file:

```
nsca 5667/tcp
```

This will indicate that TCP port 5677 maps to the service name `nsca`. This information is used later by the super-server daemons to map port numbers to names in the configuration.

For `inetd`, we also need to add the service configuration to the `/etc/inetd.conf` file—a sample definition is as follows:

```
nsca stream tcp nowait nagios /opt/nagios/bin/nsca -c /etc/nagios/
nsca.cfg --inetd
```

The following entry should be written to the inetd.conf file as a single line. Next, we should restart inetd by running:

```
/etc/init.d/inetd reload
```

This will cause it to reload the service definitions. NSCA should be run whenever a connection on port 5667 comes in.

Setting up NSCA using xinetd is very similar. All that's needed is to create a file, /etc/xinetd.d/nsca, with the following contents:

```
service nsca
{
        flags            = REUSE
        socket_type      = stream
        wait             = no
        user             = nagios
        group            = nagioscmd
        server           = /opt/nagios/bin/nsca
        server_args      = -c /etc/nagios/nsca.cfg --inetd
        log_on_failure  += USERID
        disable          = no
}
```

Next, we need to reload xinetd by running:

```
/etc/init.d/xinetd reload
```

And after that the NSCA should also be run when a connection on port 5677 comes in. You might add the only_from statement in the xinetd service definition to limit IP addresses from which a connection can come in. It works differently from server_address in the NSCA configuration. The only_from option specifies the addresses of the remote machines that will be allowed to connect. On the other hand, the server_address option is used to specify the IP addresses that NSCA will listen on.

When running under inetd or xinetd, the NSCA server ignores the server_address, server_port, nsca_user, and nsca_group parameters from the configuration files. These attributes are configured at the inetd/xinetd level. These attributes are only meaningful when running NSCA in standalone mode.

Sending results over NSCA

Now that our NSCA server is up and running, we can continue with actually submitting results over the network. We will need the send_nsca client binary on all of the machines that will report passive check results to Nagios.

There are various prebuilt binaries available at NagiosExchange, including a native Win32 binary, which allows the sending of results from any check using NSCA. As it is a prebuilt version, there is no need to compile or install it. Simply copy the binary to a Windows machine, and it can be used with any valid NSCA client configuration.

As with the NSCA server, the client uses a configuration file. This requires the specification of the `password` and `encryption_method` parameters. A sample configuration that can be used in conjunction with the configuration for a server created earlier:

```
password=ok1ij2uh3yg
encryption_method=1
```

The NSCA client accepts the status results that should be sent out to the server on standard input. Each line indicates a single result from a check. The syntax of the host check result that should be passed to `send_nsca` is as follows:

```
<hostname>[TAB]<return code>[TAB]<plugin output>
```

The return code is the same as that for sending passive checks—0 for `UP`, 1 for `DOWN`, and 2 for `UNREACHABLE`.

Sending a passive service check result requires the specification of the service name as well:

```
<hostname>[TAB]<service name>[TAB]<return code>[TAB]<plugin output>
```

In this case, the return codes are the same as the exit codes for checks, and are 0 for `OK`, 1 for `WARNING`, 2 for `CRITICAL`, and 3 for `UNKNOWN`. Exit codes have been explained in more detail in Chapter 4, *Overview of Nagios Plugins*. The command differentiates the host and service checks by the number of fields that are passed in a line.

The NSCA client command has the following syntax:

```
send_nsca -H <host_address> [-c config_file]
          [-p port] [-to to_sec] [-d delim]
```

The `-H` option specifies the name of the NSCA server that messages should be transmitted to. The option specifies `-p` the port to send messages on; the port defaults to 5667 if nothing is specified. The timeout in seconds is specified using the `-to` flag. A field delimiter can also be specified using the `-d` option; if this is omitted, it defaults to tab-delimited.

The easiest way to test if you can send data to NSCA correctly is to try to send a host status for a valid computer. As `send_nsca` accepts information on standard input, it is enough to run an echo command and send its output to the NSCA client.

A sample script is provided as follows:

```
#!/bin/sh

HOST=localhost
NSCAHOST=127.0.0.1

echo -e "$HOST\t1\tHost temporarily down" | \
     /opt/nagios/bin/send_nsca -H $NSCAHOST
     -c /etc/nagios/send_nsca.cfg

exit 0
```

The script will send a report that the host, `localhost`, is currently down with the status description, `Host temporarily down`. The `NSCAHOST` variable is used to specify the destination to which the NSCA server should send messages. While the example above is set to `127.0.0.1`, it should be replaced with the actual IP address of your Nagios server.

A similar script can be written for sending service related reports to Nagios. The only difference is that the return codes mean something different, and that the service name is sent along with the host name.

The following is an example that sends a warning state:

```
#!/bin/sh

HOST=localhost
SERVICE="NSCA test"
NSCAHOST=127.0.0.1

echo -e "$HOST\t$SERVICE\t1\tService in warning state" | \
     /opt/nagios/bin/send_nsca -H $NSCAHOST
     -c /etc/nagios/send_nsca.cfg

exit 0
```

This example sends out a `warning` status to Nagios over NSCA. The parameters are very similar and the main difference is in the return codes. Morever, a service description also needs to be passed; in this case, it is `NSCA test`.

> If the service has `max_check_attempts` set to anything other than 1, the script above needs to send out multiple status messages to Nagios. This can be done by piping multiple echo commands into a single `send_nsca`.

Applications that pass multiple results over a short period of time might pass multiple status results without having to re-run `send_nsca` for each of the result. Instead, you can simply send multiple lines to the same `send_nsca` process, and it will send information on all of the status to Nagios. This approach reduces the overhead of spawning multiple new processes.

Security Concerns

Both passive checks and NSCA allow the sending of the status about machines and applications to Nagios. This produces several types of security concerns. If a malicious user is able to send reports to Nagios, he or she can force a change to the status of one or more objects by frequently sending its status. He or she can also flood Nagios or NSCA with a large number of invalid requests that might cause performance problems. This might stop Nagios from receiving actual passive check results. For example, SNMP traps may not be passed to Nagios and, therefore, an event handler will not be triggered to fix a problem when it should have been.

This is why being able to send results to Nagios should be made as secure as possible, so that only authorized applications can communicate with it. Securing passive checks that are sent directly over external commands pipe is relatively easy. It only requires the external commands pipe to be accessible to Nagios and to the applications that are allowed to send data to it.

Securing NSCA is a more complex issue and requires ensuring that every step of the communication is secure. The first step = is to make sure that the NSCA configuration files have adequate access rights. They should be set so that the NSCA daemon and clients are able to read them, but other users cannot. In the client case, the issue is that all users who invoke `send_nsca` should be able to read its configuration file. This will ensure that your NSCA password and encryption methods cannot be read by unauthorized users.

Another thing that affects your setup security is whether the password used for communications is strong. It is recommended that you use a random password composed of lower case and upper case letters, as well as digits. It is also recommended that you use one of the MCrypt based algorithms, and not use the simple XOR algorithm.

The next step is to make sure that only authorized IP addresses are allowed to send information to the NSCA server. This can be done either through `xinetd` configuration or by using a system firewall such as **netfilter** ot **iptables**(`http://www.netfilter.org/`) for Linux. In both cases, it is best to define a list of allowed IPs and automatically reject connections from unknown hosts.

Summary

Nagios allows both the monitoring of services on its own, and the receipt of information about computer and service statuses from other applications. Being able to send results directly to Nagios creates a lot of opportunities for extending how Nagios can be used.

Nagios can be integrated with external applications so that they report the status of certain hosts and services. It also allows applications to report the status of services that they use on the fly. This can be used to make Nagios instantly aware of any failures that occur within the IT infrastructure.

Passive checks can also be used for performing long-running tests and reporting the the results of these to Nagios. Active checks usually have a very short timeout for the check commands, whereas some tests require several minutes or even hours to complete. In such cases, it is possible to schedule them outside Nagios and report the results as passive checks.

Nagios also offers an additional component that can be used when tests need to be performed on multiple computers. NSCA allows the sending of passive check results over the Internet and the local area network. This makes it possible to pass results that are gathered from different computers and report them directly to Nagios. NSCA is designed in such a way that it can be easily integrated with other applications, and all of the burden of authentication and encryption is left in the NSCA client application.

NSCA is also used to report results when using multiple Nagios instances on different computers. In these setups, the performance of checks is usually split between different machines and reports are sent to a central Nagios server.

Pushing passive checks to Nagios also introduces security issues that should be addressed when implementing such a set-up. Both the external commands pipe and the NSCA that is used to send results to Nagios need to be set up in a secure manner to avoid issues such as unauthorized results being retrieved by Nagios.

8

Monitoring Remote Hosts

Nagios offers various ways of monitoring computers, and the services offered by them. Depending on how you need to check if your services are running correctly, one of these ways will work best for you. The first and the easiest way is to set up a check that is performed from the Nagios server. This is a great way of monitoring services that work over the network. Another possibility is to run applications on one or more machines that report to the Nagios server using passive checks.

This chapter talks about another approach to service status checking. It uses Nagios active checks that run the actual check commands on different hosts. This approach is most useful in cases where resources local to a particular machine are to be checked. A typical example is monitoring a disk or memory usage. Checking if your operating system is up-to-date is also an example of such a test. This type of information is usually only available by reading special files or calling system commands, and cannot be checked without running commands on the target computer.

These tests can be done using two approaches. The first approach is to use the SSH protocol (Secure Shell; `http://en.wikipedia.org/wiki/Secure_Shell`) to connect and run the Nagios plugins on the remote host. Here, the main advantage is that no other additional server application needs to be run on remote machines. Therefore, in some cases, it does not even require access to the administrative account to be set up. It is also easier to have the installation done in the companies that have restrictive network connectivity, as it uses only the SSH connection, and no other port for communication.

Another approach is to use **NRPE** (**Nagios Remote Plugin Executor**) server application on remote machines that will run Nagios plugins and pass results. This requires the installation of additional software that needs to be run on remote hosts, but has the advantage of greater configuration options in terms of which checks can be performed and which cannot be. NRPE daemon listens for connections, and allows running tests on the machine it is running on, based on certain predefined criteria.

In both the cases, the situation might seem a bit similar to passive checks as applications or computers report check results to Nagios. There is a great difference between passive checks and remote checks. While passive checks require the external applications to schedule checks by themselves, with remote checks, Nagios is responsible for scheduling them. Checks can also be performed using the same command plugins as the active checks. So migrating checks to remote hosts is a relatively easy task.

Remote checks are usually used combined with the `nagios-plugins` package using either SSH or NRPE to run the plugins on the remote machine. This makes monitoring remote systems very similar to monitoring local computer, with a difference only in how the commands are actually run on the remote machine.

Monitoring over SSH

Very often, Nagios is used to monitor computer resources such as CPU utilization, memory, and disk space. One way in which this can be done is to connect over SSH and run a Nagios check plugin.

This requires setting up SSH to authenticate using public keys. This works so that Nagios server has an SSH private key, and the target machine is configured to allow users with that particular key to connect without prompting them for password.

Nagios offers a plugin, `check_by_ssh`, that takes the host name and the actual command to run on the remote server. It then connects using SSH, runs the plugin, and returns both output and exit code from the actual check performed on the remote machine to Nagios running on the local server. Internally, it runs SSH client to connect to it and runs the actual command to run along with its attributes. After the check has been performed, the output, along with the check command's exit code, is passed back to Nagios.

Thanks to this, regular plugins can be run from the same machine as the Nagios daemon, as well as remotely over SSH without any changes to the plugins. Using SSH protocol also means that authorization process can be automated using key based authentication so that each check is done without any user activity. This way Nagios is able to log in to remote machines automatically without using any passwords.

The following is an illustration of how such a check is performed:

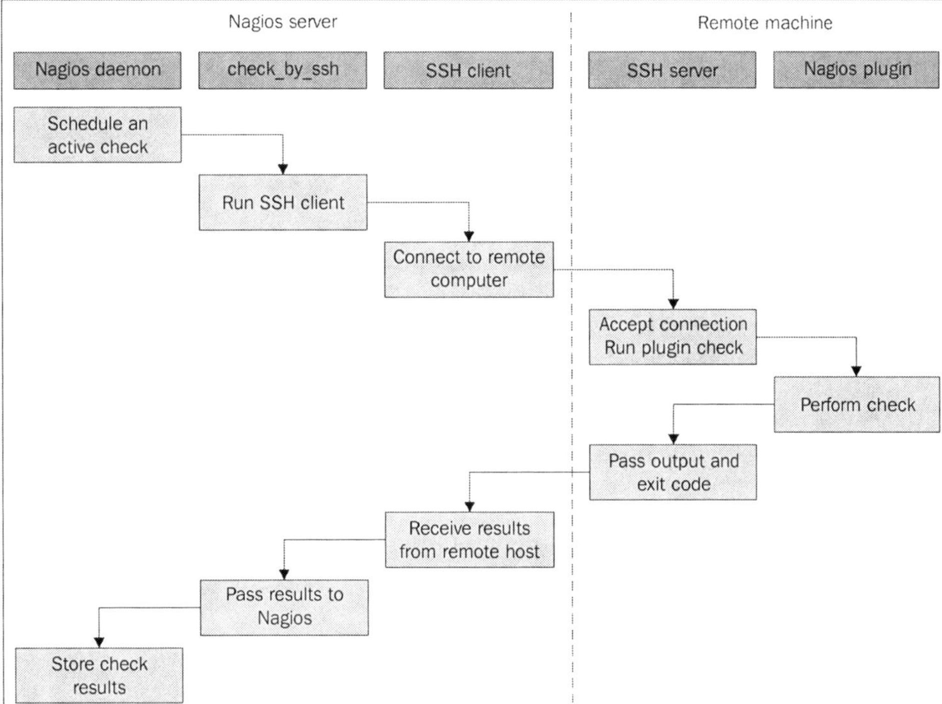

Once Nagios schedules an active check to be performed, the `check_by_ssh` plugin runs the `ssh` command to connect to the remote host's SSH server. It then runs the actual plugin, which is located on the remote host, waits for the result, and passes it back over to the SSH protocol. SSH client passes this information down to the `check_by_ssh` plugin which, in the end, passes it back to the Nagios daemon.

Even though the scenario might seem a bit complicated, it works quite efficiently and requires little setup to work properly. It also works with various flavors of UNIX systems as both SSH protocol, clients, and the shell syntax for commands used by the `check_by_ssh` plugin is the same on all the systems.

Configuring SSH

Setting up remote checks over SSH requires a few steps. The first step is to create a dedicated user for performing checks on the machine that they will be run on. We will also need to set up directories for the user. This is very similar to the steps performed for the entire Nagios installation.

The first thing that needs to be performed on the Nagios server is to create a private and public key pair that will be used to log into all remote machines without using a password. We will need to execute the `ssh-keygen` command to generate it. A sample session is shown below:

```
root@nagiosserver:~# su -s /bin/bash nagios
nagios@nagiosserver:~$ ssh-keygen
Generating public/private rsa key pair.
File in which to save the key (/opt/nagios/.ssh/id_rsa): <enter>
Created directory '/opt/nagios/.ssh'.
Enter passphrase (empty for no passphrase): <enter>
Enter same passphrase again: <enter>
Your identification has been saved in /opt/nagios/.ssh/id_rsa.
Your public key has been saved in /opt/nagios/.ssh/id_rsa.pub.
The key fingerprint is:
c9:68:47:bd:cd:6e:12:d3:9b:e8:0d:cf:93:bd:33:98 nagios@nagiosserver
nagios@nagiosserver:/root$
```

As in most cases, it was not possible to log in as user `nagios` directly, we used the `su` command to switch users along with the `-s` flag to force the shell to be `/bin/bash`. `<enter>` text means that the question was answered with the default reply.

The private key is saved as `/opt/nagios/.ssh/id_rsa`, and the public key has been saved in the `/opt/nagios/.ssh/id_rsa.pub` file.

Next, we need to set up remote machines that we will monitor. All the following commands should be executed on the remote machine that is to be monitored, unless explicitly mentioned.

First, let's create user and group named `nagios`:

```
groupadd -g 5000 nagios
useradd -u 5000 -g nagios -d /opt/nagios nagios
```

We do not need the `nagioscmd` group as we will need only the account to be able to log into the machine. The computer that only performs checks does not have a full Nagios installation along with the external command pipe that needs a separate group.

The next thing that needs to be done is to compile Nagios plugins. You will probably also need to install prerequisites that are needed for Nagios. Detailed instructions on how to do this can be found in Chapter 2, *Installation and Configuration*.

For the rest of the section, we will assume that the Nagios plugins are installed in `/opt/nagios/plugins` directory, similar to how they would be installed on the Nagios server.

It is best to install plugins in the same directory on all the machines they will be running on. In this case, we can use the `$USER1$` macro definition when creating the actual check commands in the main Nagios configuration. `USER1` macro points to the location where Nagios plugins are installed in the default Nagios installations. This is described in more detail in Chapter 2.

Next, we will need to create the `/opt/nagios` directory and set its permissions:

```
mkdir /opt/nagios
chown nagios.nagios /opt/nagios
chmod 0700 /opt/nagios
```

You can make Nagios permissions less restrictive by setting the mode to `0755`. But it is recommended not to make the users' home directories readable by all users.

We will now need to add the public key from the `nagios` user on the machine that is running the Nagios daemon.

```
mkdir /opt/nagios/.ssh

echo 'ssh-rsa … nagios@nagiosserver' \
     >>/opt/nagios/.ssh/authorized_keys

chown nagios.nagios /opt/nagios/.ssh /opt/nagios/.ssh/authorized_keys
chmod 0700 /opt/nagios/.ssh /opt/nagios/.ssh/authorized_keys
```

When actually running the command, you should replace the entire text, `ssh-rsa … nagios@nagiosserver`, with the actual contents of the `/opt/nagios/.ssh/id_rsa.pub` file on the computer running the Nagios daemon. If your machine is maintained by more than one person, you might replace the `nagios@nagiosserver` string to a more readable comment such as `Nagios on nagiosserver SSH check public key`.

Make sure to change permissions of both the `.ssh` directory and the `authorized_keys` file as many SSH server implementations ignore public key based authorization if the files' permissions are too wide.

In order to configure multiple remote machines to be accessible over `ssh` without a password, you will need to perform all the steps mentioned earlier except for key generation at the computer running Nagios server, as a single private key will be used to access multiple machines.

Assuming everything was done successfully, we can now move on to testing if the key based authorization actually works. To do that, we will try to run the `ssh` client in verbose mode and see whether using the previously generated key works fine.

In order to check that our connection can now be successfully established, we need to try to connect from the computer that has the Nagios daemon running to the remote machine. We will use the `ssh` client with the verbose flag to be sure that our connection works properly:

```
nagios@nagiosserver:~$ ssh -v nagios@192.168.2.1
OpenSSH_4.6p1 Debian-5ubuntu0.2, OpenSSL 0.9.8e 23 Feb 2007
debug1: Reading configuration data /etc/ssh/ssh_config
debug1: Applying options for *
debug1: Connecting to 192.168.2.1 [192.168.2.1] port 22.
debug1: Connection established.
debug1: identity file /opt/nagios/.ssh/id_rsa type 1
(...)
debug1: SSH2_MSG_KEXINIT sent
debug1: SSH2_MSG_KEXINIT received
debug1: kex: server->client aes128-cbc hmac-md5 none
debug1: kex: client->server aes128-cbc hmac-md5 none
debug1: SSH2_MSG_KEX_DH_GEX_REQUEST(1024<1024<8192) sent
debug1: expecting SSH2_MSG_KEX_DH_GEX_GROUP
debug1: SSH2_MSG_KEX_DH_GEX_INIT sent
debug1: expecting SSH2_MSG_KEX_DH_GEX_REPLY
The authenticity of host '192.168.2.1 (192.168.2.1)' can't be
established.
RSA key fingerprint is cf:72:1e:40:03:a4:e0:9b:6c:84:4e:e1:2d:ea:56:
fc.
Are you sure you want to continue connecting (yes/no)? yes
Warning: Permanently added '192.168.2.1' (RSA) to the list of known
hosts.
debug1: ssh_rsa_verify: signature correct
debug1: SSH2_MSG_NEWKEYS sent
debug1: expecting SSH2_MSG_NEWKEYS
debug1: SSH2_MSG_NEWKEYS received
debug1: SSH2_MSG_SERVICE_REQUEST sent
debug1: SSH2_MSG_SERVICE_ACCEPT received
debug1: Authentications that can continue: publickey,password
debug1: Next authentication method: publickey
debug1: Offering public key: /opt/nagios/.ssh/id_rsa
debug1: Server accepts key: pkalg ssh-rsa blen 277
debug1: read PEM private key done: type RSA
debug1: Authentication succeeded (publickey).
debug1: channel 0: new [client-session]
debug1: Entering interactive session.
debug1: Sending environment.
debug1: Sending env LANG = en_US.UTF-8
$
```

As we were connecting to the remote machine for the first time, ssh prompted us to check whether we had accepted the remote machine's key to a list of known hosts. This needs to be done only once for a specific host.

Also, note that we need to test the connection from the nagios account so that the keys that are used for authentication, as well as the list of known hosts are the same ones that will be used by the Nagios daemon later.

Assuming we have Nagios plugins installed on the remote machine in the /opt/nagios/plugins directory, we can try to use check_by_ssh plugin from the computer running Nagios to the remote machine by running:

```
nagios@nagiosserver:~$ /opt/nagios/plugins/check_by_ssh \
      -H 192.168.2.1 -C "/opt/nagios/plugins/check_apt"
APT OK: 0 packages available for upgrade (0 critical updates).
```

We are now sure that the checking itself works fine, and we can move on to how check_by_ssh can be used and what its syntax is.

Using the check_by_ssh Plugin

As mentioned earlier, Nagios uses a separate check command that connects to a remote machine over SSH and runs the actual check command on it. The command has very powerful features and can be used to query a single service status by using active checks and can be used to perform and report multiple checks at once as passive checks.

The following is the syntax of the command:

```
check_by_ssh -H <host> -C <command> [-fqv] [-1|-2] [-4|-6]
             [-S [lines]] [-E [lines]] [-t timeout] [-i identity]
             [-l user] [-n name] [-s servicelist] [-O outputfile]
             [-p port] [-o ssh-option]
```

The following table describes all options accepted by the plugin. Items required are marked in bold:

Option	Description
-H, --hostname	The host name or IP address of the machine to connect to; this option must be specified
-C, --command	The full path of the command to be executed on the remote host along with any additional arguments; this option must be specified
-l, --logname	Log in as a specific user name; if omitted, it defaults to the current user (usually nagios) or any other specified in the per-user SSH client configuration file

Option	Description
-I, --identity	Path to the SSH private key to be use for authorization; if omitted then `~/.ssh/id_rsa` is used by default
-o, --ssh-option	Allows passing SSH specific options that will be passed as the `-o` option to the `ssh` command
-q, --quiet	Stops SSH from printing a warning and information messages
-w, --warning	Specifies time in seconds after which the connection should be terminated and a warning should be issued to Nagios
-c, --critical	Specifies time in seconds after which the connection should be terminated and a critical should be issued to Nagios
-t, --timeout	Specifies time in seconds after which the connection should be terminated and checks should be stopped; defaults to 10 seconds
-p, --port	Port to connect over SSH to; defaults to 22
-1, --proto1	Use SSH protocol version 1
-2, --proto2	Use SSH protocol version 2; this is the default
-4	Use IPv4 protocol for SSH connectivity
-6	Use IPv6 protocol for SSH connectivity
-S, --skip-stdout	Ignore all or the provided number of lines from standard output
-E, --skip-stderr	Ignore all or the provided number of lines from standard error
-f	Tells SSH to work in the background just after connecting instead of using a terminal

The only required flags are `-H` for specifying the IP address or host name to connect to as well as `-C` for specifying the command to be used. The remaining parameters are optional. If they are not passed, SSH defaults and the timeout of 10 seconds will be used.

The `-S` and `-E` options are used to skip messages that are written by the SSH client or by the remote machine regardless of the commands executed—for example, to properly check machines printing MOTD, even for non-interactive sessions, it is required to skip it by using one of the options.

When specifying commands, they usually need to be enclosed in single or double quotation marks. This is because the entire command that should be run needs to be passed to `check_by_ssh` as a single argument. If one or more arguments contain spaces, single quote characters will have to be used.

For example, when checking for disk usage remotely, we need to quote the entire command as well, as it's safer to quote the path to the drive we're checking as shown here:

```
nagios@nagios1:~$ /opt/nagios/plugins/check_by_ssh -H 192.168.2.1 -C \
    "/opt/nagios/plugins/check_disk -w 15% -c 10% -p '/'"
DISK OK - free space: / 243 MB (17% inode=72%)
```

The preceding example is a typical usage of `check_by_ssh` plugin as an active check. It performs a single check and returns the status directly using standard output and exit code. This is how it is used as an active check from within Nagios.

If you want to use `check_by_ssh` to deploy checks locally on the same machine as Nagios is running, you will need to add the SSH key from `id_rsa.pub` to the `authorized_keys` file on that machine as well. In order to verify that it works correctly, try logging in to the local machine over SSH.

Now that the plugin works when invoked manually, we need to configure Nagios to make use of it.

Usually, for commands that will be performed both locally and remotely, the approach is to create a duplicate entry for each command with a prefix, for example, `_by_ssh`. Assuming we have the following command that checks swap usage locally, the definition is as follows:

```
define command
{
  command_name  check_swap
  command_line  $USER1$/check_swap -w $ARG1$ -c $ARG2$
}
```

Then assuming we will also check the swap usage on remote machines, we need to define the following remote counterpart:

```
define command
{
  command_name  check_swap_by_ssh
  command_line  $USER1$/check_by_ssh -H $HOSTADDRESS$ -C
                "$USER1$/check_swap -w $ARG1$ -c $ARG2$"
}
```

Usually, services are defined for groups — for example, a service should be defined to check swap space usage on all Linux servers. In such cases, you can use the check_swap_by_ssh command even for checking the local machine — the overhead for such a check is larger than the one for calling the plugin directly. But in many cases, it makes managing the configuration much easier. You can also set up two sets of services similar to the following example:

```
define service
{
  use                    generic-service
  host_name              localhost
  service_description    SWAP
  check_command          check_swap
}

define service
{
  use                    generic-service
  host_name              !localhost
  hostgroup_name         linux-servers
  service_description    SWAP
  check_command          check_swap_by_ssh
}
```

This way, localhost will use the check_swap command and all the remaining machines that are part of the linux-servers host group will use the check_swap_by_ssh check command.

This way, you can slightly reduce the overhead related to monitoring the machine Nagios is running on.

Performing Multiple Checks

A completely different approach is to make check_by_ssh perform multiple tests and report them directly to Nagios over the external command pipe. This way, the results are sent to Nagios as passive check results. So, specified services need to accept passive check results.

The reason for this approach is that SSH protocol negotiations introduce a lot of overhead related to the protocol itself. For hosts with heavy load, it is more efficient to log in once and run all the checks instead of performing a complete login for each check.

A drawback of doing multiple checks is that it is not trivial to schedule these directly from Nagios. The typical approach to passive checks is to schedule checks from an external application such as `cron` (`http://man.linuxquestions.org/index.php?query=cron`).

An alternate approach is to create a dummy service that will launch passive checks in the background. The actual result for this service would also be to check whether running the tests was successful or not. Another benefit of this approach is that the checks will be performed even if the `cron` daemon is currently disabled, as Nagios will still take care of scheduling the checks by itself.

When using `check_by_ssh` to report multiple results as passive checks, the following options need to be specified:

Option	Description
-n, --name	The short name of the host that the tests refer to; this is the name of the host that will be used when sending the results over the external command pipe
-s, --services	The names of the services that the tests refer to, separated by colon; these are the names of services that will be used when sending results over the external pipe; separated by colon
-O, --output	Path to the external command pipe that the results of all the checks should be sent to

The options above are specific to performing multiple checks only. The remaining options described earlier must also be specified—especially the `-H` and `-C` options. The second one needs to be specified multiple times, each for one check.

The number of `-C` parameters must match the number of entries in the `-s` parameter so that each result can be mapped to a service name.

The following example reports disk check results for three partitions:

```
/opt/nagios/plugins/check_by_ssh -H 192.168.2.1 -O /tmp/out1 -n
ubuntu1 \
     -s "DISK /:DISK /usr:DISK /opt" \
     -C "/opt/nagios/plugins/check_disk -w 15% -c 10% -p /" \
     -C "/opt/nagios/plugins/check_disk -w 15% -c 10% -p /usr" \
     -C "/opt/nagios/plugins/check_disk -w 15% -c 10% -p /opt"
```

This command will put the output into `/tmp/out1`, similar to the following example:

```
[1206096000] PROCESS_SERVICE_CHECK_RESULT;ubuntu1;DISK /:DISK
CRITICAL...
[1206096000] PROCESS_SERVICE_CHECK_RESULT;ubuntu1;DISK /usr:DISK OK
...
[1206096000] PROCESS_SERVICE_CHECK_RESULT;ubuntu1;DISK /opt:DISK OK
...
```

As mentioned previously, it is very common to write a script that is run as an active check. This script is set up as a service that is only responsible for running multiple checks for other services. Results from those services are passed as passive check results.

The following is a sample script that runs several tests and reports their results back to Nagios:

```
#!/bin/sh

COMMANDFILE=$1
HOSTNAME=$2
HOSTADDRESS=$3
PLUGINPATH=$4

$PLUGINPATH/check_by_ssh -H $HOSTADDRESS -t 30 \
    -o $COMMANDFILE -n $HOSTNAME \
    -s "SWAP:Root Partition:Processes:System Load" \
    -C "$PLUGINPATH/check_swap -w 20% -c 10%" \
    -C "$PLUGINPATH/check_disk -w 20% -c 10% -p /" \
    -C "$PLUGINPATH/check_procs -w 100 -c 200" \
    -C "$PLUGINPATH/check_load -w 5,3,2 -c 10,8,7" \
       (
        echo "BYSSH CRITICAL problem while running SSH"
        exit 2
       )

echo "BYSSH OK checks launched"
exit 0
```

For the remaining part of the section, let's assume the script is in the `/opt/nagios/plugins` directory and is called `check_linux_services_by_ssh`.

The script will perform several checks, and if any of them fail, it will return a critical result as well. Otherwise, it will return an `OK` status and the remaining results will be passed as passive check results.

We will also need to configure Nagios, both services that will receive their results as passive checks, and the service that will actually schedule the checks, properly.

All the services that are checked via the `check_by_ssh` command itself have a very similar definition. They only need to accept passive checks and don't have any active checks scheduled.

The following is a sample definition for the SWAP service:

```
define service
{
  use                     generic-service
  host_name               !localhost
  hostgroup_name          linux-servers
  service_description     SWAP
  active_checks_enabled   0
  passive_checks_enabled  1
}
```

All other services will also need to have a very similar definition. We might also define a template for such services and only create services that use it. This will make the configuration more readable.

Now, we need to define a command definition that will launch the passive check script written earlier:

```
define command
{
  command_name    check_linux_services_by_ssh
  command_line    $USER1$/check_linux_services_by_ssh
  "$COMMANDFILE$"
                  "$HOSTNAME$" "$HOSTADDRESS$" "$USER1$"
}
```

All the parameters that are used by the script are passed directly from Nagios configuration. This makes reconfiguring various paths easier to manage.

The next step is to define an actual service that will run these checks:

```
define service
{
  use                         generic-service
  host_name                   !localhost
  hostgroup_name              linux-servers
  service_description         Check Services By SSH
  active_checks_enabled       1
  passive_checks_enabled      0
```

```
    check_command                  check_linux_services_by_ssh
    check_interval                 30
    check_period                   24x7
    max_check_attempts             1
    notification_interval          30
    notification_period            24x7
    notification_options           c,u,r
    contact_groups                 linux-admins
  }
```

This will cause the checks to be scheduled every 30 minutes. It will also notify Linux administrators if any problem occurs with scheduling the checks.

An alternative approach is to use the `cron` daemon to schedule the launch of the previous script. In such a case, the `Check Services By SSH` service is not needed. In this case, scheduling of the checks is not done in Nagios, but we will still need to have the services for which the status will be reported defined.

In such a case, we need to make sure that `cron` is running to have up-to-date results for the checks. Such verification can be done by monitoring the daemon using Nagios and the `check_procs` plugin.

The first thing that needs to be done is to slightly adapt the script not to print out results in case everything worked fine, and to hardcode paths to the Nagios files:

```
#!/bin/sh

COMMANDFILE=/vat/nagios/rw/nagios.cmd
PLUGINPATH=/opt/Nagios/plugins
HOSTNAME=$1
HOSTADDRESS=$2

$PLUGINPATH/check_by_ssh -H $HOSTADDRESS -t 30 \
    -o $COMMANDFILE -n $HOSTNAME \
    -s "SWAP:Root Partition:Processes:System Load" \
    -C "$PLUGINPATH/check_swap -w 20% -c 10%" \
    -C "$PLUGINPATH/check_disk -w 20% -c 10% -p /" \
    -C "$PLUGINPATH/check_procs -w 100 -c 200" \
    -C "$PLUGINPATH/check_load -w 5,3,2 -c 10,8,7" \
    || (
        echo "BYSSH CRITICAL problem while running SSH"
        exit 2
    )

#echo "BYSSH OK checks launched"
exit 0
```

Actual changes have been highlighted.

The next step is to add entry to the Nagios user, `crontab`. This can be done by running the `crontab -e` command as the `nagios` user, or `crontab -u nagios -e` command as the administrator. Assuming the check should be performed every 30 minutes, the `crontab` entry should be as follows:

```
*/30 * * * * /opt/nagios/plugins/check_linux_services_by_ssh
```

For more details on how an entry in `crontab` should look like, please consult the corresponding manual page (`http://linux.die.net/man/5/crontab`).

Troubleshooting SSH-Based Checks

If you have followed the steps from the previous sections carefully, then most probably, everything should be working smoothly. However, in some cases, your setup might not be working properly, and you will need to find the root cause of the problem.

The first thing that you should start with is to use the `check_ssh` plugin to make sure that SSH is accepting connections on the host we are checking. For example, we can run the following command:

```
root@ubuntu1:~# /opt/nagios/plugins/check_ssh -H 192.168.2.51
SSH OK - OpenSSH_4.7p1 Debian-8ubuntu1.2 (protocol 2.0)
```

Where `192.168.2.51` is the name of IP address of the remote machine we want to monitor. If no SSH server is set up on the remote host, the plugin will return `Connection refused` status, and if it failed to connect, the result will state `No route to host`. In these cases, you need to make sure SSH server is working, and that all routers and firewalls do not filter out connections for SSH—which is TCP port 22.

Assuming SSH server is accepting connections, the next thing that can be checked is whether SSH key-based authorization works correctly. To do this, switch to the user the Nagios process is running as. Next, try to connect to the remote machine. The following are sample commands to perform this check:

```
root@ubuntu1:~# su nagios -
$ ssh -v 192.168.2.51
```

This way, you will check the connectivity as the same user that Nagios is running checks at. You can also analyze the logs that will be printed to the standard output as described earlier in this chapter. If SSH client will prompt you for a password, then your keys are not set up properly. It is a common mistake to set up keys on the `root` account instead of setting them up on the `nagios` account. If this is the case, then create a new set of keys as a correct user and verify whether these keys work correctly now.

Assuming this step worked fine, the next thing to be done is to check whether invoking an actual check command produces correct results. For example:

```
root@ubuntu1:~# su nagios -
$ ssh 192.168.2.51 /opt/nagios/plugins/check_procs
PROCS OK: 51 processes
```

This way, you will check the connectivity as the same user that Nagios is running checks at.

The last check is to make sure that the `check_by_ssh` plugin also returns correct information. An example of how to do this is as follows:

```
root@ubuntu1:~# su nagios -
$ /opt/nagios/plugins/check_by_ssh -H 192.168.2.1 \
    /opt/nagios/plugins/check_procs
PROCS OK: 52 processes
```

If the last step also worked correctly, it means that all check commands are working correctly. If you still have issues with running the checks, then the next thing you should investigate is if Nagios has been properly configured, whether all commands, hosts, and services are set up in the correct way.

Introduction to NRPE

Nagios Remote Plugin Executor (NRPE) is a daemon for running check commands on remote computers. It is designed explicitly to allow the central Nagios server to trigger checks on other machines in a secure manner.

NRPE offers a very good security mechanism along with encryption mechanisms. It is possible to specify a list of machines that can run checks via NRPE, and which plugins can be run along with aliases that should be used by the central Nagios server.

The main difference is that the communication overhead is much smaller than for the SSH checks. This means that both central Nagios server and the remote machine need less CPU time to perform a check. This is mainly important for Nagios servers that deal with a lot of checks performed remotely on machines. If the SSH overhead compared to NRPE is only one second, then for performing 20,000 checks, it is 5.5 hours spent on negotiations that can be saved.

It also offers a better level of security than using SSH mechanisms in terms of the remote machine's safety. It does not provide complete access to the destination machines from the Nagios central server and forbids running any commands outside predefined check commands. This is very important in situations where Nagios is monitoring machines that might store sensitive information. In such a case, SSH based solution might not be acceptable due to security policies.

NRPE checks work similar to SSH checks in many aspects. In both the cases, the Nagios check command connects to the remote machine and sends a request to run a plugin installed on that machine. NRPE uses a custom protocol. It offers more flexibility in terms of what can be executed and what not, as well as which hosts can connect to the NRPE daemon running on the remote machine. It also requires much less overhead to send the command to NRPE and receive output from it.

Another difference compared to the SSH-based checks is that NRPE allows running only a single command and can be used so that results are passed back as active checks. The feature of performing multiple checks that the `check_by_ssh` plugin offers is not possible using NRPE.

NRPE uses the TCP protocol with **SSL** (**Secure Socket Layer**) encryption on top of it. Enabling encryption is optional, but it is recommended for companies that require security to be at a high level. By default, NRPE communicates on port 5666. The connection is always made from the machine running Nagios daemon to the remote machine. If your company has firewalls set up for local connectivity, make sure that you allow communications from port 5666 that originate from your Nagios servers. The following is an illustration of how such a check is performed.

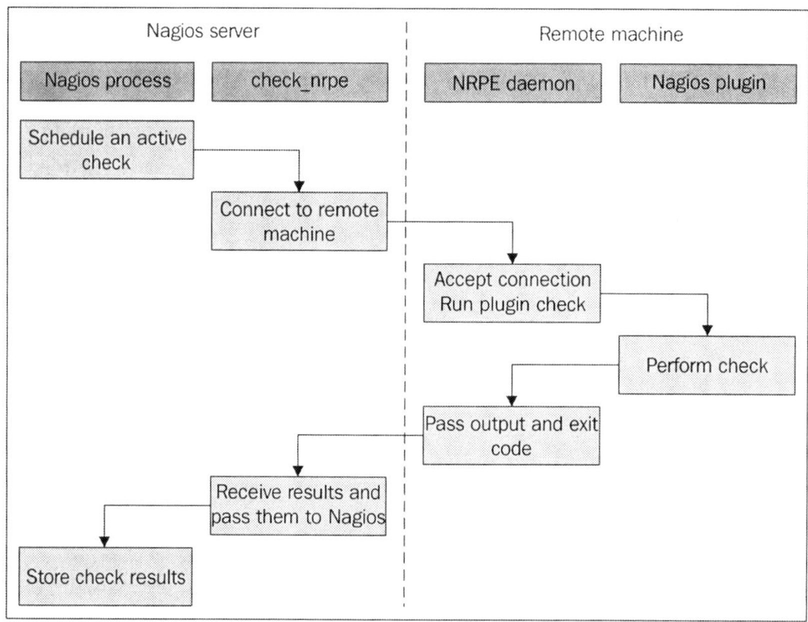

Nagios determines that an active check should be performed. It runs the `check_nrpe` plugin that connects to the remote host's NRPE daemon. After the NRPE daemon accepts this as a valid host to send commands to, `check_nrpe` sends the command to be run along with any parameter to the remote machine.

Next, the NRPE daemon translates these into the actual system command to be run. In case the specified command is not configured to be run, NRPE daemon will reject this request. Otherwise, it will run the command and pass the results back to `check_nrpe` on the machine hosting the Nagios daemon. This information is then passed back to the Nagios daemon and stored in the data files and/or databases.

The NRPE package consists of two parts—the NRPE daemon and the NRPE check command. The first one needs to be running on all remote machines that are to be monitored using this method. The NRPE check command (`check_nrpe`) is a Nagios plugin for performing active checks and needs to be installed on the machine on which Nagios daemon is running.

Obtaining NRPE

NRPE is a core add-on for Nagios, and is maintained by the Nagios development team. NRPE can be downloaded as both source code and binary packages. In the first case, you can compile NRPE from sources by yourself; in the latter, you have a ready-to-use set of binaries.

The NRPE source package can be downloaded from the Nagios download page (`http://www.nagios.org/download/`). NRPE can be found in the `Addons` section of the page. The file is named in the form of `nrpe-2.1.12.tar.gz`.

Many Linux distributions already contain prebuilt NRPE binaries. If you want to use precompiled packages instead of building them yourself, then this is the way to go.

For Ubuntu Linux, the package names are `nagios-nrpe-server` and `nagios-nrpe-plugin` for the daemon and client respectively.

For Ubuntu, the command to install the client and the server is as follows:

```
apt-get install are nagios-nrpe-server nagios-nrpe-plugin
```

For **RHEL** (**Red Hat Enterprise Linux**), CentOS, and Fedora systems that have `yum` installed, the package names are `nagios-nrpe` and `nagios-plugins-nrpe` for the daemon and the client respectively.

The command to install both client and server is as follows:

```
yum install nagios-nrpe nagios-plugins-nrpe
```

Microsoft Windows of the NRPE daemon can be found in the NRPE_NT (`http://sourceforge.net/projects/nrpent/`) project on SourceForge. It offers the same functionality as its UNIX version and is configured in the same way.

The main difference in the Microsoft Windows version is that the Nagios plugins do not provide the Windows version, so you will need to compile Nagios plugins using the Cygwin package (visit `http://www.cygwin.com/`).

You can also provide only your own check commands and set up NRPE_NT to use those. In the case of Microsoft Windows, it is important to remember that your plugins need to be command line tools and cannot be created as GUI-based tools.

Compiling NRPE

If you are using NRPE from prebuilt packages, you can skip this section and resume with the NRPE configuration information.

Compiling NRPE requires a standard compiler, linker, and similar tools to be present on your system. It also needs the OpenSSL package along with the actual `openssl` command line, which is used to generate the Diffie-Hellman key for each instance.

On an Ubuntu Linux system, installing the prerequisite packages can be done by performing the following command:

```
apt-get install gcc make binutils cpp pkg-config libc6-dev \
        libssl-dev openssl
```

For other systems, the commands and package names might differ a bit, but should be very similar.

It is also recommended to install the same prerequisites as those for compiling Nagios and the Nagios plugins. These packages should already be there from when the actual plugins were built, but in case the compilation fails, it would be a good idea to install all packages that were also used for the Nagios build.

For Ubuntu Linux, this would require running the following command:

```
apt-get install gcc make binutils cpp libpq-dev libmysqlclient15-dev \
                libssl0.9.8 libssl-dev pkg-config apache2 \
                libgd2-xpm libgd2-xpm-dev libgd-tools \
                libpng12-dev libjpeg62-dev \
                perl libperl-dev libperl5.8 libnet-snmp-perl
```

More information on what packages should be installed on other operating systems, and how to do this, can be found in Chapter 2, *Installation and Configuration*.

Now that our packages are set up, the next step is to run the `configure` script that will set up the NRPE parameters and create the Diffie-Hellman key.

For standard paths and users that were used in Chapter 2, the command is as follows:

```
sh configure \
    --sysconfdir=/etc/nagios \
    --libexecdir=/opt/nagios/plugins \
    --prefix=/opt/nagios \
    --localstatedir=/var/nagios \
    --with-nrpe-user=nagios \
    --with-nrpe-group=nagios \
    --with-nagios-user=nagios \
    --with-nagios-group=nagios \
    --enable-ssl
```

If running the configure script failed, it is probably because one or more required packages are missing. If this happens, verify whether all packages mentioned earlier in the chapter have been installed, and then try again.

The next step is to actually build the NRPE client and daemon. To do this, run the following command:

```
make all
```

This command will build both binaries and create sample configuration files for the NRPE daemon.

It is a very common problem that the build fails, claiming that the `get_dh512` function could not be found. The problem is not obvious. In this case, please make sure that the `openssl` command is installed and the directory where it is located is added to the `PATH` environment variable, and then run all of the steps, starting with the `configure` script, again.

The problem is that the `configure` script tries to generate a Diffie-Hellman key—if a problem exists during this step. Then the script itself does not fail to complete, but the build process eventually fails. Please make sure that somewhere at the end of the output from the configure script, a text similar to the one that follows is printed out:

```
*** Generating DH Parameters for SSL/TLS ***
Generating DH parameters, 512 bit long safe prime, generator 2
This is going to take a long time
+.............+..........+........++*+*++*++*++*++*
```

If the `openssl` command is not present, the following error will show up instead:

```
*** Generating DH Parameters for SSL/TLS ***
configure: line 6703: /usr/bin/openssl: No such file or directory
```

If the compilation process fails for any other reason, it is most probably due to missing libraries or header files. In this case, installing the packages mentioned earlier will help.

Assuming that the build succeeded, the next step is to install either the NRPE client or the daemon. On the machine that is running the Nagios daemon, we need to install the client (`check_nrpe`) command. To do this, type the following command:

```
make install-plugin
```

This command will copy the `check_nrpe` command to the `/opt/nagios/plugins` directory. NRPE does not require any configuration file for the NRPE client and, hence, no additional file needs to be copied.

For all of the remaining machines, please run the following command to install the NRPE daemon:

```
make install-daemon
```

This command will copy the `nrpe` binary to the `/opt/nagios/bin` directory.

Because the NRPE daemon requires configuration, it is recommended that you copy the `sample-config/nrpe.cfg` file as `/etc/nagios/nrpe.cfg`.

Configuring the NRPE Daemon

Our NRPE daemon is now built and ready to be deployed on the remote machines. We need to configure it and set up the system so that it accepts connections from other computers.

The NRPE daemon should use a separate user and password.

First, let's create a user and a group named `nagios`:

```
groupadd -g 5000 nagios
useradd -u 5000 -g nagios -d /opt/nagios nagios
```

We also need to create a home directory for the user, and it is a good idea to lock out access for that user if no checks are to be performed over SSH. To do this, run the following commands:

```
mkdir /opt/nagios
chown nagios.nagios /opt/nagios
passwd -l nagios
```

There are many ways of setting this up—NRPE can work either as a standalone process that handles incoming connections, or as part of the `inetd` (`http://en.wikipedia.org/wiki/inetd`) or the `xinetd` (`http://www.xinetd.org/`) setup. In all cases, a configuration file is needed. This file specifies the commands to be used and the additional options for running the NRPE daemon standalone.

The configuration file is similar to the main Nagios configuration file—all parameters are written in the form of `<name>=<value>`. If you have compiled NRPE from the source, then a default configuration can be found in the `sample-config/nrpe.cfg` file.

A sample NRPE configuration script that will work for both standalone installations as well as under `inetd` is as follows:

```
log_facility=daemon
pid_file=/var/run/nrpe.pid
server_port=5666
nrpe_user=nagios
nrpe_group=nagios
allowed_hosts=192.168.2.51
command_timeout=60
connection_timeout=300
debug=0
```

The first series of parameters includes information related to logging. NRPE uses standard UNIX logging mechanisms. The `log_facility` parameter specifies the syslog facility name to be used for logging. The default value is `daemon`, but it can be set to any of the predefined syslog facility names.

A standalone NRPE daemon also allows the setting up of the IP address and the port to listen to, as well as the user and group names to be used. In order to specify that NRPE should listen only on a specific IP address, you need to use the `server_address` parameter. If this parameter is omitted, then the NRPE will listen on all network interfaces. The `server_port` parameter is used to specify the port number NRPE should listen on. If NRPE should accept connections only from a predefined list of machines, you need to specify the `allowed_hosts` parameter, which will contain a list of all the IP addresses of these machines, separated by commas.

For security reasons, NRPE usually runs as a separate user. The options to specify the user and group names that should be used by NRPE are `nrpe_user` and `nrpe_group` respectively.

We can also specify the file to which NRPE should write the PID of the daemon process—this is useful in the startup scripts that can read this file to terminate any NRPE processes during a restart of the service. The option name is `pid_file`.

We can also tell NRPE how long a command can run for. The first option is `command_timeout`, and it tells NRPE how many seconds a command can run before it should be stopped. If a command is running for more than the specified number of seconds, it is terminated, and a `CRITICAL` status is sent back to the NRPE client.

The `connection_timeout` option specifies the time in seconds after which a connection should be closed if no data has been received. This does not change the way the command times out, and only specifies how much time NRPE should wait for a command to be sent.

NRPE also offers a `debug` option that can specify whether it should record a large amount of information in the system log. A value of 1 enables verbose logging and 0 disables it. This should be disabled in production, but can be useful during the initial runs in case you run into a problem.

The next step is to configure the commands that can be used by the other machines. The NRPE commands define aliases for the actual commands that will be executed. All commands have a unique name and the actual command line to be run.

Usually, command names are the plugin names or the plugin names with some description appended. For example, the `check_disk` based command that checks the `/home` directory could be called `check_disk_home`.

Each command is defined as `command[<command_name>]=<command_to_execute>`. Each `command_name` can be used only once, and there is no possibility of defining which hosts can run which commands. The same set of commands can be run by all hosts specified in the `allowed_hosts` parameter.

An example command definition to use `check_disk` to verify the space on the root partition is as follows:

```
command[check_disk_sys]=/opt/nagios/plugins/check_disk -w 20% -c 10%
                        -p /
```

It would be a good idea to create a template configuration that will contain the typical checks and the hosts that should be allowed to run the checks. These can be modified later for individual hosts, but using a template makes it easier to deploy for a large number of boxes. A typical set of commands would be as follows:

```
command[check_rootdisk]=/opt/nagios/plugins/check_disk -w 20% -c 10%
                        -p /
command[check_swap]=/opt/nagios/plugins/check_disk -w 40% -c 20%
command[check_sensors]=/opt/nagios/plugins/check_sensors
command[check_users]=/opt/nagios/plugins/check_users -w 10 -c 20
command[check_load]=/opt/nagios/plugins/check_load -w 10,8,5 -c
                    20,18,15
command[check_zombies]=/opt/nagios/plugins/check_procs -w 5 -c 10 -s
                       Z
command[check_all_procs]=/opt/nagios/plugins/check_procs -w 150 -c
                         200
```

Please note that the parameters for several plugins may be changed according to your preferences, but they do represent reasonable defaults.

In case you need to troubleshoot why a check is failing, it would be a good idea to set the `debug` parameter to `1` in `nrpe.cfg`. If NRPE is running in standalone mode, it will need to be restarted for the changes to take effect. An example log from a connection is as follows:

```
Apr 21 20:07:29 ubuntu2 nrpe[5569]: Handling the connection...
Apr 21 20:07:29 ubuntu2 nrpe[5569]: Host is asking for command
    'check_root_disk' to be run...
Apr 21 20:07:29 ubuntu2 nrpe[5569]: Running command:
    /opt/nagios/plugins/check_disk -w 20% -c 10% -p /
Apr 21 20:07:29 ubuntu2 nrpe[5569]: Command completed with return code
0
    and output: DISK OK - free space: / 7211 MB (90% inode=96%);|
    /=759MB;6717;7557;0;8397
Apr 21 20:07:29 ubuntu2 nrpe[5569]: Return Code: 0, Output: DISK OK -
free space: / 7211 MB (90% inode=96%);| /=759MB;6717;7557;0;8397
```

Another requirement for using NRPE is that the commands need to be specified using the full path to the plugin, and no macro substitution can take place.

Not being able to use any macro definitions requires more attention when writing macros. It also requires that any change to the command is edited in the NRPE configuration on the remote machine, not in the Nagios configurations on the central server. This introduces a very strict security model, but makes NRPE a bit harder to maintain.

In some cases, it is better to be able to pass arguments to NRPE from the Nagios server and have NRPE put these into the command definition. Even though this functionality is disabled for security reasons, it is possible to enable it. How NRPE can be set up to accept parameters from the Nagios server is described in the *NRPE and Command Arguments* section in this chapter.

Installing NRPE as a System Service

The easiest way to get NRPE up and running is to add it to startup in a standalone mode. In this case, it will handle listening on the specified TCP port and changing the user and group by itself.

To do this, simply run the NRPE binary with the following parameters:

```
/opt/nagios/bin/nrpe -c /etc/nagios/nrpe.cfg -d
```

You can also add NPRE to `init.d` file so that NPRE will start automatically at system start. Usually, this file is located in `/etc/init.d/nrpe` or `/etc/rc.d/init.d/nrpe`.

A simple script that starts up and shuts down NRPE is as follows:

```
#! /bin/sh

case "$1" in
  start)
        echo -n "Starting NRPE daemon..."
        /opt/nagios/bin/nrpe -c /etc/nagios/nrpe.cfg -d
        echo " done."
        ;;
  stop)
        echo -n "Stopping NRPE daemon..."
        pkill -u nagios nrpe
        echo " done."
        ;;
  restart)
        $0 stop
        sleep 2
        $0 start
        ;;
  *)
        echo "Usage: $0 start|stop|restart"
        ;;
esac

exit 0
```

The next step is to set up a system to stop and start this service when changing to appropriate runlevels. Depending on your system, the command to add `nrpe` as a service can be one of the following:

```
chkconfig --add nrpe ; chkconfig nrpe on
update-rc.d nrpe defaults
```

NRPE can also be run either from `inetd` or `xinetd`. To do this, we first need to add the following line to the `/etc/services` file:

```
nrpe 5666/tcp
```

This will indicate that the TCP port 5666 maps to the service name, `nrpe`. This specification is used by both `inetd` and `xinetd` to map the service name to the actual protocol and port definition.

If we're using `inetd`, we need to add the following service configuration to the `/etc/inetd.conf` file—a sample definition is as follows:

```
nrpe stream tcp nowait nagios /opt/nagios/bin/nrpe -c /etc/nagios/
nrpe.cfg -i
```

The entry above should be stored as a single line.
Next, we should restart `inetd` by running the following command:

```
/etc/init.d/inetd reload
```

This will make `inetd` reload the service definition. The NRPE daemon should now be accepting connections whenever one comes in on TCP port 5666.

Configuring the NRPE daemon for `xinetd` is very similar. We will need to create a file called `/etc/xinetd.d/nrpe` with the following contents:

```
service nrpe
{
        flags           = REUSE
        socket_type     = stream
        wait            = no
        user            = nagios
        group           = nagios
        server          = /opt/nagios/bin/nrpe
        server_args     = -c /etc/nagios/nrpe.cfg -i
        log_on_failure  += USERID
        disable         = no
}
```

Next, we need to reload `xinetd` by running:

```
/etc/init.d/xinetd reload
```

As with the previous reloading of `inetd`, the NRPE daemon should now accept connections on port 5666.

When NRPE is working under `inetd` or `xinetd`, the server ignores the `server_address`, `server_port`, `nrpe_user` and `nrpe_group` parameters from the configuration files. This is because `inetd` and `xinetd` handle these internally.

NRPE also ignores the `allowed_hosts` directive when running from any `inetd` flavor. In this, you can configure which hosts are allowed to access this particular service in the `inetd/xinetd` file. For `xinetd`, this can be done by using the `only_from` statement in the service definition. For `inetd`, this can be done using the `tcpd` wrapper (`http://linux.about.com/library/cmd/blcmdl8_tcpd.htm`) to achieve this.

Configuring Nagios for NRPE

The next step is to set up Nagios to use NRPE for performing checks via a remote machine. Using NRPE for performing checks requires creating one or more commands that will use the check_nrpe plugin to send actual check requests to a remote machine.

The syntax of the plugin is as follows:

```
check_nrpe -H <host> [-n] [-u] [-p <port>] [-t <timeout>]
          [-c <command>] [-a <arglist...>]
```

The following table describes all of the options accepted by the plugin. The items required are marked in bold:

Option	Description
-H, --host	The host name or IP address of the machine to connect to; this option must be specified
-c, --command	The name of the command that should be executed; the command needs to be defined in the nrpe.cfg file on the remote machine
-n, --no-ssl	Disables SSL for communication
-p, --port	Connects to the specified port; defaults to 5666
-t, --timeout	The number of seconds after which a connection will be terminated; defaults to 10
-u, --unknown-timeout	If a timeout occurs, will return an UNKNOWN state; if not specified then CRITICAL status is returned in case of timeout

The only two required attributes are -H and -c, which specify the host and the command alias to run on that machine.

The next thing we should do is to make sure that the NRPE server on the remote machine is working correctly. Assuming that check_swap is a valid command defined in NRPE on a remote machine, we can now try to connect from the Nagios server. The first thing that's worth checking is whether calling check_nrpe directly works:

```
$ /opt/nagios/plugins/check_nrpe -H 192.168.2.52 -c check_swap
SWAP OK - 100% free (431 MB out of 431 MB) |swap=431MB;86;43;0;431
```

In our example, 192.168.2.52 is the IP address of the remote computer. As the connection was successful, NRPE passed the actual plugin output to the standard output.

After a successful check, we can now define a command in the Nagios configuration that will perform a check over NRPE.

```
define command
{
  command_name     check_swap_nrpe
  command_line     $USER1$/check_nrpe -H "$HOSTADDRESS$"
                   -c "check_swap"
}
```

We can then use the `check_swap_nrpe` command in a service definition.

NRPE has a much lower overhead as compared to SSH. So in some cases, it would be a good idea to use NRPE even for performing local checks.

In case we are defining a service for a group of hosts, we can use the same trick as those for checks over SSH to perform checks on a local machine-using the plugins directly and checking all of the remaining machines using NRPE. This will reduce the overhead related to monitoring the local machine, and will remove the requirement to install NRPE on local host.

The following is a sample configuration that defines a check for swap usage locally for the computer on which it is defined, and over NRPE for all the remaining machines:

```
define service
{
  use                    generic-service
  host_name              localhost
  service_description    SWAP
  check_command          check_swap
  normal_check_interval  15
}

define service
{
  use                    generic-service
  host_name              !localhost
  hostgroup_name         linux-servers
  service_description    SWAP
  check_command          check_swap_nrpe
  normal_check_interval  30
}
```

NRPE and Command Arguments

By default, NRPE is configured to run only the predefined commands, and it is not possible to pass any arguments to the commands that will be run. In some cases, s for example with a large number of partitions mounted on various servers, this is hard to manage as changes to the command configurations need to be done at the remote machine level, not at the central Nagios server level.

In such cases, it might be worth investigating an option included in NRPE to pass arguments to commands. This option is disabled by default as it is considered to be a large security concern. This is because is possible to send malicious arguments to a check command and make it perform actions other than the ones it should be doing. It is recommended that you keep the option disabled as this is a more secure option. However, if lowering the level of security is not a concern, it is possible to enable this functionality within the NRPE daemon. It allows easier management of NRPE and Nagios configuration.

The first thing that needs to be done is to rebuild the NRPE daemon with this option enabled. To do this, run the `configure` script again with the `--enable-command-args` flag added. For the same invocation that was used previously to build NRPE, the command would be:

```
sh configure \
    --sysconfdir=/etc/nagios \
    --libexecdir=/opt/nagios/plugins \
    --prefix=/opt/nagios \
    --localstatedir=/var/nagios \
    --with-nrpe-user=nagios \
    --with-nrpe-group=nagios \
    --with-nagios-user=nagios \
    --with-n agios-group=nagios \
    --enable-command-args \
    --enable-ssl
```

Of course, it is also necessary to rebuild the NRPE daemon and reinstall the binary. If you are running NRPE as a standalone daemon, then you need to restart the daemon after overwriting the binary.

Only the daemon on remote machine needs to be reconfigured and recompiled. It is not necessary to rebuild the NRPE client as it always supports the passing of arguments to the NRPE daemon.

The next step is to add the `dont_blame_nrpe` option to the `nrpe.cfg` file and set it to 1. This option, despite its strange name, enables the functionality to use arguments in the command definitions. When both NRPE is compiled with this option and the option is enabled in the NRPE configuration, this option is enabled.

After that, it is possible to use `$ARGn$` macros in the NRPE configuration, similar to how they are defined in Nagios. This works similarly to Nagios, where `$ARG1$` indicates the first argument, `$ARG2$` the second one, and so on for up to 16 arguments. For example, a `check` command that checks the disk space on any partition looks like this:

```
command[check_disk]=/opt/nagios/plugins/check_disk -w $ARG1$ -c $ARG2$
-p $ARG3$
```

This requires that warning and critical levels are passed during the check. The actual path to the mount point, specified as a third parameter, is essential.

Arguments are passed to `check_nrpe` by specifying the `-a` flag and passing all required arguments after it, with each argument as separate parameter.

An example invocation of the check command as a standalone command would be as follows:

```
$ /opt/nagios/plugins/check_nrpe -H 10.0.0.1 -c check_disk -a 10% 5%
/usr
DISK OK - free space: /usr 7209 MB (90% inode=96%)
```

After making sure that the check works, we can now define a command and a corresponding service definition. The command will pass the arguments specified in the actual service definition:

```
define command
{
  command_name    check_disk_nrpe
  command_line    $USER1$/check_disk -H "$HOSTADDRESS$"
                  -c "check_disk" -a $ARG1$ $ARG2$ $ARG3$
}
```

And the actual service definition is as follows:

```
define service
{
  use                  generic-service
  host_name            !localhost
  hostgroup_name       linux-servers
  service_description  Disk space on /usr
  check_command        check_disk_nrpe!10%!5%!/usr
}
```

This way, you can define multiple partition checks without any modifications on the remote machines.

Of course, arguments can also be used for various plugins, for example, to be able to configure the load, user, and process thresholds in a central location.

Passing arguments to NRPE is a very useful feature. But it comes at the price of a lower security level. If the machines you deploy NRPE on do not require very strict limitations, then it would be a good idea to enable it.

Having a strict source IP address policy in both the firewalls and the remote machine is a good way of limiting security issues related to the passing of arguments down to the actual check commands.

Other Approaches

This chapter focuses mainly on using SSH and NRPE for performing remote checks. This is because Nagios is widely used to perform checks on remote machines.

There are also various alternate approaches that people take to invoke checks remotely. A very popular approach is to use frameworks for working remotely. In such cases, you might need to create some scripts or jobs that perform the checks, but the entire network communication along with authentication and authorization are already implemented in them.

One such framework is the **Software Testing Automation Framework** (**STAF**; `http://staf.sourceforge.net/`). This is a peer-to-peer based framework that allows you to write code that performs specific jobs on remote machines. As the system is not centralized, there is no critical resource that can make your entire system malfunction if it is down.

STAF can be used from various languages, including Java, Perl, Python, Tcl, and Ant. This means that pieces of the checks can be done in languages that best fit a specific scenario.

Another approach is to use `check_http` and web-based communication. This is a very common scenario when doing a check for web applications. This way, you can invoke a specific URL that will perform a check on the remote machine and provide the results over the HTTP protocol.

In such a case, an application can have a URL that is accessible only from specific IP addresses and returns diagnostic information about the website. This can mean performing a test SQL query to the database and checking the file permissions and available disk space. The application can also perform a sanity check of critical data either in files or in a database.

The web page can return a predefined string if all of the tests are passed correctly and will return an error message otherwise. In this case, it is possible to perform the check with the `check_http` plugin.

A typical scenario is when a check is done for both the string preset in the answer and a page size range. For example, a check for the `OK` string combined with a page size ranging from two to eight will check whether the result contains information about the correct test and will also detect any additional messages preset in the output.

Troubleshooting NRPE

Our NRPE configuration should now be complete and working as expected. However, in some cases, for example, if there is a firewall issue or an issue of invalid configuration, the NRPE based checks may not work correctly. There are some steps that you can take to determine the root cause of the problem.

The first thing that should be checked is whether Nagios server can connect to the NRPE process on the remote machine. Assuming that we want to use NRPE on `192.168.2.1`, we can check if NRPE accepts connections by using `check_tcp` from the Nagios plugins. By default, NRPE uses port `5666`, which we'll also use in the following example, which shows how to check this:

```
$ /opt/nagios/plugins/check_tcp -H 192.168.2.1 -p 5666
TCP OK - 0.009 second response time on port 5666|time=0.008794s;;;0.00
0000;10.000000
```

If NRPE is not set up on the remote host, the plugin will return `Connection refused`. If the connection could not be established, the result will be `No route to host`. In these cases, you need to make sure that the NRPE server is working and that, the traffic that the TCP port NRPE is listening on is not blocked by the firewalls.

The next step is to try to run an invalid command and check the output from the plugin. The following is an example that assumes that the `dummycommand` is not defined in the NRPE configuration on the remote machine:

```
$ /opt/nagios/plugins/check_nrpe -H 192.168.2.1 -c dummycommand
NRPE: Command 'dummycommand' not defined
```

If you received a `CHECK_NRPE: Error - Could not complete SSL handshake` error or something similar, it means that NRPE is not configured to accept connections from your machine—either via the `allowed_hosts` option in the NRPE configuration, or in the `inetd` configuration.

In order to check this, log on to the remote machine and search the system logs for nrpe. For example, on most systems, this would be:

```
# grep nrpe /var/log/syslog /var/log/messages
(...)
ubuntu1 nrpe[3023]: Host 192.168.2.13 is not allowed to talk to us!
```

This indicates that your Nagios server is not added to the list of allowed hosts in the NRPE configuration. Add it in the allowed_hosts option and restart the NRPE process.

Another error message that could be returned by the check_nrpe command is CHECK_NRPE: Received 0 bytes from daemon. Check the remote server logs for error messages. This message usually means that you have passed arguments or invalid characters in the command name and the NRPE server refused the request because of these.

Looking at the remote server's logs will usually provide more detailed information:

```
# grep nrpe /var/log/syslog /var/log/messages
(...)
ubuntu1 nrpe[3023]: Error: Request contained command arguments!
ubuntu1 nrpe[3023]: Client request was invalid, bailing out...
```

In this situation, you need to make sure that you enable arguments or change the Nagios configuration not to use arguments over NRPE.

Another possibility is that the check returns CHECK_NRPE: Socket timeout after 10 seconds or a similar message. In this case, the check command has not been completed within the configured time. You may need to increase the command_timeout in the NRPE configuration.

Summary

Checking whether a service is available over a network can be done from a single machine. In such cases, using a single dedicated machine to do all of these checks would be a good idea as it also reduces the burden and load to be on just a single computer on your network. In reality, this is not enough for a robust computer and failure monitoring solution.

In many cases, performing checks on machines other than the Nagios server is a necessity. this is the case for the simplest tasks, such as making sure you have enough storage space on a database server. It is also needed for more complex checks such as monitoring the load of machines and being able to react to unbalanced loads across machines. Nagios offers ways to do these types of checks and to set them up in an easy manner. Depending on what the critical issues are for your network, the choice is usually to either use SSH or NRPE to perform the checks on other machines.

The first is easier to set up from a network and administrative perspective. All that is needed is to put a set of plugins on the machine, create a public key based authentication, and you are all set to go! The main advantage of this method is that it uses the existing network protocol, which is usually running and enabled on all Unix based machines. This way it is not necessary to configure firewalls to pass traffic related to Nagios checks.

Security and performance are the trade-offs. As SSH is a generic protocol, the Nagios server can run any command on any of the machines it has access to. Many institutions may consider using a generic service such as SSH. One way of limiting this problem is to set up a restricted shell for the user that performs the checks, which will make sure that only Nagios plugins are run.

Another problem with this approach is that SSH is a complex protocol, and the overheads related to connecting to a remote machine and running a plugin are high. The main problem occurs where one central Nagios server performs a large volume of tests over SSH. The problem will not be significant on remote computers, but the central server will require more processing power to handle all of the checks in a timely manner.

NRPE is an alternative to SSH. It is a daemon that is installed on remote computers that allow the running of checks. The main advantage of this approach is that it offers much better security. The administrator of the remote computer can configure NRPE to accept only connections from certain IP addresses and to only allow the execution of predefined commands. By default, it is not even possible to pass any arguments to them. So there is very little chance of a security issue on account of NRPE. Another advantage is that the NRPE protocol requires much less overheads, and more frequent checks do not affect the central Nagios server too much.

There are some flip sides to NRPE. The first one is that it needs to be set up on all of the machines that will be monitored in a remote manner. In addition, all configuration for the checks is kept on the remote machines. In such cases, it is much harder to maintain changes in the configuration when monitoring multiple computers.

There are many other options for monitoring machines and the services on them. They are not as popular, but can be also used to get the job done. There are various agent-based systems that offer running commands remotely. They can be used to create check commands that are executed on remote machines. Another approach is to use existing protocols such as HTTP for deploying checks on remote host. Common solutions, such as PHP, CGI, or various scripting languages, can be leveraged to perform these kinds of tests. This is mainly useful if you already have a stable web server that is also used for other purposes. All that is needed is to install the scripts and configure the server to accept connections, either from all addresses or just from specific ones.

Usually, it is quite obvious which solution should be used in which case. There may be cases where it's easier to use existing SSH daemons. In other cases, security or performance is more of an issue and NRPE is a better choice. In still other cases, a custom solution will work best. How you should proceed is a matter of knowing the best tool for a particular case.

In all cases, doing checks from remote computers is not as easy as doing it locally. But, it is also not very difficult if you use the right tools!

9
SNMP

The previous chapter talked about different approaches to verifying remote computers and the services they offer. This chapter covers another way of monitoring remote machines and devices.

Simple Network Management Protocol (SNMP) is a protocol that is designed to monitor and manage various devices connected to a network. Its main purpose is to create a standardized way of getting and setting parameters regardless of the underlying hardware. The protocol allows the retrieval of information from a device, setting options, and also covers the means for a device to notify other machines about a failure.

SNMP is an industry standard, and all major hardware and software vendors support it. All commonly-used operating systems can provide information using SNMP. Microsoft offers SNMP for their Windows platform; all UNIX systems have SNMP daemons that receive requests from the other machines.

SNMP also offers a standardized, hierarchical way to group and access information, called **MIB** (**Management Information Base**). This defines which attributes can be accessed, and what data types are associated with them. This allows the creation of attributes that all devices should use for providing information on standard parameters such as network configuration, usage, and potential threats. It also allows custom parameters to be created so that they will not interfere with other devices' data.

Most operating systems come with various utilities that allow communication with other devices over SNMP. These utilities can be used to verify which attributes are available on specific devices and what their values are at the moment.

Introduction to SNMP

SNMP is designed to be easy to implement and to provide a uniform way to access information on various machines.

It is designed so that the footprint of the SNMP services is minimal. This allows devices with a very limited size of storage and operating memory to still use the protocol. SNMP uses the **UDP** protocol (**User Datagram Protocol**; see `http://en.wikipedia.org/wiki/User_Datagram_Protocol`), which requires much less resources than TCP. It also uses one packet for sending a single request or response operation, so the protocol itself is stateless.

Each machine that is managed by SNMP has an application that responds to requests from this and other computers. Such an application is called an **agent**. For UNIX systems, it is usually a daemon working in the background. Many devices with embedded systems have SNMP support included in the system core. In all of these cases, a device needs to listen for SNMP requests and respond accordingly.

All agents are usually managed by one or more machines called the SNMP **manager**. This is a computer that queries agents for data; it might also set their attributes. Usually, this is an application running in the background that communicates over SNMP and stores the information in some data storage.

Usually, SNMP uses UDP port 161 to communicate with the agent and port 162 for sending information from the agent to the manager. In order to use SNMP, these ports need to be passed correctly by all network routers, and should not be filtered by the firewalls.

There are two types of communication that are done by SNMP; the first one is when a manager sends requests to an agent. These can be **get** requests, in which case the manager wants to retrieve information from an agent. If the information needs to be modified, a **set** request is sent out.

Another type of communication is where an agent wants to notify a manager about a problem. In such cases, an SNMP **trap** is sent out. An agent needs to know the IP address of the manager to send the information out to. A manager needs to be listening for SNMP traps, and should react on the issue.

The following is an illustration of possible SNMP communication types:

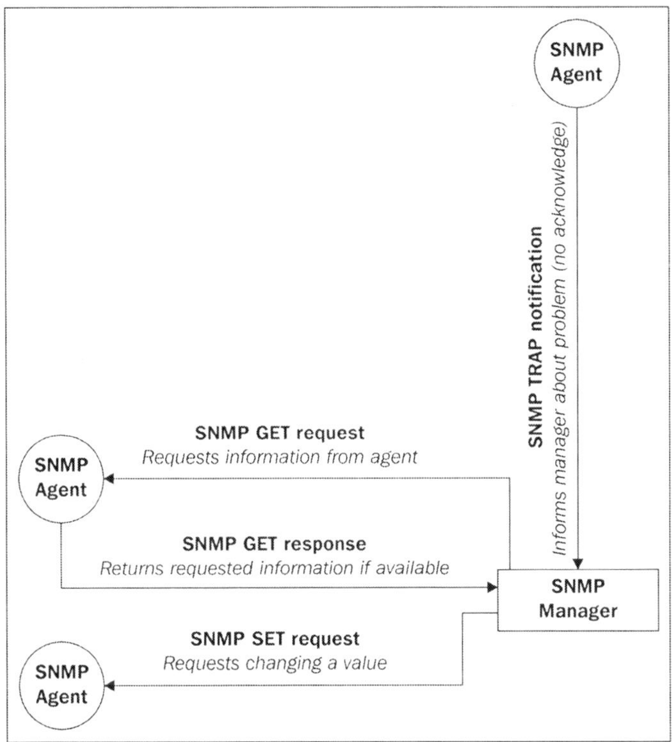

SNMP has several versions that an agent can communicate over. **SNMPv1** was the first version of the protocol. This featured get, set, and trap operations. The standard defined scalar data objects as well as tabular objects. It also featured the **getnext** operation, which allows iterating over the tables of data objects.

The security model related to SNMPv1 is relatively unsophisticated. A **get**, **set**, or **getnext** request is authenticated based on the IP address of the manager and the community string that it uses. All SNMP devices communicating over SNMPv1 use the community string for verifying that the request—whether none, only get, or both get and set operations-can be performed. By default, the `private` community string allows both reading and writing information and the `public` community string only allows reading them.

SNMP version 2 introduced improvements in terms of both performance and security. Instead of using get and getnext, it had a **getbulk** operation. This allows the retrieval of all entries in a table in a single operation. It also introduces an **inform** packet—this is a trap that requires acknowledgement from the manager. This avoids the problem where a single UDP packet gets lost, preventing a trap from being received by the manager. This version also introduced a party-based security model, which did not gain wide acceptance due to its complexity.

The most common version 2 implementation is **SNMPv2c – Community-Based Simple Network Management protocol 2**. It uses the features of version 2 without implementing the new security model, but using the community string mechanism that was introduced in SNMPv1.

User-Based Network Management Protocol version 2, or **SNMPv2u**, is another variant of SNMP version 2. This includes greater security than SNMPv2c, but does not include all of security features originally developed for SNMPv2.

SNMP version 3 introduces an improved security model, including authentication, privacy, and access control. This version introduced more security than was available in SNMPv2, and one of the security frameworks uses the functionality from SNMPv2u. This standard is now gaining more attention than SNMPv2, mostly because it offers better security without the high level of complexity that SNMPv2 introduced.

Most SNMP server implementations that come integrated with operating systems support SNMPv1, SNMPv2c, and SNMPv3. Some devices only support SNMPv1 while others also offer SNMPv2. Packets from different SNMP versions are incompatible, so a device using only SNMPv1 will not recognize a SNMPv2c packet.

In many cases, devices that are used across your network will offer a different subset of versions that they support. There are two ways to work in such an environment.

The first approach is to use a proxy agent. Some SNMP management software uses SNMPv3, and devices that do not support this version will need to have the packets translated. In such cases, all requests from the manager are received by the proxy agent; this translates and passes them to the actual agent, and sends the results back to the manager. The proxy agent receives traps from the actual agent. It then passes them to the manager as a trap or translates the packet using a newer SNMP version. A proxy agent is usually an application on a computer or a physical device.

Often, SNMP managers allow the configuration of which SNMP version should be used for specific devices.

Data Objects

SNMP uses **OIDs** (**Object Identifiers**; see `http://en.wikipedia.org/wiki/Object_identifier`) to identify the data objects that it refers to. OIDs define a unique object for a specified SNMP agent. They are identified using a hierarchical definition, similar to how domains work on the Internet.

Object identifiers are a series of numbers separated by periods. Each number represents a part of the tree. Often, the first number in the series is also preceded by a period to indicate that this is an OID—this is not necessary, though. An example of an OID is `.1.3.6.1.2.1.1.5.0`, which maps to the system name of a machine.

As it is very hard to memorize, read and compare OIDs written as a series of numbers, there is a standard for naming and describing the MIB tree.

The standard is called **MIB** (**Management Information Base**; see `http://en.wikipedia.org/wiki/Management_Information_Base`), and it defines how various parameters are defined—how they are named, as well as what types of values these objects might return. Each MIB definition is a text file written in a subset of ASN.1 notation (`http://en.wikipedia.org/wiki/ASN.1`). A file can describe a small or large subset of the MIB trees.

Currently, the standard is MIB SMIv2, and it defines all commonly-used attributes along with additional information that can be used by visualization applications.

MIB files describe fields that can be used in SNMP. They define parent nodes in the hierarchy, the numeric identifier, and the type of data that this field is associated with. SNMP uses the following basic data types:

- String—a string, written as bytes, that can have 0 to 65535 bytes
- Integer and Integer32—a signed 32 bit integer value
- Counters32, Counter64—non-negative integers that increase, and are reset to 0 after they reach maximum value
- Gauges—non-negative integers that can increase and decrease within a defined minimum-maximum range
- Time tick—defines a time span, where the value of 100 represents one second
- IP address—represents an address from a protocol family; SNMPv1 only supports IPv4

In many cases, a field is returned as an enumeration type integer. This means that some predefined numbers represent several predefined values. A good example is the `ifType` field when defining network interfaces—it specifies the type of network interface. Some examples are `23` for a **PPP** (**Point-to-Point Protocol**; see `http://en.wikipedia.org/wiki/Point-to-Point_Protocol`) connection or `6` for Ethernet interfaces.

An example OID is `.1.3.6.1.2.1.1.5.0`. The following is a table describing each element, both as string and as corresponding numbers:

Identifier	Description
1	**iso**—iso standard tree
3	**org**—Organizations; this node is a placeholder for all national and international organizations
6	**dod**—Department of Defense; this is the node for U.S. Department of Defense
1	**internet**—Subnode for the Internet; since originally Internet was a project for U.S. military defense, its placeholder is under **dod** subtree
2	**mgmt**—Systems management node
1	**mib-2**—Management Information Base, version 2 root node
1	**system**—Operating system information
5	**sysName**—Name of this machine; usually a fully qualified domain name
0	Index of the elements; in this case it is always 0

The string representation of this OID is `iso.org.dod.internet.mgmt.mib-2.system.sysName.0`. Often, it is also referred to as `SNMPv2-MIB::sysName.0`.

The `.1.3.6.1.2.1` part of the OID defines the root elements for all MIB-2 standardized parameters. All of the standard SNMP parameters that various devices use are under this OID node or its descendants. This node is also called the `SNMPv2-MIB` namespace; hence, the `SNMPv2-MIB::sysName.0` OID also maps to the same object.

The MIB tree has a few major nodes that are the base for many other subtrees that might be significant to you under various circumstances, which are as follows:

- `.1.3.6.1.2.1` stands for `iso.org.dod.internet.mgmt.mib-2`. This is the base for all of the attributes that are available on the majority of SNMP-aware devices.
- `.1.3.6.1.4.1` stands for `iso.org.dod.internet.private.enterprise`. This is a root node for all corporations and companies that use private objects; this is used by companies such as Microsoft, Motorola and many other hardware and software vendors.
- `.2.16.840.1.113883` stands for `joint-iso-itu-t.country.us.organization.hl7`. This is a root node for Health Level 7, and is used mainly in health care and public health informatics.

The most important node is `.1.3.6.1.2.1`, which is used by all SNMP-aware devices to report information. This part of the MIB tree is the root node for the majority of standard objects. It is also mandatory for all SNMP-enabled devices to provide at least the basic part of information in this subtree. For example, information such as contact information, location, system name, and the type should be provided by all SNMP-aware devices.

SNMP can be used to retrieve different kinds of information. This information is usually grouped into various categories. All categories also have corresponding aliases they are usually referenced with, to avoid putting the entire structure in every OID definition or MIB name. All applications that offer communication over SNMP allow the specification of attributes using both OID and MIB names. Let's go over a few of the most important sections of the MIB tree.

Information in `IF-MIB`, `IP-MIB`, `IPv6-MIB`, `RFC1213-MIB`, `IP-FORWARD-MIB`, `TCP-MIB`, and `UDP-MIB` describe network connectivity—interfaces, IP configuration, routing, forwarding, and the TCP and UDP protocols. They allow the querying of the current configuration as well as currently active and listening sockets.

Data contained in `SNMPv2-MIB` and `HOST-RESOURCES-MIB` describes system information and current parameters. This can include information on disk storage, current processes, installed applications, and the hardware that the computer is running on.

Working with SNMP and MIB

Different operating systems can come with different SNMP applications. Many hardware vendors also offer additional software that manages multiple machines using SNMP—for example, HP OpenView or Sun Management Center. For this section and the following ones, the Net-SNMP package (see `http://net-snmp.sourceforge.net/`) will be used. This package is included in all Linux distributions and works with almost all UNIX operating systems.

In order to install this package on Ubuntu Linux, we need to run the following command:

```
apt-get install snmp
```

For `yum`-based Linux distributions, the package is called `net-snmp` and the command to install it is as follows:

```
yum install net-snmp
```

The Net-SNMP project homepage also offers binaries for several platforms, including HP-UX and Fedora Linux. Fedora packages should also work on Red Hat Enterprise Linux systems.

It is also possible to build everything from the source for various UNIX operating systems such as AIX, HP-UX, and Solaris. Exact instructions are provided on the project page.

After a successful installation, we should be able to run any SNMP-related command, such as `snmpget`, and check the Net-SNMP version by doing the following:

```
root@ubuntu:~# snmpget -V
NET-SNMP version: 5.3.1
```

Assuming we do have a host with the SNMP agent set up, and it is accepting the SNMP protocol version 1, we can now try to communicate with it and query a few parameters:

```
root@ubuntu:~# snmpget -v 1 -c public 192.168.2.2 \
    iso.org.dod.internet.mgmt.mib-2.system.sysName.0
SNMPv2-MIB::sysName.0 = STRING: WAG354G
```

As you can see, the device returned that the system name is WAG354G. This is actually a Linksys/Cisco router and the only way to access its information is over the web interface or SNMP.

The Net-SNMP package comes with a couple of very useful commands that can be used to check current values, as well as perform a dump of a part or the whole MIB tree. These vary from simple tools for querying a single attribute to very complex ones that print out a `df`-like report of partitions on a remote system. There are also commands for displaying tables and for setting parameters remotely.

Throughout this section and the next ones, we'll mainly use SNMP version 1, as this is supported by almost all SNMP-enabled devices. When using SNMP in production, it's better to check which devices accept the SNMP versions, and use the most recent one a device handles correctly.

The first command that's worth getting familiar with is `snmpget`. This allows the querying of single or multiple attributes over SNMP.

The syntax of the command is as follows:

```
snmpget [options] IP-address OID [OID] ...
```

All of the Net-SNMP commands accept a huge number of parameters. The following parameters are the ones we will be using throughout this chapter, and they are worth knowing:

Option	Description
-h	Provides help
-V	Prints the Net-SNMP version
-c	Specifies the community name to use
-v	Specifies the SNMP version to be used; should be one of `1`, `2c` or `3`
-r	Specifies the number of retries
-t	Timeout in seconds
-O	Output options; should be one or more of the following: `n` - print OIDs as numerical values without expanding them from MIB `e` - print enum and OID fields as numbers instead of string values `v` - print values only instead of `name = value` format `f` - print full OID names; disallows shortcuts such as `SNMPv2-MIB`

The `-O` option allows the retrieval of values without having to apply MIB shortcuts; hence, being able to see the entire branch. It also allows output to be changed so that only values along with data types are printed out, instead of the object names themselves.

An example of this command is as follows:

```
# snmpget -O ef -v 1 -c public rtr SNMPv2-MIB::sysObjectID.0
.iso.org.dod.internet.mgmt.mib-2.system.sysObjectID.0 =
OID: .iso.org.dod.internet.private.enterprises.ucdavis.
ucdSnmpAgent.linux
```

All of the options above can also be used with other Net-SNMP commands.

Net-SNMP also offers a command to iterate through the entire MIB tree, or only a part of it. The `snmpwalk` command accepts the same options as shown earlier. Most versions of Net-SNMP's `snmpwalk` command do not require the passing of any OID to work. For older versions, in order to list the entire tree ,`.1` can be specified as the OID.

The following command will list the entire MIB tree of an SNMPv1 agent:

```
root@ubuntu:~# snmpwalk -v 1 -c public 192.168.2.2
```

Depending on the underlying operating system and the SNMP agent itself, the actual data may be different. Please note that if the device is not on a local network, then this operation might take a very long time to complete.

In order to retrieve only a part of the MIB tree, simply pass the prefix of the tree you are interested in. For example:

```
root@ubuntu:~# snmpwalk -v 1 -c public 192.168.2.2 1.3.6.1.2.1.1
```

The command above will limit the query to `iso.org.dod.internet.mgmt.mib-2.system` node and its children. It will also complete much faster than querying the entire tree.

Walking over a part of a tree is mainly useful when trying to check the objects that are available on a remote device that does not respond quickly to SNMP requests—either because of network lag or because of the computations required for some objects. It is also commonly used to find out which values are available in a specified part of the MIB tree.

Another useful utility is the `snmptable` command. It allows the listing of various SNMP tables, and shows them in a human readable form. The syntax is as follows:

```
snmptable [options] IP-address OIDprefix
```

For example, to list all TCP/IP connections, the following command can be used:

```
root@:~# snmptable -v 1 -c public 192.168.2.2 tcpConnTable
SNMP table: TCP-MIB::tcpConnTable

connState connLocalAddress connLocalPort connRemAddress connRemPort
   listen          0.0.0.0            23        0.0.0.0           0
   listen          0.0.0.0            80        0.0.0.0           0
   listen          0.0.0.0           199        0.0.0.0           0
```

Net-SNMP also allows the setting of new object values that can be used to reconfigure various devices. The `snmpset` command can be used to perform this. The syntax is as follows:

```
snmpset [options] IP-address OID type value [OID type value] ...
```

This command accepts all of the same standard options as the `snmpget` command. A single command invocation can be used to set more than one parameter, by specifying more than one set of OIDs to be set. Each set operation needs to specify the new value along with the data type it should be set to.

The value type can be one of the following:

Type	Description
i	Integer
u	Unsigned integer

Type	Description
s	String
x	Hex string - each letter is specified as 2 hex digits
d	Decimal string - each letter is specified as a 1-2 digit
n	NULL object
o	OID - for objects that accept object
t	Timeticks
a	IP address
B	Series of bits

The most common types are String, Integer, and OID. The first two require the passing of either a number or a text that the object's value should be set to. Setting an OID type of object requires either providing a full OID identifier or any string that can be matched by the MIB definitions.

An example to set a system's contact name and host name is as follows:

```
root@ubuntu:~# snmpset -v 2c -c private 192.168.2.2 \
    SNMPv2-MIB::sysContact.0 s admin@net.home \
    SNMPv2-MIB::sysName.0 s RTR
SNMPv2-MIB::sysContact.0 = STRING: admin@net.home
SNMPv2-MIB::sysName.0 = STRING: RTR
```

Some attributes cannot be set via SNMP. For example, it is not possible to modify objects that are used for the monitoring system. These unsettable attributes usually include the IP address configuration, counters, or diagnostic information, for example, TCP/UDP connection tables, process lists, installed applications, and performance counters. Many devices tend to support command line administration over SNMP, and in this case, the parameters might be read-only.

MIB definitions specify which attributes are explicitly read-only. Using a graphical tool to find out which attributes can be modified will ease automatic device configuration over the SNMP protocol.

Graphical Tools

Using SNMP and the MIB tree is not a simple task. Many people, not very familiar with command line tools and the large amounts of information returned, might feel a bit overwhelmed by it. This is where graphical tools come in handy. And there are lots of freely-available tools that can visualize SNMP. We will discuss only a few of them.

The first tool is called `mbrowse` (see `http://www.kill-9.org/mbrowse/`). It is a graphical tool for browsing the MIB tree, querying attributes, and running a complete or partial walk through the MIB tree. This tool uses the SNMPv1 and the SNMPv2c protocols. It uses the Net-SNMP libraries and shares the same MIB definitions.

The following is a screenshot of the tool with a result from a walk and an expanded TCP tree:

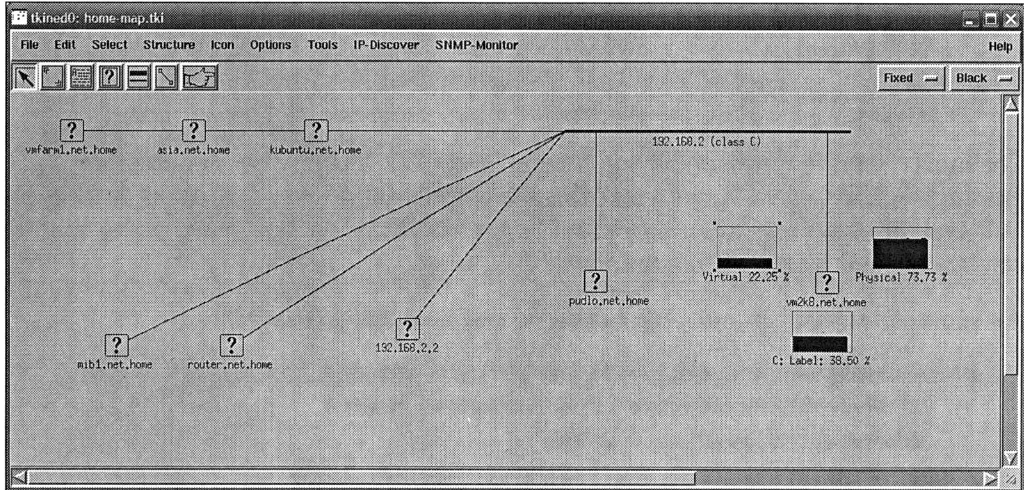

Another interesting tool is **TkIned (Tcl/tK based Interactive Network EDitor)** from the Scotty package (`https://trac.eecs.iu-bremen.de/projects/scotty/`). This is a graphical tool that uses Tk for the graphical interface and Scotty for the SNMP protocol. It allows browsing of the MIB tree, the monitoring of hosts over SNMP, and the visualization of your network by clicking on the layout.

This tool also has another very interesting feature. Based on one or more IP network addresses, it can automatically detect your networks and try to find hosts that respond to SNMP requests. It uses the default `public`/`private` community pair, and communicates over the SNMPv1 and SNMPv2c protocols. This allows the detection of various operating systems and devices that are configured to respond to these communities, which are still the default ones in many cases.

The tool can be configured to monitor various parameters such as disk usage or system load over SNMP. The results are graphed and updated in real time. This can serve as a backup system to verify up-to-date values for various attributes. Once the SNMP or ICMP checks are set up, they will be done periodically until they are removed from the map.

The following is a screenshot of the tool after an **IP-discover** option has been run, where the tool has been configured to monitor the disk and memory usage of a Windows machine.

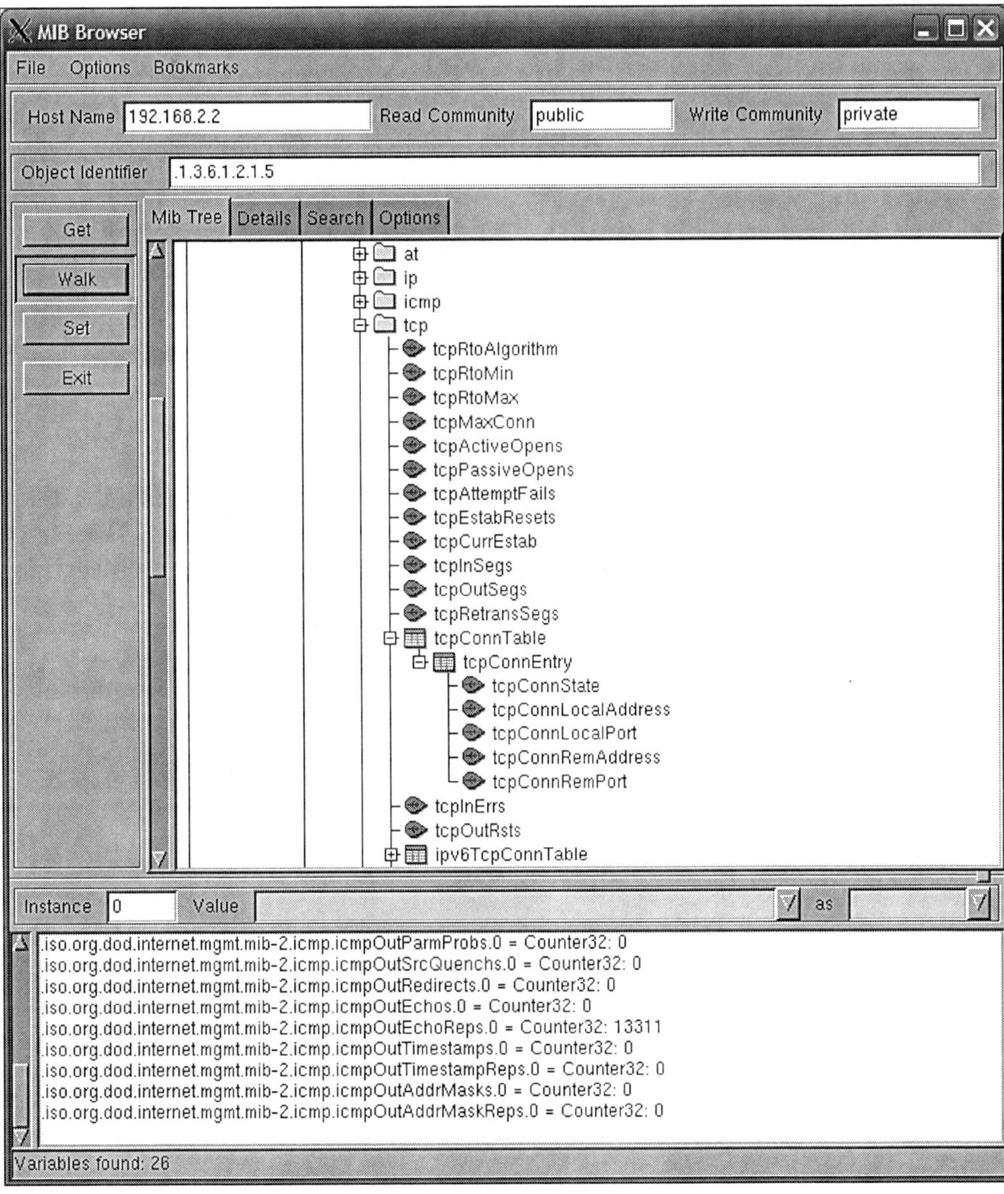

The layout of the machines on the chart can be freely edited. There is also a wide set of icons that can be associated with particular hosts.

Setting up an SNMP Agent

The previous section talked about how to communicate with SNMP agents. If you have a network device such as a router or WiFi, WiMax, or DSL gateway, most probably it will also come with a built-in SNMP agent.

The next step is to set up the SNMP agent on one or more computers so that we can use SNMP to monitor servers or workstations. In this way, a majority of the networked equipment will allow monitoring from a single machine using the SNMP protocol.

Let's start with various UNIX boxes. The SNMP agent is a part of Net-SNMP, and several distributions come with the command line tools, libraries, and the SNMP agent, usually as optional packages.

In our case, we will install the SNMP agent on Ubuntu Linux. We will run the following command:

```
apt-get install snmpd
```

This will cause the SNMP daemon which is a part of Net-SNMP, to be installed. By default, Ubuntu Linux SNMP agent only accepts connections on 127.0.0.1. This is for security reasons—in many cases, an SNMP agent is used mainly by tools such as MRTG to gather usage statistics.

To change it, we will need to either specify the IP address that SNMP agent should listen on in the `/etc/default/snmpd` file, `SNMPDOPTS` variable, or remove it completely.

If the SNMP agent should listen on all available IP addresses, then the line should look similar to the following example:

```
SNMPDOPTS='-Lsd -Lf /dev/null -u snmp -I -smux -p /var/run/snmpd.pid'
```

Changing this option requires restarting the SNMP agent by invoking the `/etc/init.d/snmpd restart` command.

After a successful installation, the SNMP agent should be up and running, and making a walk over the entire tree should produce some output.

To test the SNMP agent, simply launch the following command on the same machine, assuming through the Net-SNMP command line tools are installed:

```
snmpwalk -v 1 -c public 127.0.0.1
```

The agent that we have just installed supports the SNMPv1, SNMPv2c, and SNMPv3 protocol versions. It also features an extensive security model that you can configure to provide a more secure setup.

Net-SNMP agent allows you to define one or more OIDs along with all subnodes that can be retrieved, by specific security groups. These groups can be mapped to specific communities that originate from all or specific IP addresses. Security groups are also mapped using SNMP versions used by the remote machine.

A sample configuration that allows only read-only access from all of the hosts is as follows:

```
com2sec readonly default public
group readonlyGroup v1  readonly
group readonlyGroup v2c readonly
group readonlyGroup usm readonly
view all    included  .1                              80
access readonlyGroup "" any noauth    exact  all    none   none
syslocation Home
syscontact Administrator <admin@yourcompany.com>
```

The first line defines a mapping between the community and a security group `readonly`. The next lines assign `readonlyGroup` access rights to this group. Then it is granted access to read all objects from the `.1` OID node and its children. The last two lines specify the system administrator and the location where the machines are stored.

For SNMPv3 model, it is also possible to specify one or more users by calling the `snmpusm` command (`http://linux.die.net/man/1/snmpusm`). It allows real-time configuration of the user list for local or remote SNMPv3 agents.

SNMP can also be set up on all modern Microsoft Windows operating systems. Similar to UNIX systems, it is necessary to install an SNMP agent. In order to do this on Windows XP and Windows 2003 Server, we first need to go to the **Control Panel** first. Next, we need to select the **Add or Remove Programs** applet and select the **Add/Remove Windows Components** option. The following window will be displayed:

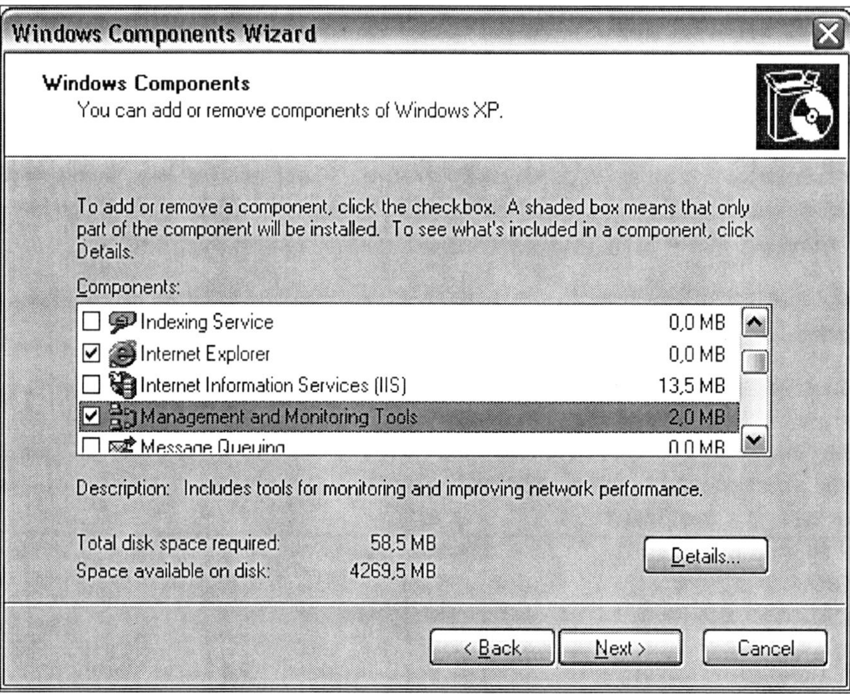
Windows Components Wizard
Windows Components
You can add or remove components of Windows XP.
To add or remove a component, click the checkbox. A shaded box means that only part of the component will be installed. To see what's included in a component, click Details.
Components:
Indexing Service 0,0 MB
Internet Explorer 0,0 MB
Internet Information Services (IIS) 13,5 MB
Management and Monitoring Tools 2,0 MB
Description: Includes tools for monitoring and improving network performance.
Total disk space required: 58,5 MB
Space available on disk: 4269,5 MB
Details...
< Back
Next >
Cancel

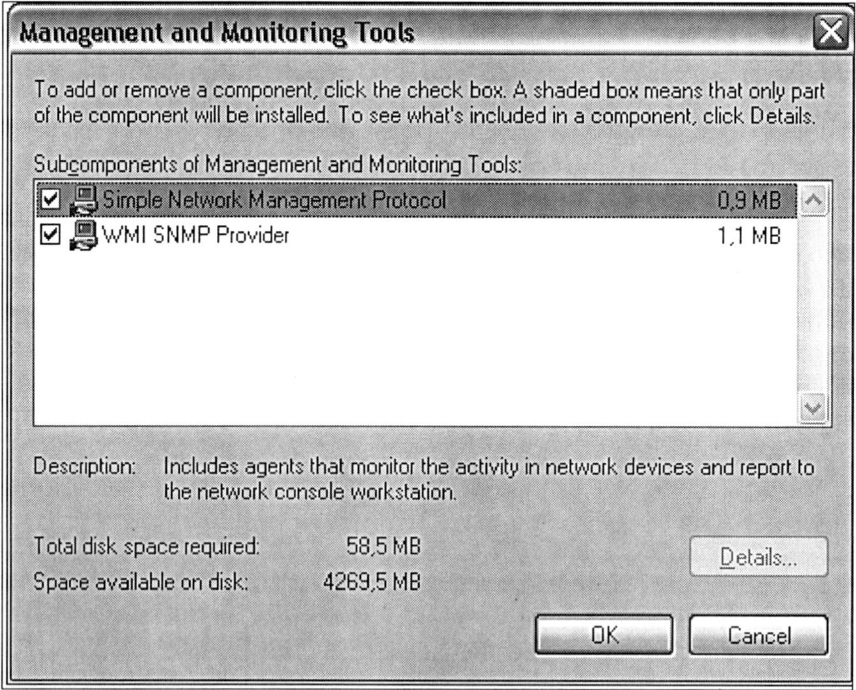
Management and Monitoring Tools
To add or remove a component, click the check box. A shaded box means that only part of the component will be installed. To see what's included in a component, click Details.
Subcomponents of Management and Monitoring Tools:
Simple Network Management Protocol 0,9 MB
WMI SNMP Provider 1,1 MB
Description: Includes agents that monitor the activity in network devices and report to the network console workstation.
Total disk space required: 58,5 MB
Space available on disk: 4269,5 MB
Details...
OK
Cancel

Next, we need to select **Management and Monitoring Tools**, as shown in the screenshot above. We can also select the **Details** button and choose **Simple Network Management Protocol**. The **WMI SNMP Provider** allows the retrieval of the SNMP parameters over WMI and can be left unchecked if you do not need it.

Windows SNMP agent exports information about the system in a similar way to other platforms. You can use it to query the underlying hardware, the operating system version, and the network configuration along with the currently-active connections. It is also possible to list active processes and monitor the systems load. The Windows SNMP agent also exports details of all of the installed applications along with security patches from Microsoft. This mechanism can be used to monitor whether all critical system patches are installed or monitor compliance with software licenses.

After a successful installation, we can go to the **Administrative Tools** folder and run the **Services** applet. When selecting **SNMP Service** and choosing **Properties**, the following service properties window, along with the SNMP configuration, is displayed:

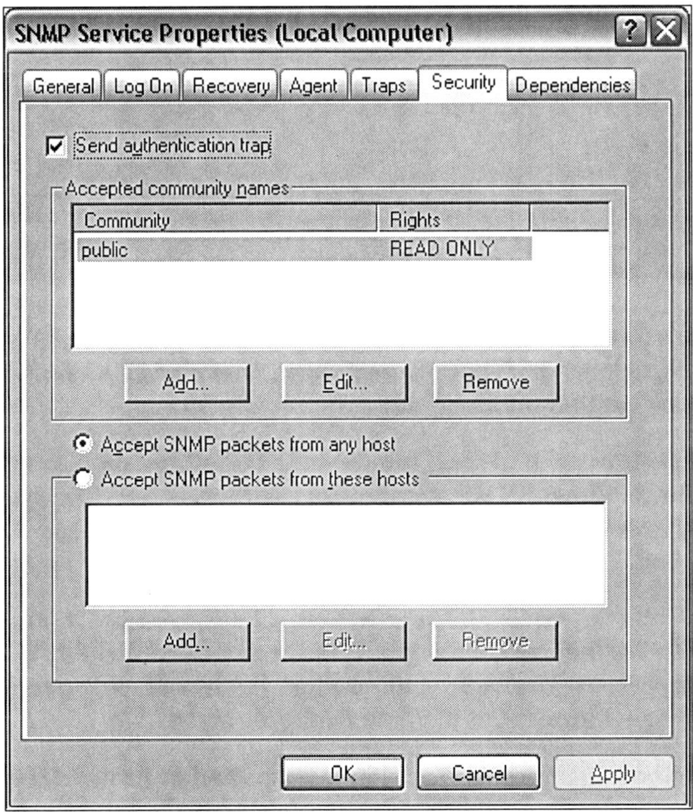

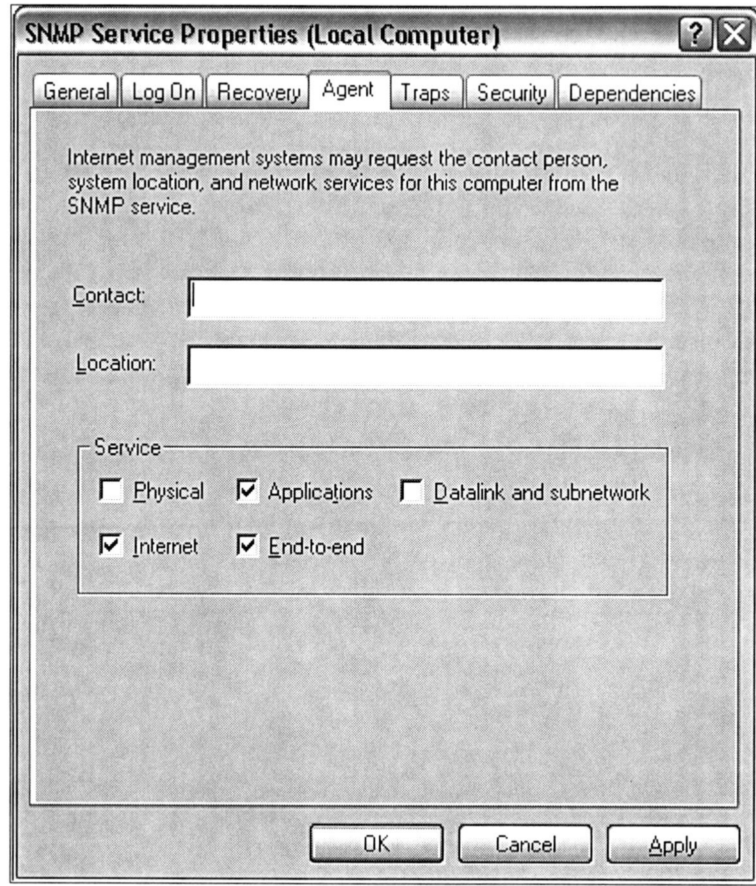

The window has three additional tabs—Agent, Traps, and Security. The **Agent** tab allows you to configure which parts are exported over SNMP, and offers the setting up of contact and location information.

The **Security** tab allows you to configure how SNMP information from this host can be accessed. The Windows SNMP agent offers support for SNMPv1 and SNMPv2c, so the security model is based on a community string and IP addresses for authentication.

The agent can either accept SNMP queries from all hosts or only from the specific hosts listed in the bottom part of the tab. There is also the possibility of specifying one or more readable and writable communities. By default, only queries on `public` community string are accepted and allow read-only access.

The **Traps** tab allows configuration of Windows to send or forward traps to specific IP addresses, and indicate which SNMP community is to be used for communication.

Using SNMP from Nagios

Now that we are able to query information from Windows and UNIX boxes, it would be good to know how to integrate SNMP checks with Nagios. The Nagios plugins package comes with a plugin called `check_snmp` for checking SNMP parameters and validating their value. The plugin uses the `snmpget` and `snmpgetnext` commands from Net-SNMP, and it does not work without these commands.

The following is the syntax of the command:

```
check_snmp -H <ip_address> -o <OID> [-w warn_range] [-c crit_range]
          [-C community] [-s string] [-r regex] [-R regexi]
          [-l label] [-u units] [-d delimiter]  [-D output-delimiter]
          [-t timeout] [-e retries] [-p port-number]
          [-m miblist] [-P snmp version] [-L seclevel] [-U secname]
          [-a authproto] [-A authpasswd] [-X privpasswd]
```

The following table describes the commonly-used options accepted by the plugin. Options that are required are marked in bold:

Option	Description
-H, --hostname	Host name or IP address of the machine to connect to; this option must be specified
-o, --oid	OID to get from the remote machine; can be specified either as dot-separated numbers or as a name; multiple elements can be specified and need to be separated with commas or spaces
-w	Specified the `min:max` range of values outside of which a warning state should be returned; for integer results only
-c	Specified the `min:max` range of values outside of which a critical state should be returned; for integer results only
-P, --protocol	Specifies the SNMP protocol version; accepted values are `1`, `2c` or `3`
-C, --community	Specifies the community string to be used; for SNMPv1 and SNMPv2c this defaults to `public`
-s, --string	Returns a critical state unless the result is an exact match of value specified in this parameter
-r, --regex	Returns a critical state if the result does not match the specified regular expression; is case sensitive
-R, --eregi	Returns a critical state if the result does not match the specified regular expression; is case insensitive
-t, --timeout	Specifies the period in seconds after which it is assumed that no response has been received and the operation times out

Option	Description
-e, --retries	Specifies the number of retries that should be performed if no answer is received
-n, --next	Uses the `getnext` request instead of `get` to retrieve the next attribute after the specified one
-d, --delimiter	Specifies the delimiter which should be used to match values in the output from the Net-SNMP commands; defaults to an equal sign: =
-D, --output-delimiter	Specifies the character used to separate output if multiple OIDs are provided

Depending on which exact flags are passed, the plugin behavior is different. In all cases, the plugin will return `critical` if the SNMP agent could not be contacted, or if the specified OID does not exist. If none of the flags `-s`, `-r`/`-R`, `-w`, and `-c` are specified, the plugin will return `OK` as long as the OID is not retrieved. Specifying `-s` will cause the check to fail if the value returned by the SNMP get request is different from the value supplied to this option. It is worth noting that this option uses an exact match, not a substring.

An example would be to make sure that the exact location is specified in an SNMP agent. This can be checked by the following command:

```
root@ubuntu:~# /opt/nagios/plugins/check_snmp -H 10.0.0.1 -P 2c \
    -o SNMPv2-MIB::sysLocation.0 -s "Miami Branch"
SNMP OK - VMware | SNMPv2-MIB::sysLocation.0=Miami Branch
```

Matching a part of text can be done with the `-r` or `-R` option. The first one is a case-sensitive match. The latter option ignores the case while matching the resulting value. Similarly, when making sure that the contact information field contains email information, the following command can be used:

```
root@ubuntu:~# /opt/nagios/plugins/check_snmp -H 10.0.0.1 -P 2c \
    -o SNMPv2-MIB::sysContact.0 -r "@"
SNMP OK - root@company.com | SNMPv2-MIB::sysContact.0=root@company.com
```

It is also possible to match the specific value ranger for integer results. Checks work in such a way that the acceptable ranges for specific values are specified. If the result is outside of a specified range, a `warning` or `critical` state is returned. It is possible to specify separate ranges for critical and warning checks.

Typical usage can be to monitor system load or the number of processes running on a specific host.

The following is an example of how to check if the number of system processes is less than 20:

```
root@ubuntu:~# /opt/nagios/plugins/check_snmp -H 10.0.0.1 -P 2c \
    -o HOST-RESOURCES-MIB::hrSystemProcesses.0 -w 0:20 -c 0:30
SNMP CRITICAL - *33* | HOST-RESOURCES-MIB::hrSystemProcesses.0=33
```

The check will return `CRITICAL` status if the number of processes is `30` or more. A `WARNING` status will be returned if the number of processes is `20` or more. If the number is less than `20`, an `OK` status will be returned.

In all cases, it is advised that you first use the `snmpwalk` command and check which objects can be retrieved from a specific agent.

Nagios also comes with SNMP plugins written in Perl that allow the checking of network interfaces and their statuses. These plugins require the installation of the Perl Net::SNMP package. For Ubuntu Linux, the package name is `libnet-snmp-perl`.

The syntax of the plugins is as follows:

```
check_ifstatus -H hostname [-v version] [-C community]
check_ifoperstatus -H hostname [-v version] [-C community]
                   [-k index] [-d name]
```

The following table describes the options accepted by the plugins. Required options are marked in bold:

Option	Description
-H, --hostname	The host name or the IP address of the machine to connect to; this option must be specified
-v, --snmp_version	Specifies the SNMP protocol version to be used; acceptable values are `1` and `2c`
-C, --community	Specifies the SNMP community string to be used
-k, --key	Specifies the index of the network interface to be checked (`ifIndex` field)
-d, --descr	Specifies the regular expression to match the interface description (`ifDescr` field) against

The `check_ifstatus` plugin simply checks if the status of all of the interfaces is up, or if they are administratively down. If at least one interface is set up correctly, even if all other interfaces are down, a critical status is reported.

The `check_ifoperstatus` plugin allows you to check the status of a specific network interface. It is possible to specify either the index of the interface or an expression to match the device name against. An example to check the `eth1` interface is as follows:

```
root@ubuntu:~# /opt/nagios/plugins/check_ifoperstatus -H 10.0.0.1 \
     -d eth1
OK: Interface eth1 (index 3) is up.
```

As we also checked the index that `eth1` is associated with, we can now use the `-k` option to check the interface status:

```
root@ubuntu:~# /opt/nagios/plugins/check_ifoperstatus -H 10.0.0.1 -k 3
OK: Interface eth1 (index 3) is up.
```

The main difference is that by using the `-d` flag, you make sure that changes to the indexes of the network interfaces shifting your configuration are not affected. On the ther hand, using the `-k` flag is faster. If you are sure that your interfaces will not change, it's better to use `-k`; otherwise `-d` should be used.

The next step is to configure the Nagios commands and services for the SNMP usage. We will define a command and a corresponding service. We will also show how custom variables can be used to standardize command definitions.

The following is a generic command used to query SNMP:

```
define command
{
  command_name check_snmp
  command_line $USER1$/check_snmp -P 1 -H $HOSTADDRESS$
               -o $ARG1$ $ARG2$
}
```

Using the Nagios 3 functionality, we can also define the `_SNMPVERSION` and `_SNMPCOMMUNITY` parameters in the host object for all of the devices that are SNMP-aware, and use them in the command:

```
define host
{
  use                             generic-host
  host_name                       linuxbox01
  address                         10.0.2.1
  _SNMPVERSION                    2c
  _SNMPCOMMUNITY                  public
}
```

```
define command
{
  command_name check_snmp
  command_line $USER1$/check_snmp -H $HOSTADDRESS$ -o $ARG1$
               -P $_HOSTSNMPVERSION$ -C $_HOSTSNMPCOMMUNITY$ $ARG2$
}
```

Next, we should define one or more services that will communicate over SNMP.

Let's check for a number of processes and add some constraints that we want to be monitored:

```
define service
{
  use                   generic-service
  hostgroup_name        snmp-aware
  service_description   Processes
  check_command         check_snmp!HOST-RESOURCES-
                        MIB::hrSystemProcesses.0!-w 0:250 -c 0:500
}
```

Please note that the `check_command` statement above needs to be specified on a single line. The above check will monitor the number of processes running on a system.

It's worth mentioning that for Microsoft Windows systems the number of processes that should trigger a warning and critical state should be much lower than shown in the above example.

Receiving Traps

SNMP traps work in opposite ways to get and set requests. That is, the agent sends a message, as a UDP packet, to the SNMP manager when a problem occurs. For example, a link down or system crash message can be sent out to the manager so that administrators are alerted instantly. Traps differ across versions of the SNMP protocols. For SNMPv1, they are called *traps*, and are messages that do not require any confirmation by the manager. For SNMPv2, they are called *informs* and require the manager to acknowledge that it has received the *inform* message.

In order to receive traps or informs, the SNMP software needs to accept incoming connections on UDP port 162, which is the standard port for sending and receiving SNMP trap/inform packets. In some SNMP management software, trap notifications are handled within separate applications, while in others, they are integrated into an entire SNMP manager back-end.

For a Net-SNMP trap, the daemon is a part of the SNMP daemons, but is a separate binary, called `snmptrapd`, which, by default, is not started. To change this, we will need to modify the `/etc/default/snmpd` file and change the `TRAPDRUN` variable to *yes*, as shown here:

```
TRAPDRUN=yes
```

Changing this option requires restarting the SNMP agent by invoking the `/etc/init.d/snmpd restart` command.

On Ubuntu Linux, the trap listening daemon keeps its configuration file in `/etc/snmp/snmptrapd.conf`. For other systems, it may be in a different location.

The daemon can log specified SNMP traps/informs. It can be configured to run predefined applications or to forward all or specific packets to other managers.

A sample configuration that logs all incoming traps but only if they originate from the SNMPv1 and SNMPv2c `private` community would look like this:

```
authCommunity log,execute,net private
```

This option enables the logging of traps from the private community originating from any address. It also allows the execution of handler scripts and forwarding of them. But this requires additional configuration directives.

Each change in the `snmptrapd.conf` file requires a restart of the `snmpd` service.

Usually, traps will be received from a device such as a network router or another computer from which we want to receive traps. We will need two machines with Net-SNMP installed—one for sending the trap and another that will process it. The one processing it should be the one where Nagios is installed, so we can pass it on later. For the purposes of this section, we will use another computer and define a test MIB definition.

We need to create an MIB file called `NAGIOS-TRAP-TEST-MIB.txt` that will define the types of traps and their OIDs. On Ubuntu, the file should be put in `/usr/share/snmp/mibs`; for other platforms, it should be in the same location as the `SNMPv2-SMI.txt` file.

The contents of the file should be as follows:

```
NAGIOS-TRAP-TEST-MIB DEFINITIONS ::= BEGIN
       IMPORTS enterprises FROM SNMPv2-SMI;

 nagiostests OBJECT IDENTIFIER ::= { enterprises 0 }
 nagiostraps OBJECT IDENTIFIER ::= { nagiostests 1 }
 nagiosnotifs OBJECT IDENTIFIER ::= { nagiostests 2 }
```

```
nagiosTrap TRAP-TYPE
      ENTERPRISE nagiostraps
      VARIABLES { sysLocation }
      DESCRIPTION "SNMPv1 notification"
      ::= 1

nagiosNotif NOTIFICATION-TYPE
      OBJECTS { sysLocation }
      STATUS current
      DESCRIPTION "SNMPv2c notification"
      ::= { nagiosnotifs 2 }
END
```

This contains definitions for both the SNMPv1 trap called `nagiosTrap` and the inform packet for SNMPv2c called `nagiosNotif`. The file should be copied to all of machines that will either send or receive these trap/inform packets. In this example, we are using a subtree of the enterprises branch in SNMPv2-MIB, but this should not be used in any production environment as this is a reserved part of the MIB tree.

In order to send such a trap as an SNMPv1 packet, we need to invoke the following command on the machine that will send the traps, replacing the IP address with the actual address of the machine that is running the `snmptrapd` process.

```
root@ubuntu2:~# snmptrap -v 1 -c private 192.168.2.51 \
    NAGIOS-TRAP-TEST-MIB::nagiostraps "" 6 nagiosTrap "" \
    SNMPv2-MIB::sysLocation.0 s "Server Room"
```

Sending an SNMPv2c notification will look like this:

```
root@ubuntu2:~# snmptrap -v 2c -c private 192.168.2.51 "" \
    NAGIOS-TRAP-TEST-MIB::nagiosNotif \
    SNMPv2-MIB::sysLocation.0 s "Server Room"
```

Please note that, in both the cases, there is no confirmation that the packet was received. In order to determine this, we need to check the system logs—usually the `/var/log/syslog` or `/var/log/messages` files. The following command should return log entries related to traps:

```
root@ubuntu:~# grep TRAP /var/log/syslog /var/log/messages
```

Now that we know how to send traps, we should take care to handle them properly. The first thing that needs to be done is to add scripts as event handlers for the traps that we previously defined. We need to add these handlers on the machine that has the Nagios daemon running.

To do this, add the following lines to `snmptrapd.conf`, and restart the `snmpd` service:

```
traphandle NAGIOS-TRAP-TEST-MIB::nagiostraps /opt/nagios/bin/
passMessage
traphandle NAGIOS-TRAP-TEST-MIB::nagiosnotifs /opt/nagios/bin/
passMessage
```

We now need to create the actual `/opt/nagios/bin/passMessage` script that will forward information about the traps to Nagios:

```
#!/bin/sh

CMD=/var/nagios/rw/nagios.cmd

read ORIGHOSTNAME
read ORIGIP
# parse IP address
IPADDR='echo "$ORIGIP" | sed 's,^...: \[,,;s,\]:.*$,,''
HOST=""

# map IP address to host and service definition
case $IPADDR in
  192.168.2.52)
    HOST=ubuntu2
    SVC=TrapTest
    ;;
  esac

if [ "x$HOST" = "x" ] ; then
  exit 1
fi

# send check result to Nagios
CLK='date +%s'
echo "[$CLK] PROCESS_SERVICE_CHECK_RESULT;$HOST;$SVC;2;Trap received"

exit 0
```

When used for a volatile service, this offers a convenient way to track SNMP traps and notifications in Nagios. Such a service will remain in a state until a problem is acknowledged via the web interface.

Using Nagios to track SNMP traps also allows you to merge it with powerful event handling mechanisms inside Nagios. This can cause Nagios to perform other checks, or try to recover from the error, when a trap is received.

Additional Plugins

NagiosExchange hosts a large number of third-party plugins under the **Check Plugins, Software, SNMP** category (visit `http://www.nagiosexchange.org/cgi-bin/page.cgi?g=Check_Plugins/Software/SNMP/index.htm`). These allow the monitoring of the system load over SNMP, the monitoring of processes, and storage space, and the performance of many other types of checks. You can also find checks that are dedicated to specific hardware, such as Cisco or Nortel routers. There are also plugins for monitoring bandwidth usage.

There are also dedicated SNMP-based check plugins that allow the monitoring of many aspects of Microsoft Windows, without installing dedicated Nagios agents on these machines. This include checks for IIS web server, checking whether WINS and DHCP processes are running, and so on.

The Manubulon site (`http://nagios.manubulon.com/`) also offers a very wide variety of SNMP plugins. These offer checks for specific processes that are running, monitoring the system load, CPU usage and network interfaces, and options specific to routers.

Another interesting SNMP use is to monitor the network bandwidth usage. In this case, Nagios can be integrated with the **MRTG** package (see `http://www.mrtg.org/`). This is a utility that allows the creation of graphs of bandwidth usage on various network interfaces that also use SNMP to gather information on traffic. Nagios offers a `check_mrtg` plugin (see `http://nagiosplugins.org/man/check_mrtg`) that can be used to retrieve bandwidth usage information from the MRTG log files.

Most companies that need bandwidth monitoring already use MRTG, as it is the de-facto standard. That is why, it is a good idea to integrate Nagios if you already have MRTG set up. Otherwise, it is better to use a dedicated bandwidth monitoring system.

Summary

SNMP can be used by Nagios in various ways. As the protocol is widely supported by operating systems and network devices, it is a great choice for monitoring a wide variety of machines. SNMP features a standardized way to describe typical parameters that describe a device—hardware, network connectivity, applications and services, and much more. This makes accessing this information from Nagios very easy. SNMP is enabled by default on many operating systems and most network devices, which makes it very easy to monitor such devices in Nagios.

The SNMP protocol has three popular versions—SNMPv1, SNMPv2c, and SNMPv3. Luckily, Nagios can be made to talk to devices using any of these versions as long as the plugins themselves allow the use of a specific version. SNMP version 3 can even be used to put more focus on security in many internal networks using SNMPv1 or SNMPv2c protocols as these are the more widely-supported version. Furthermore, from a Nagios perspective no functionality is gained by using a newer version. SNMP is mostly used on a company's intranet, which makes transmission very secure and less prone to various attacks.

Nagios comes with several plugins that allow the performing of checks using SNMP. They can be used to query specific Object Identifiers and verify whether the value is as expected or within specified ranges. There are also additional plugins that can be used to perform specialized checks and make sure that essential services are working on Microsoft Windows machines, and to monitor system load, CPU utilization, storage and memory usage, and network bandwidth usage. In most cases, there is already at least one plugin that does the job well. Otherwise, the generic `check_snmp` plugin will work in the majority of cases.

Nagios can also be integrated with SNMP traps. These are messages that other devices will send to Nagios and/or other machines on your network that will then be treated as check results inside Nagios. This allows the monitoring of SNMP traps in Nagios, which in turn allows the creation of a more complex event handling mechanism. It also helps with the integration of all other information, so that Nagios can be used as a single point for storing all network management information.

Nagios can also be integrated with SNMP using third-party applications that already communicate over SNMP and store their information as files on a machine. A good example is MRTG, which monitors network bandwidth usage. Nagios can be set up so that it reads MRTG information directly and uses the same values.

There are also plenty of other ways that SNMP can be harnessed inside Nagios. Almost all dynamic languages, such as Perl, Python, or Tcl can communicate over SNMP, as these languages have dedicated modules for doing so. This makes it very easy to write more complex check plugins or daemons that use SNMP to monitor the parameters of various devices.

10
Advanced Monitoring

Nagios can be pushed very far in terms of what can be monitored and how this can be done. It also offers a way to balance the load of monitoring activities as well as providing a fail-safe solution by using several Nagios servers.

This chapter describes additional techniques that can be used to monitor Windows by installing and configuring a dedicated agent. It shows how to communicate both from the Nagios server to the Windows machines as well as the other way around. It describes how to communicate with such agents, in addition to describing other features.

This chapter covers a very popular agent available for Microsoft Windows—**NSClient++**. This allows the querying of various system parameters over the network, and offers multiple ways in which this information can then be received by the Nagios server. Their functionality offers much more than what can be done by querying only the SNMP.

This chapter also covers how Nagios can be configured so that it notifies other Nagios instances about the current status of all hosts and services. These techniques can be used to create a central Nagios server that receives notifications from other machines.

Notifying other instances also allows the setting up of a fail-safe configuration where several instances each monitor a part of the entire IT infrastructure, and this information is gathered at a central server.

This may also be a good solution to a problem when the Nagios server is not able to directly communicate with the checked machines being checked over a TCP/IP connection. In such cases, another server can monitor these and report back to Nagios.

This chapter also covers the basics of setting up Nagios so that it handles problems in receiving information from other Nagios instances. If one of your Nagios monitoring systems is down or unreachable, you would want another Nagios instance to detect this and report it to you.

Monitoring Windows Hosts

Nagios was originally designed to monitor UNIX operating systems. The plugins package that is developed along with Nagios cannot be used on Microsoft Windows systems. As mentioned in the previous chapter, SNMP can be used to monitor Windows, and this requires installing an SNMP agent on the system.

The SNMP agent on a Microsoft Windows system allows checking for a large number of parameters. There are, however, things that cannot be easily checked using SNMP and the standard Nagios plugins. This includes running external processes, gathering information unavailable via SNMP, and checking the status of multiple parameters in a single check.

An alternative to SNMP on Microsoft Windows workstations and servers is to install a dedicated agent that is used to monitor these systems from Nagios. The most commonly-used agent is NSClient++ (visit `http://trac.nakednuns.org/nscp/`). NSClient++ was the first Windows agent to be designed to work strictly with Nagios.

Using this agent, it is possible to query the various parameters from Nagios using a special plugin. NSClient++ can also report results directly to Nagios using the NSCA protocol described in Chapter 7, *Passive Checks*, and *NSCA*. It is possible to set up the types of checks that should be performed, how often, and whether they should be reported as host or service checks. The agent will also need to know the host name of the Nagios server, the NSCA port, the encryption method, and the password.

NSClient++

NSClient++, now also known as NSCP, is a project that is based on, and extends, the NSClient concept. The original concept was to create an agent for Windows that, once installed, allows the querying of system information. NSClient created a de-facto standard protocol that offers the ability to query variables with parameters. NSClient++ also offers the ability to perform more complex checks using the NRPE protocol.

Installing NSClient++ requires passing the path where it will be installed, and choosing the features to install. Unless you need to install NSClient++ in a specific location, it is best to use the default path of `C:\Program Files\NSClient++`. The next step is to choose the features that should be installed.

NSClient++ comes with various features that can be installed—the main program and various plugins. NSClient++ can also be set up to act as the NRPE daemon and run external checks. It is also possible to make it send results over NSCA. This option is mainly useful if your network is set up in such a way that it is not possible to connect to the workstations. Otherwise, it is better for the Nagios daemon to query NSClient++.

After a successful installation, the NSClient++ registers itself as a Windows service. This has to be started by performing a reboot of the system or by going to the **Services** management console in **Administrative Tools**.

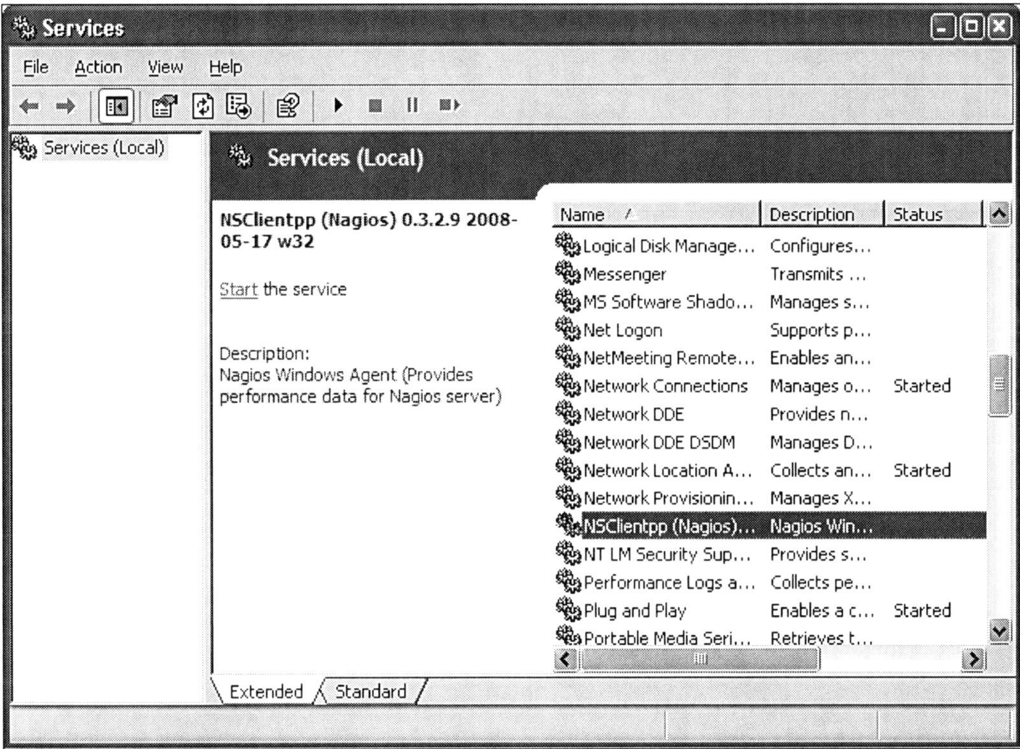

In order to start the service, select the **NSClientpp** service and click on the **Start the service** action on the left. NSClient++ comes with the main engine, the plugin that accepts checks over the network, the NRPE daemon, and the ability to perform check and reports results automatically via NSCA. It is best to choose all of the features during installation. These features also need to be explicitly enabled in the configuration file.

After being installed, NSClient++ needs to be configured. The configuration file is called `NSC.ini` and is located in the application folder by default; this is `C:\Program Files\NSClient\NSC.ini`. After a fresh installation, a default configuration is installed. This contains a list of all the available parameters along with comments for all of them. It also has all of the features disabled, so only the ones you need will be enabled. We now need to enable the features we would need to use.

The configuration is split into several sections. Each section begins with a section name enclosed in brackets. For example, the first section begins with the statement, `[modules]`. This part of the configuration defines which modules should be loaded, by simply specifying each DLL. The `Settings` section is used for specifying global parameters. The most important is `allowed_hosts`, which is a list of the IP addresses or IP ranges that can connect to the agent. The `password`, option, specifies the password that will be used for authenticating Nagios checks. If a password is not specified, then all checks will be accepted. The `NSClient` and `NRPE` sections are used for configuring the acceptance of requests from the Nagios daemon using these two protocols.

If you plan on using NSCA, then the `NSCA Commands` section allows the definition of one or more checks that should be performed and reported to the Nagios daemon over NSCA. Connectivity with the NSCA daemon can be configured in the `NSCA Agent` section.

The following is a sample configuration file that loads all types of checks, the NSCA agent, and sets up NSClient and NSCA.

```
[modules]
FileLogger.dll
CheckSystem.dll
CheckDisk.dll
CheckEventLog.dll
CheckHelpers.dll
CheckWMI.dll
CheckExternalScripts.dll
NSClientListener.dll
NRPEListener.dll
NSCAAgent.dll

[Settings]
allowed_hosts=192.168.0.0/16
use_file=1

[NSClient]
port=12489

[NRPE]
port=5666
```

```
[NSCA Agent]
interval=60
encryption_method=1
password=mysecret
hostname=windows1
nsca_host=192.168.2.51
nsca_port=5667

[NSCA Commands]
CPU Usage=checkCPU warn=80 crit=90 time=20m time=10s time=4
```

If you are not interested in using NSCA, all that you need to do is to comment out the `NSCAAgent.dll` line in `modules` section.

Performing Tests via check_nt

NSClient++ offers a uniform mechanism for querying system information. Basic system information can be retrieved using the `check_nt` command from a standard Nagios plugins package.

The syntax and options of the command is as follows:

```
check_nt -H <host> [-p <port>] [-P <password>] [-w level] [-c level]
        -v <variable> -l <arguments>
```

Option	Description
-H, --hostname	The host name or IP address of the machine to connect to; this option must be specified
-p, --port	The TCP port number to connect to; defaults to 1248; for NSClient++ it should be set to 1248, which is the default port
-P, --password	The password to use for authentication; this is optional and is needed only if a password is set up on the Windows agent
-v, --variable	The variable to query; see the list below for the possible parameters
-l, --arguments	The arguments that should be passed to the variable; this parameter is optional
-w, --warning	Specifies the return values above which a warning state should be returned
-c, --critical	Specifies the return values above which a critical state should be returned

The variables that can be checked are predefined. Most checks return both the string representation and an integer value. If an integer value is present ,then the `-w` and `-c` flags can be used to specify the values that should indicate a problem.

The first variable is `CPULOAD`, which allows the querying of processor usage over a specified period of time. The parameters are one or more series of `<time>`, `<warning>`, and `<critical>` levels, where the time is a period in minutes and the `warning/critical` values specify the CPU usage in percentage that should trigger a problem. For example:

```
# check_nt -h 192.168.2.11 -v CPUUSAGE -l 1,80,90
CPU Load 2% (1 min average) |   '1 min avg Load'=2%;80;90;0;100
```

The variable `USEDDISKSPACE` can be used to monitor space usage. The argument should be a partition letter; the `-w` and `-c` options should be used to specify the used disk space percentage that should trigger a problem. For example:

```
# check_nt -h 192.168.2.11 -v USEDDISKSPACE -l C -w 80 -c 90
C:\ - total: 24.41 Gb - used: 17.96 Gb (74%) - free 6.45 Gb (26%) |
'C:\ Used Space'=17.96Gb;0.00;0.00;0.00;24.41
```

System services can also be monitored using the `SERVICESTATE` variable. The arguments should specify one or more internal service names, separated by commas. Internal service names can be checked in the **Services** management console. For example:

```
# check_nt -h 192.168.2.11 -v SERVICESTATE -l NSClientpp,Schedule
OK: All services are running.
```

As with to services, it is also possible to monitor processes running on a Windows machine. The `PROCSTATE`, variable, can be used to achieve this. The variable accepts a list of executable names separated by commas. For example:

```
# check_nt -h 192.168.2.11 -v PROCSTATE -l winword.exe
OK: All processes are running.
```

Monitoring memory usage can also be checked this way. To perform this kind of check, use the `MEMUSE` variable. This does not require any additional arguments. The arguments `-w` and `-c` are used to specify the warning and critical limits. For example:

```
# check_nt -h 192.168.2.11 -v MEMUSE -w 80 -c 90
Memory usage: total:5891.77 Mb - used: 846.01 Mb (14%) - free: 5045.75
Mb (86%) | 'Memory usage'=846.01Mb;4713.41;5302.59;0.00;5891.77
```

Another thing that can be checked is the age of a file, using the `FILEAGE` variable. This allows the verification of whether a specified file has been modified within a specified time period. The arguments, `-w` and `-c`, are used to specify the warning and critical limits. Their values indicate the number of minutes within which a file should have been modified—a value of 240 means that a file has been modified within the last 4 hours. For example:

```
# check_nt -h 192.168.2.11 -v FILEAGE -l \
```

```
"C:\\Program Files\\NSClient++\\NSC.log" -w 5 -c 10
0 years 0 mon 0 days 0 hours 0 min 0 sec
```

It is also possible to check the version of the agent. This makes render the maintainenance of upgrades and new versions much easier. The `CLIENTVERSION`, variable, allows the retrieval of version information. For example:

```
# check_nt -h 192.168.2.11 -v CLIENTVERSION
NSClient++ 0.3.2.9 2008-05-17
```

Using `check_nt`, it is also possible to query the Windows counters for information. However, this method is deprecated, as querying **Windows Management Instrumentation** (**WMI**, visit `http://en.wikipedia.org/wiki/Windows_Management_Instrumentation`), available as NRPE, is a much more powerful feature. NPRE is described in the next section.

WMI is a mechanism that allows applications to access the system management information using various programming languages. WMI offers an extensive set of information that can be retrieved. It describes the hardware and operating system as well as the currently-installed applications and the running applications. WMI also offers a query language (visit `http://en.wikipedia.org/wiki/WQL`) very similar to the **SQL** (**Structured Query Language**; `http://en.wikipedia.org/wiki/SQL`) that makes the retrieval of specific information very easy.

Performing Checks with NRPE Protocol

Another way to communicate with NSClient++ is over NRPE (described in more detail in Chapter 8). UNIX machines offer a way to run external commands via NRPE. In this case, the protocol can be used for querying internal functions as well as running external commands or scripts.

NSClient++ requires the modification of the `NSC.ini` configuration file in order to offer querying data over NRPE. The first thing that needs to be done is to enable `NRPEListener.dll` and `CheckExternalScripts.dll` entries in the `modules` section. The first one is responsible for handling NRPE protocol, while the second module allows the creation of aliases for internal commands and external scripts.

NSClient++ can be configured to use both internal commands and external scripts to perform actual checks. Internal commands define aliases for checks that will be done internally, without launching external applications. NSClient++ allows the definition of aliases that are used later on when invoking the `check_nrpe` command from the Nagios server. The section `External Alias`, in the NSClient++ configuration allows the definition of aliases for the actual commands.

The following are some examples of aliases:

```
[External Alias]
check_cpu=checkCPU warn=80 crit=90 time=5m time=1m
check_mem=checkMem MaxWarn=80% MaxCrit=90% ShowAll type=physical
check_no_ie= CheckWMI -a 'Query:load=SELECT Caption FROM Win32_
Process' +filter-string:Caption=iexplore.exe MaxCrit=1
```

The `check_no_ie` alias needs to be put on a single line in the configuration file. The first alias is used to monitor CPU usage. The second one allows the monitoring of memory. The third example uses the WMI command to list processes and find `iexplore.exe`. It will return a critical state if at least one `iexplore.exe` process is found.

In order to perform a check from Nagios, the following command can be used:

```
# check_nrpe -h 192.168.2.11 -c check_cpu
OK CPU Load ok.|'5m'=48;80;90; '1m'=45;80;90; '30s'=45;80;90;
```

The `$IP` argument is the IP address of the remote host that a check should be performed against.

It is also possible to use direct NSClient++ NRPE commands without aliases. This requires setting the `allow_arguments` option to `1` in the `NRPE` section the `NSC.ini` file.

In such a case, it is possible to do the following:

```
# check_nrpe -h $IP -c check_cpu -a warn=80 crit=90 time=5m time=1m
OK CPU Load ok.|'5m'=48;80;90; '1m'=45;80;90; '30s'=45;80;90;
```

The commands that can be used both directly and when defining aliases in `External Alias` configuration section can be found in the commands documentation (`http://trac.nakednuns.org/nscp/wiki/CheckCommands`).

NSClient++ also allows the execution of external commands, similar to the UNIX NRPE implementations. This can be used to run various types of scripts, as well as executables. The default configuration comes with some sample definitions.

The following are a few examples that show how to use the various scripting languages:

```
[External Scripts]
check_vbs_sample=cscript.exe //T:30 //NoLogo scripts\check_vb.vbs
check_tcl_test=tclsh.exe scripts\check_tcl.tcl
check_python_test=python.exe scripts\check_python.py
```

The first check uses the standard Windows Script Host mechanism for running a Visual Basic script. In order to run Tcl or Python scripts on Windows, a distribution of these languages needs to be installed. The most popular ones are ActiveTcl (`http://www.activestate.com/Products/activetcl/`) and ActivePython (`http://www.activestate.com/Products/activepython/`), both maintained by the ActiveState company.

Running external commands does not differ from running internal ones. This makes it possible to dynamically change between internal checks and external scripts when necessary.

For example:

```
# check_nrpe -h $IP -c check_tcl_test
OK from Tcl 8.4.19 as C:/Tcl/bin/tclsh.exe (pid 1234)
```

As with to other NRPE implementations, NSClient++ also allows the passing of parameters to commands that are to be executed.

For example, the following alias allows the monitoring of the CPU adaptively:

```
[External Alias]
check_cpu2=checkCPU warn=$ARG1$ crit=$ARG2$ time=5m time=1m
```

To perform the check, the following command needs to be run:

```
# check_nrpe -h $IP -c check_cpu2 -a 80 90
OK CPU Load ok.|'5m'=48;80;90; '1m'=45;80;90; '30s'=45;80;90;
```

Passive Checks using NSCA Protocol

NSClient++ offers a way for Windows machines to send results to the Nagios server using the NSCA protocol. This is done by incorporating the sending mechanism in the agents. A very common situation is where network routers or firewalls are filtering out communication to the Windows machines. It is impossible to communicate using the `check_nt` and `check_nrpe` plugins. In such cases, sending results over NSCA is the only option.

Setting up the NSCA functionality is very simple. The first thing that needs to be done is to enable the `NSCAAgent.dll` library in the `modules` section. It is also necessary to configure the section `NSCA Agent`. This configures the checks interval (in seconds) and the connection options—encryption, password, NSCA host, and port. For details on NSCA connectivity, please refer to Chapter 7 *Passive Checks and NSCA*.

Configuration also specifies the local host name that should be used when reporting to the NSCA daemon. The section, `NSCA Commands`, specifies the list of commands that are to be checked, and services they should be reported as. The host name and services need to reflect the actual names used in the Nagios configuration. Otherwise, reports from NSClient++ will be discarded by Nagios.

The following is an example of such a configuration:

```
[NSCA Agent]
interval=300
encryption_method=1
password=test
hostname=windows1
nsca_host=192.168.2.51
nsca_port=5667

[NSCA Commands]
check_cpu=checkCPU warn=80 crit=90 time=20m time=10s time=4
check_no_ie= CheckWMI -a 'Query:load=SELECT Caption FROM Win32_
Process' +filter-string:Caption=iexplore.exe MaxCrit=1
```

NSCA check alias definitions are the same as the NRPE aliases. The commands that can be used in NSClient++ when defining NSCA commands can be found in the commands documentation (`http://trac.nakednuns.org/nscp/wiki/CheckCommands`).

In order for Nagios to accept information coming from the Windows machine, we also need to create a corresponding service for it.

The following is an example that has active checks disabled and allows only passive checks to be received.

```
define service
{
  use                         generic-service
  host_name                   windows1
  service_description         check_cpu
  active_checks_enabled       0
  passive_checks_enabled      1
}
```

We also need to have the NSCA server running on the Nagios server. This is described in more detail in Chapter 7.

Distributed Monitoring

There are many situations in which you might want to have more than one Nagios instance monitoring your IT infrastructure. One reason can be a firewall blocking all but a few machines in your company. Another reason would be the need to load-balance all checks so that they don't require an enterprise-class server. Other people may need to monitor machines in different physical locations from separate machines to be able to check what is wrong within a branch, even if the links to central servers are temporarily down.

Regardless of the reason, you may need, or want the execution of checks to be split across multiple computers. This type of setup might sound complicated and hard to configure, but with Nagios, it is not as hard as it seems. All that's necessary is to set up multiple Nagios instances along with the NSCA agents or daemons.

There are subtle the various in how the various instances need to be configured. Usually, there are one or more Nagios instances that report information to a single central Nagios instance. We will refer to an instance that reports information to another Nagios machine as a **slave**. A Nagios instance that receives reports from one or more slaves will be referred to as a **master**.

Let's consider a simple organization that has four branches and a headquarters. Each branch is connected to the main office and has a local set of computers. A typical scenario is that a local instance of Nagios monitors the computers and routers in a single branch. The results are then sent to the central Nagios server over an NSCA protocol. These are instances of slave Nagios. When a connection to one of the branches is broken, the local administrators still have access to the status of the local machines. This information is not propagated to the master Nagios server. Setting up the services on the central Nagios server to use freshness checks will cause the central Nagios server to generate an alert when no results are received within a predetermined timeframe. Combining this with parent configurations will cause Nagios to determine the root cause of the problems accurately.

The following diagram shows how a typical setup in a multiple-branch configuration is done. It shows the network topology, which machines are checked by which Nagios servers, and how this information is reported to the central Nagios server.

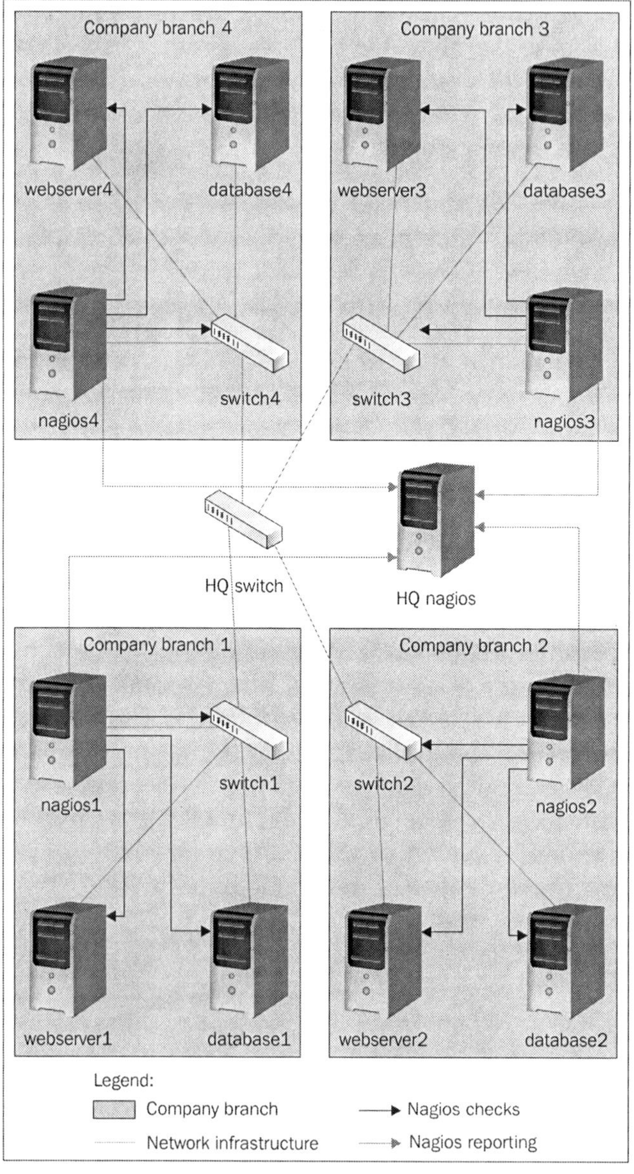

In this example, each branch has a Nagios slave server that monitors and logs information on the local computers. This information is then propagated to the master Nagios server.

Obsessive Notifications

Monitoring IT infrastructure using multiple Nagios instances requires a way to send information from slave servers to one or more master servers. This can be done as events that are triggered when a service or a host state changes. However, this has a huge drawback of necessitating the set-up of an event handler for each object. Another disadvantage is that the event handlers are only triggered on actual changes, and not after each test is done.

Nagios offers another way to do this, through **obsessive notifications**. These provide a mechanism for running commands when a host or a service status is received—regardless of whether it is a passive or active check result. The mechanism is also set up system-wide, which means that object definitions do not need to be changed in any way for Nagios to send information about their status changes.

Setting up obsessive notifications requires a couple of changes in your configuration. The first one is to define a command that will be run for each notification. An example of this is shown below:

```
define command
{
    command_name  send-ocsp
    command_line  $USER1$/send-ocsp 192.168.1.4 $SERVICESTATE$
                  $HOSTNAME$ '$SERVICEDESC$' '$SERVICEOUTPUT$'
}
```

The command line needs to be entered on a single line in your configuration file. You will also need to specify the actual IP address of the example IP of your central Nagios server in place of `192.168.1.4` in the example.

We now need to write command that simply pass the results to the other server, over NSCA.

A sample script would be as follows:

```
#!/bin/sh

# args: nsca-server hostname svcname status output

# map status to return code
RC=-1
case "$2" in
    OK)
        RC=0
        ;;
    WARNING)
        RC=1
```

```
            ;;
        CRITICAL)
            RC=2
            ;;
    esac

    echo -e "$3\t$4\t$RC\t$5" | /opt/nagios/bin/send_nsca \
        -H $1 -c /etc/nagios/send_nsca.cfg

    exit 0
```

The next step is to enable obsessive notifications for services, and to set up the correct commands to be run in the main Nagios configuration file.

The following are the required parameters, along with example values that should be set:

```
obsess_over_services=1
ocsp_command=send-ocsp
```

The command name should match the name in the command definition.

That's it! After reloading your Nagios configuration, the `send-ocsp` script will be run every time a check result comes in.

Configuring Nagios to send host status information is very similar to setting up service status to be sent. The first thing that we need to set up is the command that will be run for each notification. It is as follows:

```
define command
{
    command_name  send-ochp
    command_line  $USER1$/send-ochp 192.168.1.4 $HOSTSTATE$
                  $HOSTNAME$ '$HOSTOUTPUT$'
}
```

Please note that the `command_line` directive above needs to be specified on a single line.

The script to send information will look exactly like the one for sending the host status information except that the actual command sent over NSCA would be generated a bit differently, by sending only the host name, to indicate that it's a host check result:

```
echo -e "$3\t$RC\t$4" | /opt/nagios/bin/send_nsca \
    -H $1 -c /etc/nagios/send_nsca.cfg
```

In order for Nagios to send notifications to another Nagios instance, we also need to enable obsessing over hosts, and specify the actual command to use.

Here are some example directives in `nagios.cfg`:

```
obsess_over_hosts=1
ochp_command=send-ochp
```

After these changes have been made to the configurations, Nagios needs to be restarted. After that, Nagios should start sending notifications.

A good thing to do is to check the `nagios.log` file to see if notifications are being sent out after a check has been made. By default, the file is in the `/var/nagios` directory. If the notifications are not received, it may be a good idea to make the scripts responsible for sending messages to log this information in either the system log or in a separate log file. This is very helpful when it comes to debugging instances where the notifications sent out by slave Nagios instances get lost. Writing information to the system log can be done using the `logger` command (`http://linux.die.net/man/1/logger`).

Configuring Nagios Instances

Setting up multiple servers to monitor the infrastructure using Nagios is not trivial. However, is not very hard either. It only requires a slightly different approach as compared to setting up a single machine. That said, there are issues with the configuration of hosts and services themselves. It is also necessary to set up all slave and master servers correctly, and in a slightly different way.

Distributed monitoring requires having a more mature change control and versioning process for Nagios configurations. This is necessary because both the central Nagios server and its branches need to have a partial or complete configuration available, and these need to be in sync across all machines.

Usually, it is recommended that you make the slave servers query both the service and the host status. It is also recommended that you disable service checks on the master Nagios server, but keep the host checks enabled. The reason for this is that host checks are not usually scheduled and are done only when a service check returns a `warning`, `critical` or, `unknown` status. Therefore, the load required for only checking the hosts is much lower than performing regular service checks. In some cases, it is best to also disable host checks. Either the host checks need to be performed regularly or the security policies should disallow checks being done by the central server.

Our recommendation for maintaining Nagios configurations is to set up a versioning system such as **CVS (Concurrent Versions System**—`http://www.cvshome.org/`) or Subversion (`http://subversion.tigris.org/`). This will allow you to keep track of all of the Nagios changes and make it much easier to apply configuration changes to multiple machines. Storing and managing the configuration can be done in a similar way as we had done previously. Hosts, services, and the corresponding groups should be kept in directories, separately for each Nagios slave—for example, `hosts/branch1` and `services/branch1`. All other types of objects, such as contacts, time periods, and check commands can be kept in global directories and re-used in all branches—for example, the single `contacts`, `timeperiods`, and `commands` directories.

It's also a good idea to create a small system for deploying the configuration to all the machines, along with the ability to test new configuration before applying it in production. This can be done by using a small number of shell scripts. Doing everything manually when dealing with multiple computers, locations and Nagios instances is very difficult and can get problematic over the long term. This will cause the system to become unmanageable, and can lead to errors in actual checks caused by out-of-sync configurations between the slave and master Nagios instances. A very popular tool that is recommended for this purpose is **cfengine** (`http://www.cfengine.org/`). This allows the automation of configuration deployment and ensuring that Nagios is up-to-date on all the machines. It also allows for customization—for example, a different set of files can be deployed on slave servers than on the master server.

The first step in setting up a distributed environment is to set up the master Nagios server. This will require the installation of Nagios from a binary distribution, or building it from sources. Details related to Nagios installation are described in Chapter 2.

The main differences from a single Nagios set up for a master server are defined in the main Nagios configuration file—`nagios.cfg`. This needs to contain the `cfg_dir` directives for objects related to all of the slave servers. Otherwise, the master Nagios instance will ignore the reports related to the hosts that it does not know about.

We'll also need to make sure that Nagios accepts passive check results for services, and that the master Nagios instance does not perform any active checks on its own. To do this, set the following options in the main Nagios configuration file on the master server:

```
check_external_commands=1
accept_passive_service_checks=1
execute_service_checks=0
```

If you also want to rely on passive check results for host checks, you will also need to add the following lines to your main Nagios configuration:

```
accept_passive_host_checks=1
execute_host_checks=0
```

You will also need to set up the NSCA daemon on the master Nagios server. Details of how to set this up are described in Chapter 7 *Passive Checks and NSCA*.

The next step is to set up first slave server that will report to the master Nagios instance. This also necessitates setting up Nagios from a binary or source distribution, and configuring it properly.

All of the slave Nagios instances also need to have the `send_nsca` command from the NSCA package in order to be able to communicate changes to the master instance. After setting up the NSCA client, we also need to create a configuration for sending notifications. It is also a good idea to check that sending dummy reports about an existing host and an existing service works correctly.

All of the slave instances need to be set up to send obsessive notifications to the master Nagios server. This includes setting up the OCSP and OCHP commands, and enabling them in the main Nagios configuration file. (Obsessive notifications have already been described in the previous section.)

After setting everything up, it's best to run notification commands directly from the command line to see if everything works correctly. Next, a restart of the slave Nagios server is needed. After that, it would be a good idea to check the Nagios logs to see if the notifications are being sent out.

It would also be a good idea to write down or automate all the steps needed to set up a Nagios slave instance. Setting up the master is done only once, but large networks might require the set-up of a large number of slaves.

Freshness Checking

We now have distributed monitoring set up and the slave Nagios instances should be reporting results to the master Nagios daemon. Things should be working fine, and the main Web interface will be reporting up-to-date information from all of the hosts and services being monitored.

Unfortunately, it is not always the case. In some cases, network connectivity can be down, the NSCA agents, daemon, or anything else on the network might fail temporarily, and the master Nagios instance may not even know about it. Because our basic assumption is that master Nagios instance is not responsible for monitoring the IT infrastructure, it needs to rely on other systems to do it. Configuration, as described earlier, does not take into account a situation where checks are not sent to the master instance.

Nagios offers a way to monitor whether results have come within a certain period of time. We can specify that if no report has come in within a certain amount of time, Nagios should treat this as a critical state and warn the administrators about it. This makes sense as obsessive notifications are sent out very frequently. So if no notification has come within half an hour, this means that there is a problem with some part of the distributed monitoring configuration.

Implementing this in the master Nagios configuration requires a slightly different approach to the one mentioned in the previous section. In this case, it is necessary to enable service (and host, if needed) checks on a global basis in the `nagios.cfg` file. The approach in the previous section was to disable service checks completely. That is why all services and/or hosts needed to have their active checks reconfigured in order for the new approach to work correctly.

For the reasons given above, all of the services and/or hosts that receive notifications from slave Nagios instances need to be defined differently in the master configuration to the definitions that are set for the Nagios slaves.

The first change is that active checks for these objects need to be enabled, but should not be scheduled. That is, the option `normal_check_interval` should not be set. In addition, the `check_freshness` and `freshness_threshold` options need to be specified. The first of these options enables monitoring whether results are up-to-date, and the second one specifies the number of seconds after which the results should be considered outdated.

This means that Nagios will only run active checks if there has been no passive check result for a specified period of time. It is very important that the host and service definitions on both the master and slave instances have the same value specified for the `check_period` directive. Otherwise, the master Nagios instance might raise an alert for services that are checked only during specific time periods. An example could be the `workinghours` time period, which is not checked on weekends.

For example, the following service definition will accept passive checks but will report an error if they are not present:

```
define service
{
  use                         generic-service
  host_name                   linuxbox02
  service_description         SSH
  check_command               no-passive-check-results
  check_freshness             1
  freshness_threshold         43200
  active_checks_enabled       1
  passive_checks_enabled      1
}
```

The `freshness_threshold` option specifies the number of seconds after which an active check should be performed. In this case, it is set to 12 hours.

It is also necessary to define a command that will be run if no passive check results have been provided.

The following command will use the `check_dummy` plugin to report an error:

```
define command
{
  command_name        no-passive-check-results
  command_line        $USER1$/check_dummy 2 "No passive check
                      results"
}
```

It is important to make sure that all of the services and/or hosts are defined so that no actual active checks will be performed, only dummy checks that report problems. This is different from our previous approach that made sure that active checks were not performed.

Using passive checks for regular reporting, and performing active checks when no passive results have been provided, is described in more detail in Chapter 7. The main difference is that in our case no actual checks will be performed if passive results are not available.

The main drawback of this approach is that it makes managing configurations on master and slave instances more difficult. We need to maintain the configuration for the master Nagios instance that contains the service with only the dummy freshness checks. However, slave configurations need to have complete check definitions in place.

In order to avoid reconfiguring all of the objects, and managing two sets of configurations, it is possible to use Nagios 3.x' s multiple inheritance to manage the configurations efficiently. Assuming that all checks will be put in templates, it is possible to either redefine these templates, or create a template that is inherited by all of the objects that will overwrite the various parameters. Assuming inheritance would specify something like `generic-service,check-smtp,`and `master-override`, the template could be blank on slave instances, but the master version would contain the directives to overwrite the template parameters with actual check parameters.

Summary

Nagios offers multiple ways to monitor Microsoft Windows workstations and servers. These vary from monitoring computers remotely, to querying SNMP and installing dedicated agents.

Installing agents to monitor Microsoft Windows systems may be a time-consuming task. However, the advantage is that dedicated agents such as NSClient++ can be configured to perform checks that cannot be performed otherwise. It can read WMI, and monitor system processes and services. In addition, such agents can run external binaries and scripts so that any language you are familiar with can be used to perform additional checks.

NSClient++ can also send results directly to Nagios using the NSCA protocol. This can be used to avoid problems with firewalls and security policies which may disallow connections to Windows machines.

Another very interesting feature of Nagios is its ability to configure multiple machines easily in order to perform monitoring, and also to have a single place where the results are easily available.

This can be used to split the load related to actually performing the checks. It can also be a solution to the firewall and security policies. A local instance can query all of the machines in the same location and report back to the central server.

Unlike many other systems, Nagios does not require a huge rework to allow the splitting of checks into several computers. Setting up a working, usable, and distributed monitoring system is only a little more as compared to monitoring all your resources from a single server.

Nagios can also make sure that the results sent by other instances are up-to-date. This deals with situations where a broken network connection or Nagios server causes problems to go unnoticed as no critical results are sent to the master Nagios server.

11
Extending Nagios

One of the key features of Nagios is its extensibility. There are multiple ways in which Nagios can be tailored to suit your needs. It is also possible to integrate Nagios tightly with your applications and benefit from a powerful mechanism for scheduling and performing checks.

The first and the easiest way to adapt Nagios is to perform checks customized to your company's needs. The default Nagios plugins suit most needs very well—they allow simple checking of databases, web sites, and various networked or local services. However, in many cases this may not be enough. You might want to create a script to verify that critical tables in a database are not corrupted, or that your website actually works and communicates with web services over SOAP.

Another area that can be customized in a variety of ways is how users are notified about problems. By default, Nagios is able to send emails to users when a problem occurs. There are also plugins for various protocols, such as Jabber (`http://www.jabber.org/`). However, sometimes you may need to integrate Nagios with your company's applications or the corporate instant messenger. In such cases, you're able to create scripts or binaries that will send notifications the way you want to.

If your application is already performing diagnostic checks, it can be integrated with Nagios so that the application will report the status of the checks it performs as passive check results. We'll show how this can be done. It is also possible that your application can control Nagios—telling it to perform checks.

We will also discuss how to schedule the performance of long lasting tests. These tests can be anything from verifying bad sectors on a disk to running suites of tests for your applications on a regular basis.

Finally, there's also room for using more than one of the functions mentioned above. For example, after Nagios detects a problem, an event handler may attempt to fix it and then reschedule another check to verify whether the problem still exists.

Introduction

The most exciting aspect of using Nagios is the ability to combine your programming skills with the powerful engine offered by the Nagios daemon. Your own pieces of code can be plugged into the Nagios daemon, or can communicate with it in various ways.

One of the best things about Nagios is that, in most cases, it does not force you to use a specific language. Whether the language of your choice is PHP, Perl, Tcl, Python, or Java, you can easily use it with Nagios. This is a fundamental difference between Nagios and the majority of monitoring applications. Usually, an application can only be extended in the same language it is written in.

Our code can cooperate with Nagios in various ways—either by implementing commands or by sending information to the Nagios daemon. The first case means that we create a script or executable that will be run by Nagios, and its output and exit code is then processed by Nagios. Running external commands is used for performing active checks, sending notifications, and triggering event handlers. By using macro substitutions and variables available in the current context (see `http://nagios.sourceforge.net/docs/3_0/macrolist.html`), we're able to pass down all of the information that's needed for the command to do its job.

The alternative method of extending Nagios is to send information to it from other applications. The first option is that external applications (such as Web or typical user interface) allow the configuration and management of the Nagios system. This is done by sending control commands over UNIX sockets to Nagios. Because this involves opening and writing to a UNIX socket, which works just like a file, it can be done in any programming language that handles I/O.

In this case, the final option is that the other applications reporting to your application or a system scheduling mechanism, such as `cron`, are responsible for running the checks. A test needs to be carried out on its own and the application itself is responsible for sending results back to Nagios. Results can be sent directly via a UNIX socket or via an NSCA protocol. Luckily, even sending over a network with NSCA is simple as results can be sent directly to the standard input of the `send_nsca` command.

Your software can also get information related to Nagios easily. All that's needed is to monitor Nagios's `status.dat` file for changes, and read it as if it contains all object definitions along with the current soft and hard states. The format of the file is quite simple, and the task of writing a parser for it is quite trivial. A parser for the Tcl language can be found on the TclMentor page (`http://tclmentor.kocjan.org/search/label/nagios`).

Over the course of this chapter we will use various programming languages - PHP (`http://www.php.net/`), Python (`http://www.python.org/`), Perl (`http://www.perl.org/`), Tcl (`http://www.tcl.tk/`), and Java (`http://java.sun.com/`). Even though many people do not know all of these languages, the code will only use the basic functionality of the languages so that it is understandable to nontechnical users.

Assuming that you need to write a piece of code on your own, the first thing you should start with is choosing the programming language. If you already know a language that would fit this task, stick to it. Otherwise, there are a few candidates to consider. The language I would recommend is either Python or Tcl.

Python is a very trendy language, and its syntax makes it easy to write check commands. It has a wide range of libraries that can be used to interact with other software. It also has a very pleasant syntax that will seem intuitive to people coming from C/C++ or Java.

Tcl, on the other hand, is a bit less popular, but a very powerful language in its own way. This is usually my first choice for a programming language. It features a very simple, but powerful syntax. Tcl is tightly integrated with an event loop, which is handy when programming event-driven applications. This is perfectly suitable for communicating with the Nagios server. It also comes with a huge set of protocols and libraries to use, especially the ActiveTcl distribution from ActiveState (`http://www.activestate.com/`). Throughout this book, Tcl examples will be using packages available with ActiveTcl distributions. If your Tcl interpreter does not have one or more of these packages, it is recommended that you install the ActiveTcl distribution.

People who are only familiar with PHP can also feel safe about it. It's possible to create various commands and passive check scripts in this language. It is also possible to integrate Nagios with error reporting for your web applications.

Nagios is known to integrate very well with Perl. This chapter teaches us how both Perl and other languages can be easily integrated with Nagios so that readers familiar with other languages will also benefit from it and will learn Perl just for the purpose of extending Nagios.

Even though we'll focus mainly on Perl, Python, Tcl, and PHP, there are many other possibilities that can be used—C/C++ native binaries, Java, Ruby language, shell scripts, and so on.

Active Checks

One of most common areas where Nagios can be suited to fit your needs is that of **active checks**. These are the checks that are scheduled and run by the Nagios daemon. This functionality is described in more detail in Chapter 2.

Nagios has a project that ships the commonly-used plugins and comes with a large variety of checks that can be performed. Before thinking of writing anything on your own, it is best to check for standard plugins (described in detail in Chapter 4 *Overview of* Nagios *Plugins*). It's also worthwhile to visit the NagiosExchange website to check whether somebody has already written a similar plugin for you.

The reason for this is that even though active checks are quite easy to implement, sometimes a complete implementation that handles errors and parameters is not very easy to create. Typically, proper error handling can take a lot of time to implement. Another thing is that plugins that have already existed for some time have often been thoroughly tested by others. Typical errors will have already been identified and fixed; sometimes the plugins will have been tested in a larger environment, under a wider variety of conditions. Writing check plugins on your own should be preceded by an investigation to find out whether anybody has encountered and solved a similar problem.

Active check commands are very simple to implement. They simply require a plugin to return one or more lines of check output to the standard output stream and return one of the predefined exit codes—`OK` (code 0), `WARNING` (code 1), `CRITICAL` (code 2), or `UNKNOWN` (code 3). How active check plugins work is described in more detail at the beginning of Chapter 4.

Let's start with a simple check plugin. We'll implement a simple check that connects to a MySQL database and verifies that if the specified tables are structurally correct. It will also accept connection information from command line as a series of arguments. We'll write the script in Python.

From a technical point of view, the check is quite—all that's needed is to connect to a server, choose the database, and run the `CHECK TABLE` (`http://dev.mysql.com/doc/mysql/en/CHECK_TABLE.html`) command over SQL.

The plugin requires the installation of the MySQLdb package for Python (`http://sourceforge.net/projects/mysql-python/`) to work. We will also need a working MySQL database that we can connect to, for testing purposes. It is a good idea to install MySQL server on your local machine and set up a dummy database with tables for testing.

In order to set up a MySQL database server on Ubuntu Linux, install the `mysql-server` package as follows:

```
apt-get install mysql-server
```

In Red Hat and Fedora Linux, the package is called `mysql-server` and the command is:

```
yum install mysql-server
```

After that, you will be able to connect to the database locally as root, either without a password or with the password supplied during the database installation.

If you do not have any other databases to run the script against, you can use `mysql` as the database name as this is a database that all instances of MySQL have.

The following is a sample script that performs the test. It needs to be run with the host name, username, password, database name, and the list of tables to be checked as arguments. The table names should be separated by comma.

```
#!/usr/bin/env python

import MySQLdb
import sys, string

# only perform check if we're loaded as main script
if __name__ == '__main__':
    dbhost = sys.argv[1]
    dbuser = sys.argv[2]
    dbpass = sys.argv[3]
    dbname = sys.argv[4]
    tables = sys.argv[5]
    errors = []
    count = 0

    # connect to the database
    conn = MySQLdb.connect(dbhost, dbuser, dbpass, dbname);
    cursor = conn.cursor()

    # perform check for all tables in the table list
    # (splits the table names by ",")
    for table in string.split(tables, ","):
       cursor.execute("CHECK TABLE %s" % (table))
       row = cursor.fetchone()
       count = count + 1
       if row[3] != "OK":
           errors.append(table)

    # handle output - if any errors occurred, report 2, otherwise 0
    if len(errors) == 0:
        print "check_mysql_table: OK %d table(s) checked" % count
        sys.exit(0);
    else:
```

```
        print "check_mysql_table: CRITICAL: erorrs in %s" % \
            (string.join(errors, ", "))
        sys.exit(2);
```

The code consists of four parts—initialization, argument parsing, connection, and checking each table. The first part consists of import statements that load various required modules and make sure that the code is run from the command line. In the second part, the arguments passed by the user are mapped to the various variables. After that, a connection to the database is made. If the connection succeeds, for each table specified when running the command, a `CHECK TABLE` command (`http://dev.mysql.com/doc/refman/5.0/en/check-table.html`) is run. This makes MySQL verify that the table structure is correct.

To use it, let's run it by specifying the connection information, and tables `tbl1`, `tbl2`, and `tbl3`:

```
root@ubuntu:~# /opt/nagios/plugins/check_mysql_table.py \
    127.0.0.1 mysqluser secret1 databasename tbl1,tbl2,tbl3
check_mysql_table: OK 3 table(s) checked
```

As you can see, the script seems quite easy and it is usable.

The next task is to create a check plugin that compares the local time with the time on a remote machine and issues a warning or critical state if the difference exceeds a specified number. We will use Tcl for this job.

We'll use Tcl's `time` package (`http://tcllib.sourceforge.net/doc/ntp_time.html`) to communicate with remote machines. This package comes bundled with ActiveTcl and is a part of the `tcllib` package available in many Linux distributions.

If you do not have the `tcllib` and/or `time` packages, you will need to install them. On Ubuntu Linux, the package is called `tcllib` and the following command installs it:

```
apt-get install tcllib
```

The script will accept the host name, and the warning, and critical thresholds in number of seconds. The script will use these to decide on the exit status. It will also output the number of seconds difference for informational purposes.

The following is a script to perform a check of the time on a remote machine:

```
#!/usr/bin/env tclsh

package require time

# retrieve arguments for the script
set host [lindex $argv 0]
set warndiff [lindex $argv 1]
```

```
set critdiff [lindex $argv 2]

# retrieve times
set handle [time::gettime $host]
set remotetime [time::unixtime $handle]
time::cleanup $handle
set localtime [clock seconds]

# calculate difference
set diff [expr {abs($remotetime - $localtime)}]

# decide which exit code should be used
if {$diff > $critdiff} {
    puts "check_time CRITICAL: $diff seconds difference"
    exit 2
}  elseif {$diff > $warndiff} {
    puts "check_time WARNING: $diff seconds difference"
    exit 1
}  else {
    puts "check_time OK: $diff seconds difference"
    exit 0
}
```

This command is split into three parts: initializing, parsing arguments, and checking status. The first part loads the `time` package, the second maps the arguments to variables. After that, a connection to remote host is made, the time on the remote machine is received, and this remote time compared with the local time. Based on what the difference is, the command returns either a `CRITICAL`, `WARNING`, or `OK` status.

And now let's run it against a sample machine:

```
root@ubuntu:~# /opt/nagios/plugins/check_time.tcl \
    ntp2a.mcc.ac.uk 60 120
check_time WARNING: 76 seconds difference
```

As shown, the script works properly.

Writing Plugins the Right Way

We have already created a few sample scripts, and they're working. So it is possible to use them from Nagios. But these checks are very far from being complete. They lack error control, parsing, and argument verification.

It is recommended that you write all the commands in a more user-friendly way. The reason is that, in most cases, after some time, someone else will take over your custom check commands. You might also come back to your own code after a year of working on completely different things. In such cases, having a check command that is user friendly, commented, and allows debugging will save a lot of time.

The first thing that should be done to provide the proper handling of arguments—this means using functionality such as the `getopt` package for Python (`http://www.python.org/doc/2.5/lib/module-getopt.html`) or the `cmdline` package for Tcl (`http://tcllib.sourceforge.net/doc/cmdline.html`) to parse the arguments. This way, functionality such as `--help` parameter will work properly and in a more user-friendly way.

Another thing worth considering is proper error handling. If connectivity to a remote machine is not possible, the check command should exit with a critical or unknown status. In addition, all other pieces of the code should be wrapped to catch errors depending on whether an error suggests a failure in the service being checked, or is due to a problem outside a checked service.

Using the example of the first check plugin, we can redesign the beginning of the script to parse the arguments correctly. The reworked plugin sets the values of all of the parameters to their default value and then parses the options, corresponding values based on what the argument is. The script also allows specification of the `--verbose` flag to tell the plugin that it should report more information on what it is currently doing.

Finally, the connection is wrapped in `try ... except` Python statements to catch exceptions when connecting to the MySQL server. This statement is used to detect errors when running the commands between `try` and `except`. In this case, if a connection to the database could not be established, the script will handle this and report an error, instead of returning a Python error report.

It's also a good practice to wrap the entire script in a `try ... except` statement, so that all potential errors or unhandled situations are sent to Nagios as a general error. In addition, if the `--verbose` flag is specified, more information should be printed out. This should ease the debugging of any potential errors.

The following code extract shows the rewritten beginning of a Python script that uses `getopt` to parse arguments and has used `try ... except` for handling errors in connectivity:

```
# only perform check if we're loaded as main script
if __name__ == '__main__':
    dbhost='localhost'
    dbuser=''
    dbpass=''
    dbname=''
    tables=''
    verbose = False

    try:
        options, args = getopt.getopt(sys.argv[1:],
            "hvH:u:p:d:t:", ["help", "verbose", "hostname=",
                "username=", "password=", "dbname=", "tables="]
            )
    except getopt.GetoptError:
        usage()
        sys.exit(3)

    for name, value in options:
        if name in ("-h", "--help"):
            usage()
            sys.exit(0)
        if name in ("-H", "--hostname"):
            dbhost = value
        if name in ("-u", "--username"):
            dbuser = value
        if name in ("-p", "--password"):
            dbpass = value
        if name in ("-d", "--dbname"):
            dbname = value
        if name in ("-v", "--verbose"):
            verbose = True
        if name in ("-t", "--tables"):
            tables = value

    if verbose:
        print "  Connecting to %s@%s (database %s)" % \
            (dbuser, dbhost, dbname)

    try:
        conn = MySQLdb.connect(dbhost, dbuser, dbpass, dbname);
    except Exception:
        print "Unable to connect to database"
        sys.exit(3)
```

This code also requires to define a `usage` function that prints out the usage syntax. This has been left out of our example and is left as an exercise for the reader.

Another change would be to add reporting on what is currently being done, if the `--verbose` flag is passed. This helps in determining if the script is idle or is currently trying to check specific table contents.

Similarly, For Tcl, we should use the `cmdline` package to parse arguments. It's also a good idea to check if all arguments have been specified correctly:

```
package require cmdline

array set opt [cmdline::getoptions argv {
   {host.arg     "127.0.0.1" "Host to connect to"}
   {warntime.arg "300"       "Warning threshold (seconds)"}
   {crittime.arg "600"       "Critical threshold (seconds)"}
}]

set host $opt(host)
set warntime $opt(warntime)
set crittime $opt(crittime)

if {![string is integer -strict $warntime] || $warntime <= 0} {
    puts stderr "Invalid warning time specified"
    exit 3
}

if {![string is integer -strict $crittime] || $crittime <= 0} {
    puts stderr "Invalid critical time specified"
    exit 3
}
```

This code should replace the three lines that read the `argv` variable , in the original script above. The remaining part of the check script should stay the same.

Of course, the changes mentioned here are just small examples of how plugins should be written. It's not possible to cover all possible aspects of what plugins should take into account. It's your responsibility as the command's author to make sure that all scenarios are covered in your plugin.

Typically, this means correct error handling—usually related to catching all of exceptions that the underlying functions might throw. There are also additional things to take into account. For example, if you are writing a networked plugin, the remote server can return error messages that also need to be handled properly.

An important thing worth considering is handling timeouts properly.

Usually, a plugin tries to connect in the background, and if it fails within a specified period of time, the plugin will exit the check and report an error status. This is usually done through the use of child threads or child processes. In languages that are event driven, this can be done by scheduling an event that exits with a timeout message after a specified time interval.

Checking Websites

Nagios ships with a very powerful `check_http` plugin that allows you to monitor web sites in quite a simple way. This plugin should be enough for a large variety of tasks. However, there are often situations where using only this plugin is not enough.

If you are running a website that is critical to your business, checking only that the main page is showing up correctly may not be enough. In many cases, you might actually want to be sure that the users are able to log in, orders can be sent out, and reports can be generated correctly.

In such cases, it is not sufficient just to check if a couple of pages work correctly. It might be necessary to write a more complex check that will log you into the website, fill out an order form, send it, and verify that it shows up in the order history. You may also want to check that a specified text is present on specific pages.

This task is very common when either performing automated tests during the development of a site. Not many people perform such tests regularly when the site is in production. A downside of this is that if version control of your website is not very strict, then small bug fixes can break things in a different part of the website and those might go on unnoticed for a long time.

One might argue whether this is a task for system monitoring or for the testing phase of the development and maintenance cycles. For a number of reasons, this task should be common to both development and maintenance but it should also be a part of system monitoring. The first reason is that such tests make sure that the overall functionality of the site is working as expected. Monitoring the web page's functionality should normally be performed rarely, but checks of the web server and the main page should be done more often.

There are a couple of approaches to this problem, depending on what you actually want to monitor. The first one is using the `http` or `https` protocol directly using various libraries—`urllib` for Python (`http://docs.python.org/lib/module-urllib.html`), `http` (`http://www.tcl.tk/man/tcl8.4/TclCmd/http.htm`) for Tcl/Tk, and `LWP` (`http://search.cpan.org/~gaas/libwww-perl/lib/LWP.pm`) for Perl. By deciding on the appropriate approach, you will need to hardcode your URLs along with the queries to send and, in some cases, also implement cookie handling on your own.

Another approach is to use automated test frameworks. This includes `mechanize` (`http://wwwsearch.sourceforge.net/mechanize/`) for Python, `webautotest` (`http://sourceforge.net/projects/dqsoftware/`) for Tcl, and `WWW::Mechanize` (`http://search.cpan.org/dist/WWW-Mechanize/`) for Perl. There are also multiple Java frameworks for this, such as `HttpUnit` (`http://httpunit.sourceforge.net/`) and `HtmlUnit` (`http://htmlunit.sourceforge.net/`). These packages offer the automated parsing of HTML, reading of the DOM tree, and operating similar to how a browser would work. This allows scripts to be written at a higher level without having to care about low-level things such as reading and passing values from all fields. A typical script would consist of going to an URL, locating forms, setting values, and sending these values.

The last approach is to use packages that take advantage of Internet Explorer over **COM (Component Object Model**; `http://www.microsoft.com/com/`). This approach uses an entire browser and, therefore, is the most accurate method of testing the website's correctness. It also requires a much larger set up to accomplish the same task—tests need to be performed on a Microsoft Windows system and require a separate account for proper cookie management. For example, in the cases where tests need to start after all of the cookies have been removed, Perl offers the ability to automate Internet Explorer using the `PAMIE` package (`http://pamie.sourceforge.net/`) , while for Python it is `SAMIE` (`http://samie.sourceforge.net/`). Tcl offers Internet Explorer automation in the `autoie` (`http://sourceforge.net/projects/dqsoftware/`) package. For Ruby, the most popular utility is called Watir (`http://wtr.rubyforge.org/`). In order to use IE and COM based automation, you should set up all the checks on a Microsoft Windows based machine and set it up so that the results are sent back via NSCA.

Usually, the best choice is to use automated web testing frameworks. These require much less overheads when developing the code for performing checks and tend to react nicely to small changes in the way your website works.

As an example, we will write a simple script in Tcl that communicates with a website using the `webautotest` package. The plugin logs into the backend of a Joomla! content management system (`http://www.joomla.org/`) and makes sure it that works correctly. This test checks that all Joomla! mechanisms are working correctly.

The following is the source code of the plugin:

```
package require http

# initialize Webautotest object
package require webautotest::httpclient
set o [webautotest::httpclient ::#auto]
```

```
if {$argc != 3} {
    puts "Usage: check_joomla_backend URL username password"
    exit 3
}

set url [lindex $argv 0]
set username [lindex $argv 1]
set password [lindex $argv 2]

if {[catch {
    # go to your company's Joomla backend
    $o navigate $url

    # log in and submit form
    $o setForm -name login
    $o setFormValue username $username
    $o setFormValue password $password
    $o setFormValue lang en-GB
    $o submitForm

    # check if "Logged in Users" text can be found on the page
    set result [$o regexpDataI "Logged in Users"]
} error]} {
    puts "JOOMLA UNKNOWN: error occurred during check."
    exit 3
}

if {[llength $result] > 0} {
    puts "JOOMLA OK: Administrative panel loaded correctly."
    exit 0
}  else  {
    puts "JOOMLA CRITICAL: Administrative panel does not work."
    exit 2
}
```

To check the plugin, simply run the following command:

```
root@ubuntu:~# /opt/nagios/plugins/check_joomla_backend \
    http://joomla.yourcompany.com/administrator/ admin adminpassword
JOOMLA OK: Administrative panel loaded correctly.
```

Monitoring VMware

Virtual machines are playing an important role in today's IT infrastructure. They help lower the cost of hardware by allowing multiple systems to reside and re-use resources from a single physical machine. It also allows migration from a large number of physical hardware to a small number of high-end servers with a large number of processors.

For Intel based platforms, VMware virtualization (`http://www.vmware.com/`) is one of the most advanced technologies. This spans from desktop solutions to server products. VMware also offers a free virtualization platform called VMware Server (`http://www.vmware.com/products/server/`).

Although Nagios does not offer a large variety of plugins to monitor VMware systems, VMware offers a Perl API that can easily be used to query virtual machines, along with a few of their parameters. On Windows operating systems, there is also the `VmCOM` API that allows interaction with VMware server product.

These functions allow querying of the virtual machine's status, guest parameters, as well as checking whether the virtual machine is working correctly.

The next page contains a script written in Perl that allows the querying of a particular virtual machine's state as well as making sure that it is working correctly. The script can easily be expanded to monitor CPU usage on a particular machine by querying `cpu.cpusecs` parameter using the `get_resource()` function from a virtual machine object.

Even though the script is configured to connect to a local machine, it is possible to specify different connection parameters so that it will query remote machines. In such a case, it is also necessary to specify the username and password of a user who can log into the VMware system.

For the script to work, it is necessary that the VmPerl API is configured to your Perl interpreter. In order to check this, please run the following command:

```
root@ubuntu:~# perl -e 'use VMware::VmPerl;'
```

If VmPerl libraries are correctly installed then this command should pass without any warnings or errors being generated. Otherwise, a configuration of VMware might be needed—VmPerl needs to be recompiled on each minor and major upgrade of Perl.

```
#!/usr/bin/perl

require VMware::VmPerl::VM;
require VMware::VmPerl::ConnectParams;
```

```
if (@ARGV != 2)
{
  printf "Usage: check_vmstatus <machine> <command>\n";
  exit(1);
}
($vmpath, $cmd) = @ARGV;
my $params = VMware::VmPerl::ConnectParams::new();
my $vm = VMware::VmPerl::VM::new();
$vm->connect($params, $vmpath);
my $title = $vm->get_config("displayName");

if ($cmd eq "state")
{
  if ($vm->get_execution_state() != 1)
  {
    printf "CRITICAL: %s is not running\n", $title;
    exit(2);
  }
  else
  {
    printf "OK: %s is running\n", $title;
    exit(0);
  }
}
if ($cmd eq "heartbeat")
{
  my $hb0 = $vm->get_heartbeat();
  sleep(5);
  my $hb1 = $vm->get_heartbeat();
  if ($hb0 == $hb1)
  {
    printf "CRITICAL: %s does not respond to events\n", $title;
    exit(2);
  }
  else
  {
    printf "OK: %s is alive\n", $title;
    exit(0);
  }
}

printf "UNKNOWN: invalid command\n", $cmd;
exit(3);
```

In order to test the script, simply run the following command:

```
# /opt/nagios/plugins/check_vm "/path/to/Solaris.vmx" state
OK: Solaris 10 test machine is running
```

You will need to specify the full path to the `.vmx` file, and virtual machine needs to be currently added to the VMware.

Your Own Notifications

Another part of Nagios that can be extended to fit your needs are notifications. These are messages that Nagios sends out whenever a problem occurs, or is resolved.

One way in which Nagios notification system can be expanded is to create template-based email sending. This will send notifications as both plain text and HTML messages. The of the email will be kept in separate files.

We will use Tcl for this purpose as it contains libraries for MIME (`http://tcllib.sourceforge.net/doc/mime.html`) and SMTP (`http://tcllib.sourceforge.net/doc/smtp.html`) functionality. The first one allows the creation of structured emails whereas the latter one is used to send these using an SMTP server.

Emails that contain content in multiple formats need to be wrapped in the `multipart/alternative` MIME type. This type will contain two subparts—first the plain text version, and following this the HTML version. This order makes email clients choose HTML over plain text if both the types are supported.

This part can then be wrapped in a `multipart/related` MIME type. This allows the embedding of additional files such as images that can then be used from within an HTML message. This is not used in the example shown on the next page, but can easily be added, similarly to how text and HTML parts are embedded inside the `multipart/alternative` MIME type.

In the same way as how macro substitution works in Nagios commands, templates will replace certain strings such as `$HOSTSTATE$` within the template. For example, the following can be used in a HTML template:

```
<tr><td>Notification type</td>
<td><b>$TYPE$</b></td></tr>
```

Similar macros can be used in plain text templates and will be substituted as well.

The following is a script that allows users to be notified in HTML format, through the use oftemplates:

```
#!/usr/bin/env tclsh

package require mime
package require smtp
package require fileutil

# map arguments
set mappings {TEMPLATE EMAIL TYPE
    HOSTNAME HOSTSTATE HOSTOUTPUT}

if {[llength $argv] != [llength $mappings]} {
    puts stderr "Usage: [info script] [join $mappings]"
    exit 1
}

# handle arguments
set template [lindex $argv 0]
set to [lindex $argv 1]
foreach name $mappings value $argv {
    lappend map "\$$name\$" $value
}

# read template files and map variables accordingly
set textbody [string map $map \
    [fileutil::cat $template/body.txt]]
set htmlbody [string map $map \
    [fileutil::cat $template/body.html]]
set mailsubject [string map $map \
    [fileutil::cat $template/subject.txt]]

# create a list of alternate formats (plain text and html)
set parts [list]
lappend parts [mime::initialize -canonical text/plain \
    -encoding 8bit -string $textbody]
lappend parts [mime::initialize -canonical text/html \
    -encoding 8bit -string $htmlbody]

# wrap all parts inside multipart/alternative
set parts [mime::initialize -canonical multipart/alternative \
    -header [list Subject $mailsubject] \
    -header [list To "\"$to\" <$to>"] \
    -header [list From "\"Nagios\" <nagios@yourcompany.com>"] \
    -parts $parts]
```

```
smtp::sendmessage $parts \
    -recipients $to \
    -originator "nagios@yourcompany.com" \
    -servers {localhost}

exit 0
```

To test it simply run:

```
root@ubuntu:# /opt/nagios/plugins/notify-email-fancy template1 \
    jdoe@yourcompany.com RECOVERY myhost1 OK "OK: host is alive"
```

This should cause an email to be sent to `jdoe@yourcompany.com`.

Managing Nagios

Your application might also want to have some control over Nagios. You might want to expose an interface for users to take control of your monitoring system, for example, a web interface or a client-server system. You might also want to handle custom authorization and access control list. This is something that is beyond the functionality offered by the web interface that Nagios comes with.

In such cases, it is best to create your own system for reading the current status, as well as for sending commands directly over the external command pipe. In both cases, this is very easy to do from any programming language.

The first part is showing Nagios' current status. This requires reading the `status.dat` file, parsing it to any data format, and then manipulating it. The format of the file is relatively simple—each object is enclosed in a section. Each section contains one or more `name=value` directives. For example, the following is a definition of information about the `status.dat` file:

```
info
{
   created=1214331481
   version=3.0.1
}
```

A, all hosts, services, and other objects are defined in the same way to the definition above. There can be multiple instances of a specified object type; for example, each `hoststatus` object definition specifies a single host along with its current status.

Sending commands to Nagios also seems trivial. The details and Details of the most commonly used commands were given in Chapter 6, *Notifications and Events*. Sending commands simply involves opening a pipe for writing, sending commands, and closing the pipe again.

Controlling Nagios from an external application is commonly done in PHP, to create web applications. Implementing the reading of the current status, as well as sending commands to Nagios, is relatively easier to do in PHP as PHP offers convenient functions for string manipulation, and regular expressions. Your web application also needs to limit commands that a user is able to send to Nagios as it might be a security risk if your application offers functionalities such as disabling and enabling checks for hosts and/or services.

The following is a function to read the Nagios status file and return it as an array of types of objects:

```
function readStatus($filename)
{
    $fh = fopen($filename, "r");
    $objname = "";
    while (!feof($fh))
    {
        $line = fgets($fh);
        $line = substr($line, 0, strlen($line)-1);
        if (ereg("^(.*) \{$", $line, $arr))
        {
            if ($objname != "")
                $rc[$objname][] = $ar;
            $objname = $arr[1];
            $arguments = array();
        }
        else if (ereg("^(.*)=(.*)$", trim($line), $arr))
            $ar[trim($arr[1])] = $arr[2];
    }
    return $rc;
}
```

It's also relatively easy to write a function that allows you to search for objects by their type so that they match the specified criteria, for example, all of the services associated with a host. A sample code to do this is as follows:

```
function findObject($status, $type, $match)
{
    $rc = array();
    foreach ($status[$type] as $o)
    {
        $ok = true;
        foreach ($match as $mname => $mvalue)
        {
            if ($o[$mname] != $mvalue)
```

```
                $ok = false;
        }
        if ($ok)
            $rc[] = $o;
    }
    return $rc;
}
```

Next, We can test this by reading the status, and finding all of the services on the `localhost` machine that have critical statuses by invoking the following sample code:

```
$s = readStatus("/var/nagios/status.dat");
print_r(findObject($s, "servicestatus",
    array("host_name" => "localhost", "last_hard_state" => "2")));
```

This code will print out an array of all services matching the predefined criteria. This can be used to perform complex searches and show the status depending on many configuration options.

Sending commands to Nagios from PHP is also a very simple thing to do. The following is a class that offers internal functions for sending commands, as well as two sample commands that cause Nagios to schedule the next host or service check on the specified date. If the date is omitted, then the check is run immediately.

```
class Nagios
{
    var $pipefilename = "/var/nagios/rw/nagios.cmd";
    function writeCommand($str)
    {
        $f = fopen($this->pipefilename, "w");
        fwrite($f, "[" . time() . "] " . $str . "\n");
        fclose($f);
    }
    function scheduleHostCheck($host, $when = "")
    {
        if ($when == "")
            $when = time();
        $this->writeCommand("SCHEDULE_FORCED_HOST_CHECK;" .
            $host . ";" . $when);
    }
    function scheduleServiceCheck($host, $svc, $when = "")
    {
        if ($when == "")
            $when = time();
        $this->writeCommand("SCHEDULE_FORCED_SVC_CHECK;" .
            $host . ";" . $svc . ";" . $when);
    }
}
```

A small section of code to test the functionality is as follows:

```
$n = new Nagios();
$n->scheduleHostCheck("linux1");
$n->scheduleServiceCheck("localhost", "APT", strtotime("+1 day"));
```

This initializes an instance of the Nagios class, and then schedules a host check for the `linux1` machine immediately. Next, it schedules the `APT` service check on the `localhost` machine to occur one day from now.

Implementing additional commands should be as simple as specifying new functions that send commands (`http://www.nagios.org/developerinfo/externalcommands/`) to Nagios over the external command pipe. Usually, the functionality base grows as a project grows, hence, we should not define unused functions on a *just-in-case* basis.

Using Passive Checks

Nagios offers a very powerful mechanism for scheduling tests. However, there are many situations where you might want to perform tests on your own and just tell Nagios what the result is. One of the typical scenarios for using passive tests can be when performing the actual test takes very little time, but the startup overhead is large. This is usual for languages such as Java, whose runtime initialization requires a lot of resources.

Another reason might be that checks are done on different machines where the Nagios instance is running. In many cases, due to security issues, it is not possible to schedule checks directly from Nagios, as communications not initiated by those machines are blocked. In this case, it's often best to schedule checks on your own and simply submit the results back to Nagios. In cases where such tests are going to be written by you, it's wise to integrate them with a mechanism to send the results over NSCA directly.

Passive checks are responsible for scheduling and performing tests on their own or need to be triggered by events. They can also be run as part of other applications. After a passive check is done, the result needs to be sent to the Nagios server. There are a couple of ways to do this. The easiest way is to send results over the external commands pipe, similar to how managing Nagios is done. In this case, application needs to send proper commands for submitting either service, or host check results. Nagios will then take care of incorporating results into its database.

Another approach is to use NSCA. This is a protocol for sending results over the network. NSCA provides a command for sending the results over the network and requires passing the configuration file that specifies the protocol, password, and other information. It is described in more detail in Chapter 7 *Passive Checks and NSCA*.

The next page contains an example of an application that periodically performs tests and sends their results to Nagios over the external command pipe. This code consists of a method to supply information to Nagios, and a main loop that performs tests every five minutes. It does not contain the actual test that should be performed as this might vary depending on your needs. The following is a sample Java code to perform the test and report its results using Nagios external commands pipe.

```
/* write check status to Nagios pipe */
private static void writeStatus(String host, String svc,
  int code, String output) throws Exception
{
    long time = System.currentTimeMillis() / 1000;
    FileWriter fw = new FileWriter("/var/nagios/rw/nagios.cmd");
    fw.write("[" + time +"] PROCESS_SERVICE_CHECK_RESULT;" +
        host + ";" + svc + ";" + code + ";" + output + "\n");
    fw.close();
}
public static void main(String[] args)
{
    while (true)
    {
        int code;
        StringBuffer output = new StringBuffer();
        /* perform actual test and report error if it failed */
        try
        {
            code = performTest(output);
        }
        catch (Exception e)
        {
            code = 3;
            output = new StringBuffer("Error: "+e.getMessage());
        }
        try
        {
            writeStatus("hostname","serviceDescription",
                code, output.toString());
        }
        catch (Exception e)
```

```
            {
                System.out.println("Problem sending command to Nagios:" +
                    e.getMessage());
            }
            /* wait for 5 minutes between performing tests */
            Thread.sleep(300*1000);
        }
    }
    private static int performTest(StringBuffer buf)
    {
        return 0;
    }
```

Please note that the actual implementation of the `performTest` method will perform real tests. The following is a sample test function for connecting over JDBC:

```
    int performTest(StringBuffer output)
    {
        String url = "jdbc:mysql://localhost:3306/mysql";
        String username = "root";
        String password = "yourpassword";
        Connection conn;
        try {
            conn = java.sql.DriverManager.
            getConnection(url, username, password);
            conn.close();
        }
        catch (Exception exception) {
            output.append("JDBC CRITICAL: Unable to connect");
            return(2);
        }
        output.append("JDBC OK: Connection established");
        return(0);
    }
```

To run the tests, you will first need to compile the class. Assuming the source code is called `PerformTests.java`, run the following command:

```
javac PerformTests.java
```

Now, you can run the actual test:

```
java -cp . PerformTests
```

This will send reports to Nagios, so you can check the Nagios log file to see whether it has received information from your test checker.

Very often, you will need to create or extend applications to perform checks on remote machines. In this case, NSCA is used to send the check results to Nagios server.

The following is a Python class for sending service and host results over NSCA. It uses the `popen2` API(`http://docs.python.org/lib/module-popen2.html`) and allows configuration of the path to the command, and the configuration, host, and port:

```
class nscawriter:
    def __init__(self):
        self.nscacommand = "/opt/nagios/bin/send_nsca"
        self.nscaconfig = "/etc/nagios/send_nsca.cfg"
        self.nscahost = "10.0.0.1"
        self.nscaport = 5667

    def open(self):
        (self.nscaout, self.nscain) = os.popen2(
            "\"" + self.nscacommand + "\"" +
            " -H \"" + self.nscahost + "\"" +
            " -p \"" + str(self.nscaport) + "\"" +
            " -c \"" + self.nscaconfig + "\"")

    def serviceResult(self, host, svc, code, output):
        self.nscaout.write(host + "\t" + svc +
            "\t" + str(code) + "\t" + output + "\n")
        self.nscaout.flush()

    def hostResult(self, host, code, output):
        self.nscaout.write(host +
            "\t" + str(code) + "\t" + output + "\n")
        self.nscaout.flush()

    def close(self):
        self.nscaout.close()
```

In order to test it, we can run the following code. This will send out a host notification about the `linux1` machine and submit a result for the `APT` service on that host.

```
if __name__ == "__main__":
    nsca = nscawriter()
    nsca.open()
    nsca.hostResult("linux1", 0, "Host is reachable")
    nsca.serviceResult("linux1", "APT", 0, "No upgrades available")
    nsca.close()
```

You have to open and close the handle on your own. This is because the `send_nsca` command has an internal timeout handling for reading results from the standard input. For the same reason, it is not possible to use the same NSCA instance to submit results over long periods of time.

Summary

Nagios has many places where it can be extended with external scripts or applications. We have now learned how it can be used to fit you and your company's needs. We have also learned that Nagios is not bound to any specific language and that its real power comes from the fact that you can choose the language you'll use to program your code.

One way Nagios can be made to do what you want it to do is to create your own check commands, also known as check plugins. Adding your own commands makes it possible to perform checks using techniques that might not be available using the default Nagios plugin commands. In many cases, self-created plugins are used to perform specialized checks. In this, Nagios is still responsible for planning when to perform the tests and handling their results, but it is up to you to decide how the test is going to be performed.

A similar approach is to use passive checks and supply the check results to Nagios. In such a case, you are responsible for performing the test and sending results to Nagios. Nagios will then handle all of the results of the new status for a host or service, such as triggering event handlers, sending notifications, and so on. Sending results to Nagios can be done in two different ways. If a check is performed on the same host as the one where the Nagios daemon is running, results can be written directly to the Nagios external command pipe. Nagios polls the pipe periodically for new commands and check results.

If you are performing checks on a machine different from the one where the Nagios daemon is running, you'll need to somehow send the results over the network. NSCA can be used for this purpose. It is a protocol that allows the sending of results to the Nagios daemon over the network in a secure way. It has an interface that is easy to incorporate into your application or script.

Of course, this chapter does not cover all of the aspects in which Nagios can be customized. Nagios offers an event handling mechanism that you can use for tasks such as automatic recovery or the deployment of backup configuration.

If you are serious about modifying and fine-tuning Nagios, be sure to check out the documentation on the Nagios Event Broker, available on the Nagios development pages (`http://www.nagios.org/developerinfo/`). The NEB API can be used to alter the ways in which Nagios works, and allows the integration of other ways to store status information. The Nagios Event Broker modules are written in C, and require much more coding skills than the ones that have been covered in this chapter.

Index

F

G

H

I

J

M

N

O

P

R

S

T

V

W

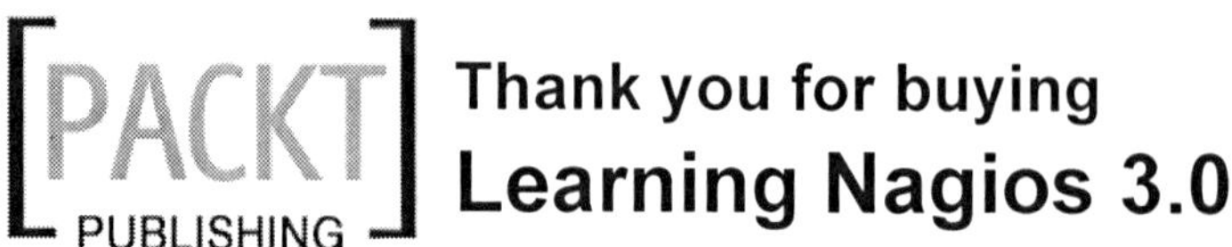

Packt Open Source Project Royalties

When we sell a book written on an Open Source project, we pay a royalty directly to that project. Therefore by purchasing Learning Nagios 3.0, Packt will have given some of the money received to the Nagios project.

In the long term, we see ourselves and you—customers and readers of our books—as part of the Open Source ecosystem, providing sustainable revenue for the projects we publish on. Our aim at Packt is to establish publishing royalties as an essential part of the service and support a business model that sustains Open Source.

If you're working with an Open Source project that you would like us to publish on, and subsequently pay royalties to, please get in touch with us.

Writing for Packt

We welcome all inquiries from people who are interested in authoring. Book proposals should be sent to `author@packtpub.com`. If your book idea is still at an early stage and you would like to discuss it first before writing a formal book proposal, contact us; one of our commissioning editors will get in touch with you.

We're not just looking for published authors; if you have strong technical skills but no writing experience, our experienced editors can help you develop a writing career, or simply get some additional reward for your expertise.

About Packt Publishing

Packt, pronounced 'packed', published its first book "Mastering phpMyAdmin for Effective MySQL Management" in April 2004 and subsequently continued to specialize in publishing highly focused books on specific technologies and solutions.

Our books and publications share the experiences of your fellow IT professionals in adapting and customizing today's systems, applications, and frameworks. Our solution-based books give you the knowledge and power to customize the software and technologies you're using to get the job done. Packt books are more specific and less general than the IT books you have seen in the past. Our unique business model allows us to bring you more focused information, giving you more of what you need to know, and less of what you don't.

Packt is a modern, yet unique publishing company, which focuses on producing quality, cutting-edge books for communities of developers, administrators, and newbies alike. For more information, please visit our website: `www.PacktPub.com`.

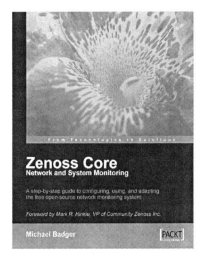

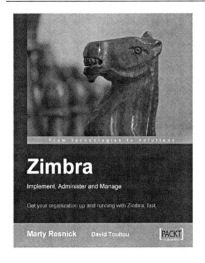

Breinigsville, PA USA
27 August 2010

244323BV00004B/10/P

9 781847 195180